The Most Beautiful Man in the World

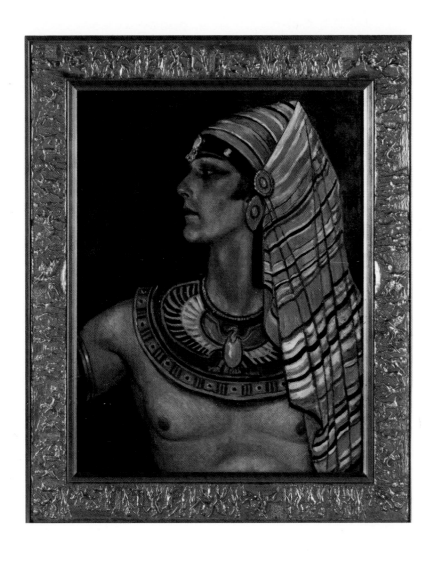

The Most Beautiful Man in the World: **Paul Swan** from Wilde to Warhol

Janis Londraville & Richard Londraville

FOREWORD BY
EMILY W. LEIDER

University of Nebraska Press
Lincoln and London

Set in Adobe Garamond by Kim Essman.
Designed by A. Shahan.
Printed by Thomson-Shore, Inc.

LIBRARY OF CONGRESS
CATALOGING-IN-PUBLICATION DATA
Londraville, Janis, 1949–

The most beautiful man in the world: Paul Swan,
from Wilde to Warhol / Janis Londraville and
Richard Londraville; foreword by Emily W. Leider.
    p.   cm.
Includes bibliographical references and index.
ISBN-13: 978-0-8032-2969-3 (cloth: alk. paper)
ISBN-10: 0-8032-2969-0 (cloth: alk. paper)
1. Swan, Paul, 1883–1972. 2. Dancers—United
States—Biography. 3. Motion picture actors and
actresses—United States—Biography. 4. Paint-
ers—United States—Biography. 5. Sculptors—
United States—Biography. I. Londraville, Richard,
1933– . II. Title.
CT275.S899L66 2006
700'.92—dc22
[B]   2005014651

Frontispiece: *Self-Portrait in Egyptian Dress* by Paul Swan,
1923. Oil on canvas (35 1/4" x 29 3/16"). Courtesy of the
collection of The John and Mable Ringling Museum of
Art, the State Art Museum of Florida. Photograph by
Giovanni Lundardi Photography.

To the Swans

Every man has his secrets, or should have. **Paul Swan**

Contents

Illustrations

Color Plates

Acknowledgments

Paul Swan's life story would not have been accessible without assistance from countless people and organizations. More than anyone else, Dallas Swan Jr., one of Paul Swan's nephews, is responsible for making this biography possible. He preserved his uncle's unpublished autobiography, scrapbooks, letters, diaries, and other primary material that allowed Paul Swan to tell much of his own story in these pages. Dallas and his wife, Margaret, opened their home to us and allowed us to photograph their collection and copy documents and letters. We recorded conversations with Mr. Swan as he shared with us his memories of his uncle. Additionally, his gifts of several paintings to The John and Mable Ringling Museum of Art in Sarasota, Florida, have helped preserve Paul Swan's name in perpetuity.

Another nephew, John Swan, and his wife, Helen, also contributed works by Swan to The Ringling Museum and gave us access to their collection of letters, photographs, and other material pertinent to this biography. Their own journals about visits to Paul Swan were invaluable.

Other family members helped at every turn, and each has our grateful appreciation: Kay Anderson, Willa Clausing, Hudson Hearst,

Laura Huff, Cynthia Swan Klemenger, Julie A. Lesser, Gregory Morris, Matthew Morris, Victoria Morris, Jane Spence Peters, Leslie Rich, Margaret Russell, and Rollin Swan. Because of the gifts of the Swan family, Swan's archive is now available at The Ringling Museum for future scholars.

Callie Angell, adjunct curator of the Warhol Film Project at the Whitney Museum of American Art, advised us on the Warhol sections and was a constant source of support and encouragement, as was Geralyn Huxley, curator of film and video at the Andy Warhol Museum. Gino Francesconi, archivist at Carnegie Hall, assisted us with documentation about the Swan works that Carnegie Hall owns. Ann Herre edited the text and was a technical adviser.

Emily Leider, whose books on Mae West, Rudolf Valentino, and other stars of yesteryear are well known, contributed the foreword, placing Paul Swan in the context of his age. Her wholehearted support of this project is deeply appreciated.

Bente Rosenkrantz Arendrup allowed us to use Baron Arild Rosenkrantz's oil portrait of Paul Swan, and she helped us research Swan's connection to her great-uncle. She provided us with material otherwise unobtainable and was generous with advice and assistance. Jacob Termansen photographed Arild Rosenkrantz's oil portrait of Paul Swan.

The staff at The Ringling Museum encouraged the project and helped at every turn with research and suggestions. Deserving special mention are curators Aaron DeGroft and Françoise Hack-Lof, library director Linda R. McKee, and assistant registrar Heidi Taylor.

Robert Barnes allowed us to use his 1958 pastel of Paul Swan and told us stories of his time at Swan's Carnegie Hall studio with Marcel Duchamp and Roberto Matta. Vince Grimaldi allowed us to use his photographs of Swan from the late 1960s and early 1970s. Gail Ambrose, Alberto Jaccoma, and Richard Nealy, three of Swan's friends, helped with research and were the source of much of the information about Swan's life in the 1960s and 1970s. Gerard Malanga also shared his memories of Swan's experiences with Andy Warhol. Cynthia Cameron, town historian of Stony Creek, and William and Caryl Hutchens, owners of Skiwaukee Farm, assisted with Swan's Adirondack history.

James Kieley allowed us to reproduce Swan's *The Three Graces*, served as a general adviser, and acted as conservator for several Swan oil paintings. Rolande Pinkerton read the chapters dealing with Swan's Paris years and corrected the French. Paul B. Franklin advised on a number of issues and edited sections of the book.

The State University of New York at Potsdam and the Associated Colleges of the Saint Lawrence Valley Independent Scholars' Center supported this project both financially and by providing superb facilities in which to work. The Computing and Technology Services staff at the college helped us with technical matters, and the Crumb Library staff were exceptional, as always. The Roland Gibson Art Gallery and the Walker Foundation at SUNY Potsdam also assisted with the project. Special thanks are given to Maggie Price, Romi Sebald, Claudette Fefee, and Tere Kirkland.

Others who helped, either directly or indirectly, include James W. Grauerholz (executor of the estate of William S. Burroughs), Ann McGarrell, Cinzia Cevinini, Bernard Cohen, Margaret Russell, Terry Gordon, Francis and Rosemarie Enzien, Curtis Farrar, Brian Gray, Cathy Fagan, Declan Foley, Richard Edwards, Arthur Collins and the late Stephanie Barber, William M. Murphy, Sheppard Ames, Brian Allison, the Percy Grainger Society, Peter Kurth, Bill Frazier, Jane Battaglia, David Garrett Izzo, Ruth Siegle, Susan Silverman, David Jacobi, Murray Glass, Bruce Posner, Wayne Koestenbaum, Michelle Scalera, Alan Steinberg, Andy McGowan, Nancy Moure, Romeyn Prescott, Ramón Santiago de Oropresa, Eileen Egan Mack, Malachy McCourt, William Name-Linich, Bonnie Jo Bell, Patricia Beckwith, Carmen Wielich Mertens, Dorothy Wielich O'Connell, Gregory Pierce, George Kahn, Chalmers H. Goodlin, and Adela Roatcap.

When Isadora Duncan encountered Paul Swan on the dance floor at a Parisian ball in the early 1920s, she greeted him with these words: "O, beautiful youth, come here to me! Where have you come from? Arcady?" Swan was already in late thirties, but he rejoiced in his ability to sustain a youthful appearance. This was a meeting of two dancers who were kindred spirits, although Swan lacked Isadora's revolutionary fervor. Restless and quintessentially American in their need for self-expression and independence, Duncan and Swan both found in early-twentieth-century Paris a haven from the provincialism and puritan inhibitions of their native land. Both regarded classical Greece as the wellspring of their art; both sensed the connection between dancing and sculpture; and both experienced their separate pilgrimages to Greece as homecomings. Champions of the unfettered body, both felt an affinity with the draped human figure in motion and with the idealized beauty celebrated in classic Hellenic art. Choreographing interpretive dances to the music of such composers as Chopin and Wagner, both saw dance not as vulgar entertainment but as temple art, a sublime manifestation of spirit and soul.

In New York, Swan admonished a jeering vaudeville audience at

Hammerstein's Victoria Theater, which had come to see "The Most Beautiful Man in the World," not to laugh at him. A serious male dance soloist had never performed in such a setting, and his scant attire and exaggerated, highly stylized gestures struck some as unmanly. They responded with rapt enthusiasm after he announced, "I am not a vaudeville performer. I hope I am an artist."

As a dancer Swan would repeatedly impersonate sandal-clad characters from the Greek myths: Narcissus, Pan, Apollo, Zeus. He would paint art collector Albert Wielich's wife and daughters as the Three Graces, and a slain World War I hero as a Greek youth from antiquity. Because of his remarkable good looks, Swan would be hailed as an Adonis, a reincarnated Greek god, the Hermes of Praxiteles come to life. Sometimes he stood before his easel barelegged and garbed in flowing, Grecian-style robes.

Isadora had studied ballet and rebelled against its rigid poses and the unnaturalness of dancing on point. Also a rebel who defined himself as an outsider, Swan had little formal training in movement and did not begin dancing in public until he was nearly thirty. For him dance was a continuation of his lifelong fascination with performance, pose, and line. Although he briefly studied privately in Europe with Diaghilev-trained Mikhail Mordkin and with onetime Pavlova partner Andreas Pavley, he was essentially self-taught.

Swan had inherent grace and an instinct for the theatrical. As a boy he staged puppet plays in an improvised corncrib theater on his family's Nebraska farm, costumed his sister as an angel, and repeatedly copied from a magazine the image of dancer Cléo de Mérode. Later he would tour with an acting company and appear in several silent movies. Celebrated performers—Alla Nazimova, John Barrymore, Raquel Meller, Nance O'Neil—were favorite and frequent subjects of his painted or sculpted portraits. Swan identified with divas. Characterizing himself as more like Sarah Bernhardt than Oscar Wilde, in his old age he began wearing theatrical makeup in everyday life, making explicit an abiding conviction that performance is not confined to theaters. For Swan, all the world was a stage, with all the limelight beamed on him.

If he lacked schooling as a dancer, the multitalented Swan could claim a more sustained grounding in the visual arts. His adored paternal grandfather, William Chapman Swan of Zenia, Illinois, was an accomplished carver in wood and horn who taught the youthful Paul how to model figures and make animals out of dry cornstalks. His mother, Adah Corson Swan, could draw and sew and had an eye for color and line that was stifled by her fervent fundamentalist Methodism and her duties as farmwife and mother of ten. Shirking farm chores, the boy would escape to his room to practice drawing. Although he would one day trace the outline of the Nebraska horizon on the blackened window of his Paris atelier, Swan never felt he belonged on a farm. When he ran away at age fifteen he set out in pursuit of a different kind of life: "I wanted to be a 'town boy' who wore his Sunday clothes every day. . . . I wanted to be far away from the smell of sweating horses. . . . I wanted to be educated and cultured, and to possess graceful, polite ways," he later wrote in his memoir. His first paying job was as a window trimmer in a department store in Lincoln.

Swan drifted to Chicago, where, after a stint as a model at the Art Institute, he was accepted as a student. Although he remained there only a few months, his teachers would leave indelible imprints. John Vanderpoel, a muralist who also once instructed Georgia O'Keeffe, trained him in figure drawing. Lorado Taft, a creator of monumental sculptures, instructed him in the simulation of textured fabric in both oils and clay.

Swan served a further apprenticeship in New York when he was hired by the pattern company Butterick to draw heads and hats. Impatient with office routine, he quit after a year, but his experience would buttress his career as a portrait artist and sculptor. The mentorship of Baron Arild Rosenkrantz, a Danish painter he met in Italy, would encourage his use of vibrant color.

Although he exhibited in major galleries, among them Macbeth, Knoedler, and Anderson, and with such contemporaries as Robert Henri and Maurice Prendergast, and although he befriended fellow artists John Butler Yeats and Charles Avery Aiken, Swan remained independent of twentieth-century artistic brotherhoods and movements. He lived in cities most of his life but proved indifferent to the gritty urban themes common to the Ashcan group, preferring to render Adirondack landscapes and to paint his daughter Paula in an idyllic pastoral setting. The cubist distortions and fragmentation that created such a furor at the Armory Show of 1913 left him unmoved.

We know nothing of his responses to Picasso and Matisse, Braque and Kandinsky, though we do know he acknowledged debts to Gainsborough and Sargent. Swan stayed faithful to the aestheticism that initially inspired him. Like the English Pre-Raphaelites whose work he admired, his figurative painting style tended toward the decorative, flat, linear, and dreamlike. In both his dancing and his art he was drawn to heroic, misty-eyed narratives. He was a storyteller. Swan did some experimental painting in the early 1930s, creating symbolist murals and improvisations in color based on music, but soon he returned to a more traditional, representational aesthetic. Most of his experimental canvases are lost or await rediscovery.

An accomplished draftsman who excelled at rendering likenesses, Swan may have been handicapped by his preoccupation with physical perfection. His own much-touted beauty of feature and form surely played a part here. He avoided naturalistic depictions of those he considered common-looking or ugly, improving on nature when his subject failed to measure up to his exalted aesthetic requirements. When he broke away from enshrining conventional beauty to produce sculptural masques influenced by Japanese theater, he produced some of his most interesting work. However, his ability to flatter helped him win commissions, which often paid handsomely. Because of his facility and popularity, he became a visual chronicler, rendering in clay or paint some of the celebrated faces of his era, among them British prime minister Ramsay MacDonald, editor Robert Underwood Johnson, Charles Lindbergh, Maurice Ravel, Claude Debussy, Willa Cather, Clare Booth Luce, Secretary of Defense James V. Forrestal, Franklin D. Roosevelt, John F. Kennedy, and Pope Paul VI.

Some of Swan's most affecting, psychologically astute portraits are of himself or people close to him: his father on his deathbed; his wife, Helen, and daughters, Paula and Flora; his sister-in-law Olivia; his friend Jeanne Robert Foster; his partner Fred Bates, probably the love of his life. Janis and Richard Londraville do an exceptional job in delineating these major relationships with honesty and compassion.

Bisexual in his younger years, Swan in middle age became exclusively homosexual while remaining emotionally if not physically devoted to his wife. Helen Gavit Swan seems to have been a model of forbearance who accepted Paul on his own terms, never demanding financial support, sexual fidelity, or even her "good-bye-saying" husband's extended presence. Whenever he turned up she welcomed him, and when he felt the need to leave, even after arthritis confined her to a wheelchair, she never questioned it. The granddaughter of sculptor Erastus Dow Palmer, she had wanted to marry an artist and to have children. Helen accomplished both goals in her marriage to Swan. During prolonged separations, she continued through her letters to provide a hearth—what Swan called "a hospital for broken wings"—and unstinting appreciation of her husband's creativity. His daughters were not always so forgiving.

Swan may have been less accepting of his sexuality than Helen was. He told a reporter in New Orleans, "I'm just a normal man. I have two daughters. Now, why do people think a male dancer is a sissy?" Perhaps his lack of forthrightness signals concern with public opinion rather than a lack of self-knowledge.

Swan could not be honest with himself about his own aging and changing appearance. He made a habit of shaving years from his date of birth and would snip off the dates from press clippings chronicling his career in his scrapbook. In his later decades he not only wore makeup daily but stuffed his pants with socks to make himself appear better endowed. He bathed in olive oil and darkened his hair.

His weekly performances at his Paris atelier in the 1930s, and after that in his studios in Manhattan, provided a way for him to come before the public in a hermetically sealed environment that evoked the past. In Paris there were painted medieval tapestries that served as stage curtains; a violet carpet striped in red and orange, and silk hangings falling from the ceiling; sculptures on pedestals abounded, and there were tables painted black and adorned with Greek-looking terra-cotta-tinted figures. In his Carnegie Hall studio, incense would burn amidst the oriental carpets and red drapes. Behind a screen, a pianist would play Chopin or Debussy. Avant-garde artists, among them Marcel Duchamp, Alexander Calder, and Robert Barnes, would visit Swan's Manhattan salon during the late 1950s and watch him do his version of the Dance of the Seven Veils, awed by his strangeness and his total immersion in himself and his anachronistic art. To Barnes and later to Andy Warhol, Swan had become an icon of the bizarre, a living relic, and a kind of performance artist who "made happenings seem mundane."

Paul Swan led an idiosyncratic life of enormous productivity and passion. In chronicling his biography, quoting his words, and assembling and helping to restore and display his body of work—much of it previously dispersed and unsung—Janis and Richard Londraville have honored Swan's singular artistic legacy and in doing so have rescued a missing chapter from the annals of American culture.

Abbreviations

DS Swan, Paul. "The Distorted Shadow" (Swan's unpublished and unfinished autobiography, written between 1926 and 1943, at RMA).

DY Londraville, Richard, and Janis Londraville. *Dear Yeats, Dear Pound, Dear Ford: Jeanne Robert Foster and Her Circle of Friends*. Syracuse: Syracuse UP, 2001.

PFR Londraville, Janis. "Paul Swan: The Life and Art of 'The Most Beautiful Man in the World.'" *Prodigal Father Revisited: Artists and Writers in the World of John Butler Yeats*. Edited by Janis Londraville. West Cornwall CT: Locust Hill P, 2001. 331–47.

RMA The John and Mable Ringling Museum of Art, the State Art Museum of Florida, Sarasota.

SB Paul Swan's scrapbooks, at RMA.

Andy Warhol and the Rebirth of Paul Swan

Fifteen Minutes of Fame

When seventy-seven-year-old Paul Swan wrote to his longtime friend American poet and journalist Jeanne Robert Foster on 28 November 1960, it was to ask her help with an autobiography that he considered his magnum opus: "Well, my book should be cut down and just the events used which contribute to the revelation of the person I am—which clarify the strangeness . . . of my personality—the soul that looks for beauty in all people and things."[1] Regardless of the judgment of others, Swan never faltered in ranking his work among the best of its kind, and he rarely felt that he was paid enough for it. In fact, the reaction of critics to his art was so favorable that Swan might be forgiven some hubris, but at this stage in his career his best work seemed behind him. Foster read the book but declined. Ultimately it would not be Swan's autobiography but a 1965 experimental film by pop artist Andy Warhol entitled, simply, *Paul Swan* that would give Swan, once hailed as "the most beautiful man in the world," a place in American cultural history.

"I am the most famous unknown person in New York," Swan says in the opening of *Paul Swan*. It is true that he was largely forgotten by the

1960s. Even his beloved Carnegie Hall pushed him aside in 1961, along with a number of other artists, when rents were raised substantially. In desperation, Swan found new digs at the Van Dyke Studios on 939 Eighth Avenue at Fifty-sixth Street in Manhattan.[2]

Once Swan had been known as "America's leading exponent of classic dancing." In the second decade of the twentieth century, while acting in silent films for Post Films, Five Star Featurettes, and the Pluragraph Company, he also dazzled audiences at Arthur Hammerstein's famous Victoria Theater in New York with performances of *The Sphinx* and *Faun Dance*. He soon became so well known that audiences readily understood Adele Astaire when she chided her brother, Fred, in one of their song-and-dance routines, "Don't think *you* look like Paul Swan!"[3] His dance performances won acclaim from Hollywood to Athens, and audiences marveled at his beauty.

As noted as Swan was for his dance, it was not his earliest artistic talent. His first published artwork appeared on the cover of *Putnam's Magazine* in December 1908. In 1909 he was chosen by Russian actress Alla Nazimova to paint five portraits of her in her various Ibsen costumes. By 1923, when he appeared in Cecil B. DeMille's original *Ten Commandments*, he was executing commissioned portraits and sculptures of some of the world's best-known figures, including actor John Barrymore and Sir Eldon Gorst, the governor of Egypt. He was hailed as one of America's leading painters, and on 21 March 1929 the *Chicago Evening American* called him "a modern Leonardo da Vinci." From New York to London, from Buenos Aires to Paris, reviewers praised his art. His portraits and photos of him dancing appeared in magazines such as *Vogue*, *Literary Digest*, *New York World*, *Spur*, *Fashion Digest*, and *Esquire*. In 1930 the *New York Times* gave equal space to Swan and French dignitary Prince Joachim Napolèon Murat in a headline announcing their arrival in France (SB).

Swan was one of a very few ever to achieve international celebrity during his life for such a combination of talents. Robert Forrest Wilson wrote in *Paris on Parade* (1925): "He follows most of the seven arts and does more in any one than most in their individual specialists. He sculptures symbolic portrait heads, and paints decorative murals for the wealthy of New York, writes verse and gives classic dancing concerts in Athens and elsewhere in Europe" (224).

But Swan eventually became a caricature of his former self. When he returned to New York in 1939 after living a decade in Paris, he found a city much different from the one he had left in 1930.[4] He was fifty-six years old, and his dance was in a natural state of decline. Unlike Japan's multitalented bisexual writer Yukio Mishima, a fellow devotee to the Greek ideal of beauty who thought his artistic life was over at forty-five (and so ended it), Swan could only remember the time he had been called the most beautiful man in the world. Most of us have some avoidance techniques to deny what we see in the mirror. Swan seemed intent on obliterating this evidence. He applied shoeblack to graying hair and improved his photographs with a black pen in order to nip his waist or lift his sagging chin.

Painting portraits still brought him commissions and exhibitions; his skills had not diminished appreciably in this area. But he continued to hold weekly dance performances into his eighties, public displays in which he unknowingly parodied his past grace. He became a character, one that New Yorkers tend to collect as evidence of the strange and complex nature of their city. Perhaps if he had retired sooner his reputation as a dancer would have been better preserved. But he chose instead to continue to dance until his daughters, Paula and Flora, finally moved him into a Bedford Hills nursing home in 1971, where he died in February 1972, at the age of eighty-eight.

By the time he met Warhol in 1964, Swan was no longer the young headliner whom Arthur Hammerstein had called "a re-incarnated Greek god."[5] Warhol then worked out of an old firehouse at East Eighty-seventh Street, a short walk from the first studio Swan had taken in New York City, on East Eighty-sixth Street, fifty years earlier. He met Warhol and his assistant, an aspiring poet named Gerard Malanga, during the filming of Gregory Markopoulos's *The Illiac Passion*, which Markopoulos based on Aeschylus's *Prometheus Bound*.[6] Swan played the role of Zeus, Warhol played Poseidon, and Malanga played Ganymede. "Illiac," although unmistakably anatomic (spelling aside) and, in this context, unmistakably gay, refers us also to Homer's poem and thus creates a circle of Greek references. Scenes in this innovative and disturbing film employ the same kind of paralysis Beckett had used on his stage: "The imagery in *The Illiac Passion* is striking in its hypnotic repetitions, particularly in a sequence where a man repeatedly attempts to walk, but finds himself unable to move, perhaps trapped in the director's powerful *mise-en-scene*. . . . [Markopoulos] reads from Thoreau's translation of *Prometheus Bound* but 'edits' the words just as he does the images, repeating phrases as if they were chants, with the repetitions alternating with silences" (Morris 2).[7]

Markopoulos was gay and wanted "to make homosexuality a beauty in life." "The average man is destroying beauty," he once said. "The average man no longer looks into another man's eyes. Everyone is afraid."[8] Swan had lived his life stubbornly, if not bravely, looking into people's eyes even in periods of self-doubt. He never wavered in his attempts to create and promote his vision of beauty. Whatever other aesthetic motives he may have had, the director admired the dancer and rewarded him with a role in his film.

At least in part because of Warhol's interest in Swan's "unswerving dedication to his increasingly anachronistic art form," the filmmaker decided to load his Auricon sound-sync camera and shoot the film *Paul Swan* (Angell, "Paul Swan" 23). Paul Morrissey, director of photography, said the movie was "a record of a kind of performing art of the early years of the century, but more fascinating being performed in the middle sixties long after it had gone out of fashion" (Morrissey). While Warhol was surgically deconstructing artistic tradition, forcing his audience to look with new eyes, Swan was hanging on blindly to the Greek ideal he had embraced as a young man, dancing for dwindling audiences who, in the 1960s, began to consist primarily of young gay men and old women with fidgety grandchildren in tow.

Warhol often focused on "reinterpreting the worth of cultural waste products" (Koestenbaum 28), whether they were soup cans or elderly artists. For those who know the story of Swan's magnificent early career, *Paul Swan* at first seems a dreary film that draws attention to the star's age. Swan has difficulty bending, kneeling, and swinging the same sword he had once wielded in *To Heroes Slain*—a dance he created half a century earlier as a tribute to soldiers killed at Flanders. It is painful to watch Swan attempt quick costume changes as Warhol's unrelenting camera lens moves just enough to observe the ordeal.

Swan's early reputation as "Greek god reincarnated," "Hermes of Praxiteles," and "Adonis" was a history long buried beneath the cultural waste Warhol wanted to excavate. This dimly lit and grainy portrayal

1. Paul Swan in his original dance *To Heroes Slain* in 1940. Twenty-five years later he performed the same dance in Andy Warhol's film *Paul Swan*. Photograph courtesy of Dallas Swan Jr.

of an eighty-two-year-old man trying to dance reminded Morrissey "of the Candid Camera TV-show in which people didn't know they were being filmed. This is the only instance . . . in any of the experiments when someone didn't know they were being filmed."

Swan did, however, know that filming continued, and he was frustrated. He complains during one difficult costume change, "Oh dear, God damn. I can't do it this way. It takes too long." Then he remarks to someone as he dons his headdress, "I look like you." Still frustrated at trying to pull on the costume, he groans, "It takes too long. It spoils it. I can't do it." He quickly reassures himself: "I suppose you can cut all that out, can't you?"

Morrissey believed that *Paul Swan* was "one of the very few times when the concept [of keeping the camera running and not editing the film later] was effective. . . . What makes this film so interesting is its combination of extreme theatrical artifice (the Paul Swan recital) and the total lack of any artifice in the intervals of the costume changes."

Swan believed—even when his skills were deteriorating—that he had something to offer those who watched him. In spite of such confidence, and even after a lifetime of performances, he still dealt with chronic stage fright. Warhol wanted to observe and record Swan as the old man confronted his demons. He may also have been attracted to Swan as a film project because of his own interest in dance. After Warhol began living in New York City in the 1950s, he associated with a number of dancers who inspired him in a variety of ways. Freddy Herko, for instance, appeared in some of Warhol's early films, but he danced himself into oblivion when, after putting Mozart's *Coronation Mass* on the hi-fi, he leaped out of a window and killed himself (Koestenbaum 24). The death must have been upsetting, even though Warhol reportedly told friends that he wished he could have filmed it. Warhol's interest in Swan—a decrepit dancer whose performance could only remind him of the body's inevitable ruin—seems to make more sense when one considers Warhol's preoccupation with last things.

Did Warhol also see himself in Paul Swan? Was he intrigued (or reassured) by Swan's stubborn decline? By the 1950s, Swan's use of theatrical makeup had increased dramatically. He began stuffing his pants with socks to make himself look more endowed; his mascara sometimes looked more like black globs than eyelashes—the result of his increasingly poor vision and palsy in one eyelid.

In the same decade, Warhol began wearing hairpieces, although he was only in his twenties. He wore pinhole cardboard glasses to try to strengthen weak eyes; he had his nose sanded (Koestenbaum 34). By 1963 he had begun wearing the now famous silver wig. Did his own uncertain health have something to do with his interest in Swan's determined denial of physical decline?[9]

Wayne Koestenbaum offers another reason. Warhol considered subjects in order "to solve one conundrum: what does it mean to exist in a body, next to another person, who also exists in a body?" (Koestenbaum 11). In *Paul Swan*, which Koestenbaum calls "more Gloria Swanson than Rudolf Nureyev" (Koestenbaum 24)—remember that the dancer was geriatric at the time—Swan was the only body, the solo performer. The body he was existing in was the distorted image of who he had been, "the most beautiful man in the world."

There are, then, two characters in *Paul Swan*: Paul Swan the old man and the memory of Paul Swan as Adonis. Swan unknowingly creates the tension in the film as these two characters battle with every lunge, every arm extension, each costume change. Just as we are often shocked by a snapshot of ourselves revealing flaws we ordinarily decide not to see, Swan's dance is a ghostly echo of the grace and beauty that once was. What at first appears as "more Gloria Swanson than Rudolph Nureyev," a spectacle for us to deride or pity, becomes a study in the capacity of the human to ignore the burdens of time. As W. B. Yeats says in "Sailing to Byzantium,"

> An aged man is but a paltry thing
> A tattered coat upon a stick, unless
> Soul clap its hands and sing
> And louder sing
> For every tatter in its mortal dress.

Swan never ceased his song, no matter how his voice cracked.

The comparison to Swanson is apt, for certainly it is not the young Gloria that Koestenbaum is referencing but rather the caricature of Norma Desmond that she created in *Sunset Boulevard*. Just as the young Gloria appears in our mind's eye when we watch that film, so does Swan's youth and skill filter through the old man's creaky performance. Warhol's unblinking camera pushes our collective noses into the ultimate end of life and art.

Further, Swanson's choice to become a caricature is clearly an artistic decision, and its execution is shared by actor, director, and writer. In Swan's case, he is more found object for Warhol, and the art that results is more precisely Warhol's alone. This intense focus removes any consideration of Swan's performance as performance and allows us to concentrate on exactly why Warhol has chosen to make this film.

The camera's focal distance varies occasionally during the film, but it returns again and again to a close-up of the face of Paul Swan, the aged Adonis. Sometimes the camera searches as it zooms, finding only part of Swan's face or briefly chopping off his head. When it ultimately locates its subject, Swan's deterioration is exposed. *Paul Swan* disturbs us. Let the movie end, and let the poor old man off the hook. But Warhol won't do that: "The more you look at the exact same thing," he said, "the better and emptier you feel."[10] After sixty-six minutes, no illusions are left.

Warhol wanted to disturb us. "Time has the power to move and the power to stand still; time's ambidextrousness thrills and kills," and so Swan's difficulty on stage is one way that "Andy pumps full-strength his experience of time as traumatic" into his film (Koestenbaum 70). He wanted to put Swan in a situation, turn the camera on, and see what happened. Swan finishes his performance, but the camera is still running. When he pokes his head out onstage, someone yells at him, "Come out and make a speech. The film is almost over." Swan questions the direction, asking if he should recite some of his poetry. The person yells again, "I just want you to make a speech, like at the end of a performance." And so Swan recites poetry until, in medias res, the film ends.

Callie Angell, adjunct curator of the Warhol Film Project at the Whitney Museum of American Art, writes that the "fluidity of Warhol's filmmaking practice, which was often serial in nature and structured around the full-length reel as the basic unit of production, has in some cases made it impossible to categorize Warhol's films in the standard filmographic terms, or evaluate them as unique art objects" ("Andy Warhol" 123). She continues: "Traditional archival methodologies became inadequate in the face of Warhol's idiosyncratic film practice. For example, the standard filmographic catalogue, which lists finished films in the year in which they were released, seriously misrepresents the actual nature of Warhol's modular and extremely flexible film production, in which individual reels often accumulated their own histories as he used and reused them under different titles and in different formats" (140).

Paul Swan is such an example. A reel was shown on KQED-TV in 1970 "as part of an exhibition of artists' films and videotapes organized by the Dilexi Gallery in San Francisco. Since no prints have been found in the collection, it seems likely that this reel of *Paul Swan* was premiered on television and never exhibited as a film" (Angell, "Paul Swan" 23). This raises certain questions: Is the KQED film a different version? Is it an altered version that may have also been presented differently because it was shown on television?

If we look only at the *Paul Swan* version restored by the Museum of Modern Art in 1994, we can at least say that Warhol's choice to use the full-length reel in this particular instance allows the physical film to function like a frame around a painting. It becomes the unifying means by which Warhol creates his art object. The opposite of Hollywood's cutting-room exercise, editing *Paul Swan* is not the shaping tool, the paintbrush, or the paint. In letting the film maintain its integrity as a whole work of art, Warhol was "restoring to film its original irrational function of presenting things to look at without any comment or artifice" (Andersen 58). For instance, we have become so inured to the scripted, edited product manufactured by Hollywood that we have forgotten the original impact produced when we, or some member of our family, waved inanely at an eight-millimeter camera.

Paul Swan was not Warhol's only film of the dancer. He also cast Swan in *Camp*, described by Angell as "a variety review apparently inspired by Susan Sontag's *Notes on Camp*" ("Paul Swan" 23).[11] Like *Paul Swan*, *Camp* consists of uninterrupted filming, except for the change of reels midway through the movie. Before *Camp*'s premiere at the Film-Makers' Cinematheque in November 1965, Warhol had enticed potential viewers with this advertisement in the *Village Voice*: "Everyone is being so creative for this festival that I thought I would just show a bad movie. The camera work is so bad, the lighting is awful, the technical work is terrible—but the people are fantastic!" (qtd. in Hoberman 136). Fantastic—bizarre, queer, freakish, grotesque—is exactly what they are. As the camera continues to roll, what first seems a dull and irritating movie becomes intriguing. The characters' foolishness, amateurish ability, and artlessness create a Warholian pathos that makes this odd group memorable in its humanity.[12]

The film opens at Warhol's Factory, with the performers in a faux *L'Atelier* pose (Anderson 58). Gustave Courbet described his 1855 painting as "the moral and physical history of my studio" (qtd. in Anderson

58), and Warhol's deliberate setting for *Camp* has the same sense, while presenting a very different collection of subjects: "There is no simple order to the arrangement: people are seated on a couch, on hard-backed wooden chairs, and on stools; they are standing against a wall in the background. The whole scene is lit with a garish melodrama created not only by stationary lights, but also by portable Sun-Guns carried about by T-shirted technicians [like the traditionally invisible black-robed stagehands in Chinese opera] who wander into the frame occasionally to light a certain spot or to move a microphone" (Anderson 58).

The fame that Paul Swan enjoyed when he won roles in movies of yesteryear, including *Narcissus*, *Orpheus*, *Diana the Huntress* (all 1916 New York films), and Hollywood's *The Ten Commandments* (1923) and *Ben Hur* (1925), was meaningful only to people who might have known who he had once been.[13] In *Camp*, he was a lost soul but didn't know it. Anderson sees Swan's role as farce: "Paul Swan in an abbreviated gladiator costume which seems to be a series of oversized diapers does a death scene to the accompaniment of Wagner. He is asked to repeat it and does so. Baby Jane Holzer, wearing a poor boy sweater and wide-wale corduroy trousers, comes forward and dances with him, then disappears" (58).

Warhol labeled another film of Swan *Paul Swan I–IV*, and though not yet restored, it is now part of Swan's official filmography. This movie consists of four 100-foot silent color rolls that probably were made around the same time *Paul Swan* was being filmed. *I–IV*, shot on Warhol's Bolex camera, shows Swan dancing again, but, different from *Paul Swan*, there is a great deal of camera movement. One roll also has some brief shots (or "single-framing") of Swan's studio, including some of his paintings. "There is no indication that these four 100 foot rolls were ever spliced together or shown publicly."[14]

No matter what one thinks of Warhol and his art, the very plethora of opinion argues his influence. His best work has a dialectic between art subject and art object, and nowhere is this clearer than in the Swan films. Swan, whose life and art was an attempt to objectify Greek ideal beauty, has devolved to the creaky old man we see on the stage. If that image were all, we might react in pity or disgust, especially because the dancer seems oblivious to the effect he is creating.[15]

But there is more. With a prescience that anticipates reality television by decades, Warhol allows us to see everything at once: Swan the dancer; Swan's idea of himself; the film as record; the film as art object. We are left with a complex and intriguing totality, one that demolishes our preconceptions of the limitations of art.

At the time the Swan films were being shot, Morrissey could still recognize the man Swan had once been: "He ran a monthly ad in the *Village Voice* for his recitals which he gave in his living-loft [Studio 508, the Van Dyke]. Underneath his photos in the ad a line appeared in quotes, 'The Most Beautiful Man in the World.' The photo of himself in profile had been taken forty years earlier, but he remained very handsome." One of Swan's friends from the 1960s recalls that even at eighty Swan "floated across a room, still moving like an elegant dancer." When his nephew Dallas Swan Jr. took him to dinner, "heads turned, as if people were trying to figure out what movie star he was." " 'Are you Francis X. Bushman?' he was asked on more than one occasion."[16]

The people who looked his way knew he was old. Makeup could not hide that, even though he rubbed olive oil over his body daily. A comb-over, for instance, may help to convince someone that he still has hair, but he is the only one fooled. Curious strangers brave enough to approach Swan never confused him with current idols of the time.

Photographer Vince Grimaldi, who knew Swan during the dancer's last years, remembers a visit to the Van Dyke on the day that Swan received a letter from Warhol's Factory: a payment for the work in the films.[17] Swan, who, according to Grimaldi, was exhibiting signs of senility and paranoia, had forgotten who Warhol was and did not even remember being filmed. Grimaldi called The Factory to get an explanation for the check and subsequently found out about the movies.

Last Art

The examples we have of Swan's painting during his last decade were not always up to his earlier range of quality. He executed several significant portrait commissions. One was of Pope Paul VI when the pontiff was in New York City to address the United Nations on 4 October 1965. According to the Vatican's secretary of state at the time, after viewing the completed work, the pope was "warmly appreciative" of Swan's sensitive depiction, "invoking upon you [Swan] and yours abundant divine graces and choicest heavenly favours."[18]

2. Paul Swan in Andy Warhol's *Paul Swan*, 1965. © 2005 The Andy Warhol Museum, Pittsburgh PA, a museum of Carnegie Institute. Film still courtesy of The Andy Warhol Museum.

Other important commissions included one for writer Malachy Mc-Court and two for Happy Rockefeller of her young children, Nelson Jr. and Mark—but not all of Swan's work was as good.[19] It may be that the infirmities of age were responsible, or perhaps some of the paintings that survive were unfinished. Swan did not have the opportunity to make a final selection of his work that might well have resulted in more representative choices. This last group of paintings from his atelier can be compared to what happens when an editor looks over unfinished manuscripts of a deceased author and pieces together a posthumous book.

Also, some of the paranoia that Grimaldi observed, evident to other friends as early as 1960, may have distracted Swan from doing his best work. When he wrote to Jeanne Foster in 1960 about the possibility of being evicted from Carnegie Hall, he was certain it was his well-to-do younger brother, Dallas Dewitt Swan, who was somehow the cause of his current misery. Dallas was purposely withholding assistance. Dallas never approved of his artistic pursuits. Dallas acted against him at every turn: "Two weeks ago he knew I hadn't a cent in my pockets and he would do nothing at all. — It is strange that now after all these years he feels called upon to take up the hateful opposition to all my dreams."[20]

Swan could not have been more wrong. Dallas thought his brother should give up dancing because he didn't get paid well enough for his performances, but he always recognized Swan's talent as a portrait artist. Because Swan was constantly asking him for money, why not translate some of this probably irrecoverable cash into something tangible? Dallas bought paintings, some of which were already in the studio, some of which he commissioned—once from an idea he had seen in another artist. One can only imagine the fury Swan felt when Dallas would asked him to provide a copy of another artist's work.

This patronage was a source of continued bad blood between them, as Swan's long resentment turned to distrust. He relinquished the paintings unwillingly, occasionally (when visiting his brother in Garden City, New York) informing Dallas that they were still his own, on loan: "I think I'll take that one back now." Dallas would then advise his brother that the works had been legally purchased. Swan would grow angry, leave the house in a huff (driven to the train station by his patient nephew Dallas Jr., who knew the routine), and storm back to New York City.[21]

After some time, in need of money again, he would offer Dallas another piece of art, repeating the inevitable, unpleasant cycle. To him, it seemed unreasonable of his brother to claim such treasure for a few hundred dollars. A portrait Swan painted of Dallas in 1953 reveals as much about the artist's emotions as it does about his brother, who was, by all accounts, a stern businessman. It was this feature that Swan took delight in preserving for all time.[22] The irony of the story is that without his brother's insistence upon getting art for money, many more of Swan's paintings and drawings might have been lost after the artist's death. Instead, Dallas Swan Jr. has meticulously preserved his father's collection of oils, drawings, watercolors, and sculptures.

However difficult he might have been, Paul Swan was often a generous and sensitive man. One of the artists living at the Van Dyke with him was Charles Avery Aiken, whose work today hangs in several important institutions, including the Brooklyn Museum of Art and the Dallas Museum of Art. "I think my uncle helped keep the old man alive," Dallas Jr. said about Swan's generosity toward Aiken.[23] Whatever money he got from Dallas Sr., Paul Swan used at least part of it to help pay Aiken's bills. Dallas Jr. lived in New York City at the time and often visited his uncle, who always wore hand-me-downs from the family, spent little on food, and slept on a couch because he did not have a bed. Dallas Jr. wisely never told his father about Swan's generous assistance to Aiken.[24]

During February 1965, the same month he was working on a portrait of Aiken, Swan received a visit from Helen Swan, the young wife of his nephew John.[25] Helen was eager but nervous about meeting her husband's eccentric uncle. Another relative had warned her that she should think twice about a visit. That lady had tried complimenting Swan's work, to which he promptly replied that she was "no artist" and that she "had no business complimenting or criticizing" his work. But Helen was determined and braved the dragon's lair. When Swan found out she was named "Helen Swan," as was his own wife (who had died in 1951), he was immediately gracious, showing her around his long, cave-like, rectangular studio, explaining the history of some of the paintings and sculptures on display.[26] Helen noticed only one window, at the far end of the room. To its left was a curtained area for dance recitals. This was the stage on which he performed in Warhol's *Paul Swan*.

Insisting that this new Helen stay for lunch, Swan disappeared behind the curtains to prepare something. She sat near a sculpture of a nude man on his back, draped over a boulder. A cockroach suddenly appeared, settling itself comfortably on the plaster. A nurse by profession, Helen began to consider the kitchen arrangement. Did he even have a refrigerator? She knew he shared a community bathroom down the hall. Was this what had become of "the most beautiful man in the world"?

Swan reappeared with two hamburgers. Not wanting to displease him, she ate with vigor, praying to be spared food poisoning. She recalls him telling her that he would be remembered for his art long after the rest of his family was forgotten. He was always convinced he would outlive his nine siblings. In fact, only one brother, Reuben, survived him.

When Helen told her father-in-law, Reuben, the story of her visit, he began to chuckle. He had long ago been the model for the nude she had sat near, and had nearly frozen in the cold at a New York beach where his brother sketched him for the sculpture. Back in the studio, Swan replaced what he thought was a less attractive face with his own beautiful one. All that discomfort, Reuben said, and he never got credit for his figure. The life-size sculpture mysteriously disappeared at the end of Swan's life, as so many things did, but a photograph remains at The John and Mable Ringling Museum of Art in Sarasota, Florida.

Three years after Helen's visit, Swan's eyesight deteriorated to the extent that he finally required surgery. By 1969 his drawings were still of excellent quality, but he found it difficult to work in oils. On the back of one painting, he wrote in black paint a quotation from *Ars Victrix*,

> All passes, art alone
> Enduring stays with us.
> The bust outlasts the throne,
> The coin, Tiberius.[27]

Twenty-nine years passed after Paul Swan's death before the first retrospective of his work was held at the State University of New York in 2001. Today, works owned by Carnegie Hall, Princeton University, the University of Virginia, the state of Nebraska, the Players theater club in New York City, and numerous private collections have begun to gather more attention. In 2003 The Ringling Museum of Art acquired seventeen portraits (oils and pencils) for its permanent collection. With the 2002 discovery in New Jersey of sixty-six lost drawings and oils, and artwork recently being found as far away as England, Denmark, and Italy, the story of Paul Swan continues long after "the most famous unknown person in New York" breathed his last.

Being born is like being kidnapped. And then sold into slavery. **Andy Warhol**

2 Cold Comfort Farm, 1880–1897

Principal Characters

On the day that Adah Corson and Randolph Swan met, the Illinois sun was relentless, and thunderheads were building on the distant horizon. Work on the farm was hot and tedious, the horses heaving and sweating as they dragged heavy plows. But the summer heat didn't stop the young people in the community from looking forward to the dance at the Grange hall that evening in Ashland. They would soon be prancing to the strains of "Turkey in the Straw" while many of their Methodist elders fretted at the sinful exhibition.

That night at the dance, a comely young lady of seventeen attended, after promises of caution to uneasy parents. Adah Corson's hair was forced into a proper bun, but it only showed her blue eyes to better advantage. A fervent Methodist, she noticed a handsome if slightly rakish-looking young man. She didn't know that Randolph had been a carefree adventurer, hiring himself out to do odd jobs around farms in several states, a jack-of-all-trades. It was perhaps fortunate that he relocated occasionally, because it provided him with an escape from ladies whom he had the occasion to befriend. But all evidence suggests that from the moment they met, he was smitten with Adah Corson.

Adah thought he might make a good penitent, and she liked the idea of rescuing someone for the Lord. "She realized herself fully at such times," Paul Swan later wrote. "It is not difficult to understand what Randolph, a normal young male of twenty-three, free and searching for ideality in a mate, should find so fully exemplified in this chaste, inexperienced young maiden—'the blue-eyed Corson girl'" (DS 12).[1]

Adah had other suitors to consider. There was an interested neighboring preacher, and even the mayor of Petersburg was a candidate for her hand. At seventeen, she was only mildly intrigued by these men, wishing to be an admired young woman rather than a wife whose dreams died with marriage. Was she also, as were many young girls before and since, intrigued by the bad boy that she thought Randolph represented? With at least some conviction, he acted the part of the remorseful reprobate, sensing that ploy to be his best chance. Adah responded with enough interest to keep him hopeful.

At the first revival meeting that Randolph attended at Adah's Methodist church in Bethel, he fell upon his knees and confessed himself a miserable, repentant sinner. "I suspect the quietness with which he conducted this effort at rebirth was not up to her precepts," their son wrote. "And I can understand Adah expressing her doubts as to the validity of this occasion; yet the honesty and justice of his nature must have hushed any doubt before all those who see with an inner eye" (14).

That same day, Randolph wrote a simple letter, asking if he might visit Adah with a view to matrimony. "He talked haltingly of the path this new vision had illuminated. . . . She knew firsthand that one must be 'born again' to be permitted the Kingdom of Heaven" (13). Her reply must have been positive, because they married two years later, on 19 February 1882. It was not a completely happy occasion. Adah's father was disappointed that his daughter had chosen beneath her. He was a hard man of God whom some thought pompous. Paul Swan remembered his grandfather as someone who had "no tentacles to his nature for a little boy to cling to. 'God's will,' a term he used so often, frightened me away" (28).

Perhaps it was the disparity in ancestors that bothered Adah's father. "Mayflower on one side; bird coop on the other" is how Paul Swan humorously explained his heritage:

I am a mythical descendant of William the Conqueror. This takes my tall tree back to 1000 AD. I do not claim this ruthless aggressor was named William Swan, for the name Swan was bestowed upon an illegitimate son because his high function for the state was as keeper of the flock of black swans at court. . . .

Perhaps the swan-coop was built near a small lagoon now effaced by the passage of time. It is possible my forebear lived not in the castle proper with other illegitimate or verified sons, but down in the village with his "back-street" mother, who must have been beauteous to the eye, since her royal lover could "pick and choose." Who knows about such domestic details? Suffice it to repeat that my name is Swan because of my forebear's occupation, and candidly I cannot imagine a more poetic or inspiring way to begin a dynasty. (8–10)

Although that cold grandfather Corson was always proud that his own great-grandfather arrived on America's shores by way of the *Mayflower*, Swan doubted the story of "that slightly overloaded vessel—how many reputed thousands claim it?" (10). (Curiously, he seemed more convinced of the equally romantic origins of the Swan name.) One story suggests that the ancestor in question was named Carsten Jansen, a Scandinavian who later settled near Cape May in New Jersey. At some point the last named changed to Corson, possibly as an evolution from Carstensen. Swan believed that another ancestor from his father's side had landed at Gravesend, Long Island, twenty years before. A Major Swan from the same family is reputed to have been a member of General Washington's staff following the Revolutionary War.[2]

For Paul Swan, however, these ancestors seemed remote and foreign, people with whom he had no connection. None were obvious artists or poets, and it seemed curious to him that he shared their blood: "Yet searching high and low I have not found hanging from the boughs of the long family tree the name of any other artist. Perhaps Conquerors and Puritans are just plain ordinaries mixed together and do not propagate the creative temperament. Who knows?" (10–11).

But two artistic families were in fact brought together in 1882 when Adah Corson and Randolph Swan wed. Everyone who knew Adah well also knew that she had a natural talent for drawing. Her religious beliefs did not allow her to value it, but her talent has been well documented by family. On the other side, Randolph's father had a similar genius.

The marriage almost didn't happen. On the day of the ceremony, an unusual midwinter rainstorm swelled the streams, and the preacher nearly drowned when he tried to cross one to reach the wedding party. Finally, to the relief of the nervous bride and groom, he arrived several hours late, disheveled and dripping, but determined.

The Swans began their life together in a little house between Ashland and Pleasant Hills, Illinois. There, on 5 June 1883, shortly after sunset, their first child was born, a son they named Paul Spencer. He always loved "the half-lights of *l'heure exquise*," and attributed this to his birth-time: "The bald glare of day distresses me. There are then only statements and no poetic suggestions" (15).

Paul wasn't an only child for long. Jesse Randolph arrived on 6 January 1885. After the Swans moved to Nebraska (when Paul was six), the rest of the cygnets were born in Crab Orchard (Johnson County): Harriet McClellan on 24 April 1887, Julia Corson on 22 February 1889, Belle Townsend on 21 November 1890, Karl Milton on 11 October 1892, Rollin Ray on 10 August 1894, Reuben Kent on 4 June 1896, Dallas Dewitt on 21 February 1898, and Eldon Wayne on 5 October 1904.[3]

A person who sought the limelight all of his life, Swan was not happy with sharing parental attention. For decades he harbored resentment toward his parents for producing "so many pilgrims," as he called his brothers and sisters. "The new fledglings crowded out the leisure for recreation, amusement, and mental improvement, and—let me use the word so lacking in our nest—sweetness. The house became too full of budding personalities" (53). Although he loved them ("because they were my brothers and sisters"), the additions only diminished the care he received from his parents: "That passionate and sense-drugged mortals can, by consummation of a sexual act, start another mortal down the current of life's dark river is, to me, more than frightening, considering how helpless we progenitors are to guide or protect or rescue the tender ignorant little flounderers" (16). Swan avoided this responsibility after he was married, for his two daughters were primarily the charge of his wife, Helen, who allowed him the freedom to travel and to pursue artistic and erotic adventures.

3. Adah Corson Swan with her son Paul about 1885. Photograph courtesy of Dallas Swan Jr.

As a little boy in Nebraska, Paul learned to keep to his room, drawing pictures of his family, or to sit outside sketching animals and trees. The farm he remembered distantly in adulthood was to the young boy a celebration of life, as long as he did not have to participate in its upkeep. Like the great Leonardo centuries before, he enjoyed watching the mighty horses at work in the field. They provided him with his first study of complex form. Next to the faces of his brothers and sisters, they were his earliest favorite subjects. When he showed his studies of horses to his mother, she was displeased and unhappy with his embarrassing depictions of "certain horsy attributes" (17). He continued his artistic experiments in secret. Years later, when newspapers labeled him "A Modern Leonardo," Swan credited old Baldie, Charlie, and Queenie with giving him the opportunity to learn "movement in art."[4]

He never drew Randolph Swan at work. It may be that he did not want to associate his father with the man who stood behind the horses, directing the plow. Randolph was "not a master unto himself," in his son's opinion. He was "the slave of all," "the butt of all professions," "the symbol of the ignorant, uninformed, ungenteel outsider": "Farmers lived in a land of fear: Poor sunburned, bony-handed slaves to sun, wind, cold, and the caprice of unfair markets, who work from dawn to dark, day in and day out for the span of their barren lives; cheated of all that make existence endurable; with no leisure, no moments of repose for the soul to look into its mirror" (53).

One day he found a headless doll discarded by his sisters and rescued it from the trash. It fascinated him — the tapering rounded line of the body, the graceful curve of the torso. His *line*, he said, his special artistic flair, "was from neck over breasts, to the point where the skirt is pleated according to the old corsets" (48). It gave him "an esthetic stimulation no one seemed to understand" and later was part of what attracted him to Greek sculpture. He began to borrow his sisters' dolls, constructing houses, carriages, churches, and even theaters in which these puppets could perform.

This was Swan's first attempt at staging; he would not see the inside of a real theater until he was seventeen. He used the empty corncrib on the farm "as a symbol of my after-life," his stage life in New York and Hollywood:

In this case my scenery was realized from the use of harvester canvas painted with the meager leavings in an old paint can. Green and red did not conform to nuance, but suggestion went far in those enthusiastic days of experimenting. Old lace curtains were part of our decor, and we [Swan and his sister Harriet] found that horse blankets had more than a thermal usage. The scene was illumined by a kerosene lantern still in use in rural parts, but we were obliged to go to bed so early in our country home that we rarely could indulge in the fullness of our effects. (49)

In one of his own plays, Paul dressed Harriet in a sheet so she would look like "the Eastern Angel on the cover of the *Christian Herald*." He cut a strip of tin roofing (without approval from his parents) for her "gold" fillet and used burnt matches as the source for makeup. He "transformed Harriet into something not real, that is to say theatrical [and] she looked amazingly the part of something far away" (50).

Swan called Harriet his "abettor" who possessed "a patient and lovable character. She was sweet and good and more understanding than any of the rest of us. She was the peace-maker, and her tears—if they did spring at some injustice or slight—moved us all to championship and rescue": "Many times I was severely scolded and accused of 'ruining' Harriet's naturalness. That is, I parted her hair and combed it flat over the ears like the photograph of my father's mother. But the beads I crowned her with made her head like that of my adored Cléo de Mérode [a dancer he admired]. In fact she was known to the corncrib theater by that assumed name. I've forgotten what mine was, but I'll wager it was something high-flown and decorative, more a thing of euphonic rhythm than an indicator of that petted word 'character'" (51).

Mommy Dearest
Adah, whose religious convictions were disturbed by the strange behavior of her oldest child, was a primary source of Swan's lifelong angst. As much as he loved her, he often criticized her behavior toward her husband and her children. Almost as soon as his parents produced siblings for him, Swan felt that he was different from them, and his mother, concerned about his "strange quirks," was often frustrated and angry with him. He seemed lazy and willful, and his brothers in

particular grew resentful. Swan had most trouble with Jesse, the next oldest, with whom he shared a room:

> He bore an unconscious contempt for my lackadaisical preoccupied, uninterested manner of getting through the long day. I dreamed night and day of other far-away things. At the first release from assigned tasks I flew upstairs, where a half-finished drawing reposed, waiting like the little toy dog for the hand that put it there. A drawing was always in process, so often interrupted, so often nearly completed. Even at noon hours, after midday dinner, while my father and Jesse slept stretched out on the floor by a cool doorway, I was sweating over some sort of creation—a drawing, a painting, or perhaps a mechanical toy. (45)

It was not beyond Adah to use fear in her attempts to control him. Once she terrified his young imagination by explaining that if he died without saying his bedtime prayer each evening, a fate far more frightening than death awaited. His little soul would be locked out of every door to salvation, and he would never see his loved ones again. "And if I forgot 'Amen' I was told to get down on my knees and append the word (whose meaning I knew not); otherwise the prayer was not valid and would remain below the ceiling" (18).

He described her in harsh terms as having "little sense of humor" or interest "in what was going on in her first child's mind." She "never tried to find out our points of view," "shouted in old-fashioned Methodist hysteria," was an "exalted, shrill-voiced woman," and too often displayed "emotional frenzy with tears and general accusation of treachery." Swan focused particularly on the religious stupidity (to him, at least) evident when she tried to frighten her children out of disobedience: "She had complete conviction that the Most High had . . . arrested his twirling of countless worlds, and had suspended himself just above the ceiling of our sitting room, and was straining his capricious ear for *her* supplications" (33). "She certainly put her Bible between herself and her children" (42).

On the other hand, some happy times were spent with Adah in her garden, where little Paul was captivated by the shapes and colors of the flowers she planted every spring. In the kitchen he liked to run his fingers over the painted designs on the pottery she used to serve her family meals; he would then reproduce them in drawings. He saved the occasional magazine, drawing the faces of people who stared back at him from the pages. They became like old friends. His favorite was the aforementioned dancer Cléo de Mérode, a mistress of King Leopold of Belgium. He had seen a photo of her in a journal and practiced drawing it over and over again until he had an exact reproduction, photographic in quality.

With the house in Crab Orchard filled with babies, Adah was too busy to spend much individual time with each child, but her son kept offering her his art to get attention, even trying his hand at several religious scenes. Once an evangelical preacher visited the family, and the young boy proudly brought forth his paintings. After looking condescendingly at the artwork, the preacher asked, "Um! What is Christ to you, my boy?" Like the toddler Pearl who was asked a similarly profound theological question in *The Scarlet Letter*, young Paul could not think of a reply. This lack of spirituality embarrassed his mother. "Instead of placating my childish disappointment, she merely said, encamped on the other side: 'Why don't you answer Brother S. when he speaks so nicely to you?' I blushed silently and with my drawings left the room. . . . My mother told me I was too much absorbed in art matters; that I was placing them between myself and God" (38).

Ironically, it was Swan's own mother who seemed to be the most direct link to his art: "When I was quite young, I remember, she would draw people's faces for me. I can see the peculiar flourish she gave to the nostrils; the ringlets of hair and the spiral curls; the ruching about the collars, which was then fashionable, and the tapering curved-lined basques" (48). But of course she never showed these to visiting preachers.

Adah had a "gift for making anything look like something." She made all of her children's clothes, even Sunday suits for her boys, and her use of color for her daughters' dresses won praise and perhaps envy from her less gifted neighbors, who sometimes called her "tony" and "stuck up." Swan did not share that opinion of his mother. In fact, he loved her most when she showed a bit of vanity, used her natural artistic genius, and painted her face or made pretty dresses. Once he watched her as she "crimped her brown hair over her too high forehead, held the second mirror the better to see her profiled effect, and in contrast to her daily housekeeping drudgery found leisure to correct with lead pencil her too-uncertain eyebrow" (52).

Swan never thought Adah cerebral and was convinced that her religion stifled any possibility for intellectual growth: "She was guileless and simple in her mental equipment as the young girl of nineteen my father married." His love for her—for in spite of their differences, he did love her—was born of pathos. "Adah the lost artist" would have had a better life, he knew, if she had let her talent direct her actions. For Swan, art was everything. When he wrote to his little brother Dallas in 1908, he told the ten-year-old, "I mean to be a great painter of beauty and nothing must come in my way."[5] He was convinced that his mother shared the same impulse but was imprisoned by her family and her religion:

> The only way to judge my mother fairly was, first, to visualize her life free from child-bearing, free also from the care and nursing of children, free from the worries of the house, with its washing, ironing, cooking, churning, and clothes-making; and secondly, to see her in robust health and with plenty of leisure and money to meet her needs. This would all have much changed the situation. She *should have had an opportunity to study art.* Pursuing art in an environment more broadly interested in the multifold aspects of life, she would not have found that it sufficed her to turn everything she experienced upon so centralized a pivot as her religious convictions. (52–53)

Adah's subconscious artistic urges served as rationale for her occasional coldness toward her firstborn. Art made him selfish; he understood that. He decided that it must be the same for her, even if she buried her passion in the deep recesses of her mind. No wonder she could not love him well enough. How could he blame her?

Although Swan thought his father had a more gentle nature, the two were never particularly close. But at six years old, Swan met the man who would be his model for life, someone who loved art—a natural, untrained talent with a kind heart and no interest in a vengeful God ("I believe he never went to church," Swan wrote in his memoir

[27]). Although Swan had only one opportunity to spend time with his paternal grandfather, William Chapman Swan had an enormous effect on him. A decorated Civil War veteran, he was well known in Zenia, Illinois, for his fiddling and wood carvings. In a few days he taught his clever grandson to play a couple of songs and to model figures. The two connected immediately:

> My grandfather carved . . . on gunpowder pouches made of cows' horns. He cut horses, Indians, deer running, birds and ornamental designs around the base and apex of the horns.
>
> I liked to watch him make these carvings. The expression of intense application on his face absorbed me. . . .
>
> This kind, knowing, Grandpa Swan also made the most wonderful animals out of dry cornstalks. He used the pithy part for heads, the section between the joints for the bodies, and splints from the bark for legs, necks, horns, ears and tails. These horses, pigs and cows would stand up on their proper four legs, and looked to me just like life.
>
> I learned to create also almost as perfectly as Grandpa did, except that his horses had better shaped heads.[6]
>
> I can still see this man, my grandfather, who, to my boyish thinking, could accomplish so many fascinating things. (28–29)

Adah didn't approve of her father-in-law's choice of "party music" and was probably distressed that her son had learned to play the fiddle so quickly. She told him more than once that "dancing was sinful amusement" (27). Had she forgotten how she met her husband, or did that memory influence her opinion? In any case, she did not encourage trips to Zenia.

First Loves, Lost Love

Disappointed in his mother's lack of affection, Swan resented his father for deferring to her when discipline was doled out. Feeling "disregarded more than abandoned" at home, the young boy instead found love elsewhere. The first occasion presented itself when the family was still in Illinois. Shortly before the move to Nebraska, Swan met Eddy McGovern, a sandy-haired, freckle-faced five-year-old classmate at Bunker Hill

4. *Adah Corson Swan* by Paul Swan. Graphite on paper, 15½ x 13 in. Swan wrote on the bottom, "Feb. 6, 1948. Adah Corson Swan—at 17." From the collection of Dallas Swan Jr. and Margaret Swan.

School. Even many decades later, Eddy's image was still clear in Swan's mind: blue eyes, "a charming *retroussé* nose," timid, shy, unassertive: "I dreamed about him at night. He occupied my waking thoughts. Oh, to be as wonderful as Eddy McGovern! He was my first adoration. I began to make an effort with my lessons to equal his perfection. I began to look forward to school, as Eddy was there, being the center of that great world of persons and new ideas" (20).

Swan drew pictures of Eddy and Eddy's friends to impress him, and it had its desired effect. "Soon the entire school, I remember, was hovering in admiration around my desk at noon-time, and thus stimulated, I was always at it, though I think the real urge came at the discovery that I could always achieve my effects, in some degree" (21). But it wasn't long before Swan was convinced that others despised him because of the attention he was getting.

> I was a favorite [of teachers] and thus not treated as the others. My gifts dug a gulf between me and my fellows. I did not know then why the mental intimacy I sought seemed always a will-o'-the wisp, or when I tried to look in the windows . . . the blinds to the windows would be quickly and tightly drawn, shutting me out. . . . Then as a little boy who thought life was fair, and living a pleasant dream, I saw only the wonder I could awaken in their eyes—the eyes of the usual, ungifted schoolmates. Being socially inclined, I have thus known bitter loneliness many times. Yet, I suppose, I learned from this loneliness all the little I know of the meaning of life. (21)

Was the jealousy more imagined than real? It was the beginning of a lifelong pattern: Swan craved attention, and when that attention was less than he considered to be his due, he often thought that others were plotting against him out of envy. Occasionally, he was right.

His attraction to Eddy was sincere but fleeting. When the Swans left Illinois, his affections easily switched to Libbie Robinson, a pretty Nebraskan redhead who made him forget the pain of lost love. He dreamed of her, too, of riding with her on a streetcar with brilliant lights, of sitting next to her with his arms around her, together "looking into a great book." He drew his fantasies on paper:

I have a feeling now that Libbie did not dream like this, or at all, of me; to be honest, I believe now that my longing glances across the schoolroom embarrassed her, even annoyed her.

The morning after the dream it was almost impossible, so vivid was the night's impression, to realize she did not know of the blissful feeling, of the streetcar, the brilliant lights, or the book, and that we were the only passengers. (31)

Stories he told to Jeanne Robert Foster, several of which are repeated in "The Distorted Shadow," suggest that such ideal childhood dreams did not last long.[7] An incident with an itinerant farmhand, coupled with religious guilt instilled in him by his mother, led to self-reproach and sexual confusion. One night when his parents were attending to one or more of their other children, a farmhand relaxing on the front porch invited little Paul to climb onto his lap. Swan always remembered the feeling of the strong arms around his small body, as if there were security and love in the man's touch. "I remember the hair on his arm, and how warm his dark face felt, and how round his thighs were under his workman's trousers." He felt guilty pleasure from the way the man stroked him. "I remember his name . . . for no other reason than the thrill of that evening's . . . experience" (24). It was a deep, secret pleasure. Swan could tell no one of his confused feelings without fear of a reprisal too horrible to imagine.

Adah's religious teachings did nothing to help him find solace. They made him at first fearful, then resentful, and finally, as an adult, enraged at the fundamentalism that he could never exorcise completely:

I was taught that anything of the flesh must be covered up as unthinkable, "do-able" only by people one didn't know, such as jailbirds and strange persons of stranger names who figured in the newspapers, and since my family subscribed to "The Christian Herald," . . . and "The Christian Advocate," the actual recounting of the unmentionable had been much diluted before our eager, questioning eyes encountered it.

Religion was a habit ingrained in the minds of my progenitors and the purification of the spirit was thought to be achieved by the complete unmentioning of the body's needs; the Puritan rigor over again, the breeder of suspicion and prying judge-of-correction attitude, the divorcement of nature from creed. (40–41)

It's easy to sympathize with Swan's predicament. Except for childhood moments with one sister, Harriet, he felt alien in his family. His own mother was too busy to spend much time with him; she had too many children. She did not help him understand his own sexuality; she was his model for religion's sublimation of natural talent: "It is a perplexing paradox that with the bearing of ten children my mother had not really the maternal instinct; that is to say, a heart understanding and sympathetic, full of instinctive protectiveness for her children's perplexities. Yet believing as she and my father did in the wickedness of contra-conception, they made way for Nature to warp their lives and ours by over-productivity" (53).

When Swan was about thirteen, his father finally decided that he must talk to his son about the natural urges of a man. He tentatively broached the subject of sex education by asking his son, "Are you pure?" It caught Swan completely by surprise. "I hope I am" was, he thought, the most appropriate answer, because he really didn't know. "Don't you know for sure?" Randolph asked. Somehow they both extracted themselves from the uncomfortable conversation, never mentioning the subject again. Later in the evening, though, he tiptoed into his father's study and removed *Dr. Gunn's Medical Book* from the shelf: "The anatomical drawings of sexual organs interested me enormously. I can clearly remember the feeling of guilt and secrecy which I experienced. To rob a strange house in the dead of night would be now a parallel feeling. Such forbidden fruit. . . . What should have been a pure ideal attitude toward one's powers was shaded by a guilty feeling of trespassing, even in possessing so natural a member—'the silent drooping poem that I carry and all men carry,' as Whitman sings" (59–61).

Shortly after his exploration into Dr. Gunn's book, Swan decided, like a child discovering there is no Santa Claus, that his parents' stories of hellfire and damnation were exactly that: stories. He observed that neighbors named Murphy, although Catholic, seemed quite human. According to Adah, to be a "Catholic" was to be lost to God's kingdom. "Her prejudice . . . was fixed and colossal, militant, active," Swan observed. Even if this harsh judgment was tainted by his flair for the dramatic and by his angry heart, he deeply felt it to be so. By the age of thirteen he refused to go to most revival meetings.

One evening Adah decided that the family would attend a meeting a short distance away, and this time Randolph insisted that Paul join them. The quiet, moonlit buggy ride gave no hint of events to come. Swan was not a belligerent passenger this time. He looked forward to watching the performance of the visiting preacher. This evangelist stood in front of his flock calling for sinners to confess. "Who here among us is on the side of the devil?" he shouted. Hoping (Swan later explained) to let others off the hook, firmly believing that "one bronco busted is worth a whole field of tame plugs," Adah Swan's eldest son arose: "I did half expect for a second or two . . . to be struck dead where I stood by a thunderbolt from the blue. It wasn't well for a jealous God to be napping at that instance, for I, like the fable of Aesop's camel, began to push my lenient master out of the tent." But, "The admonition I received on my way homeward through the peaceful country night was a contrasting event. Even their deity's tempering the wind to the shorn lamb was dreadfully taxed that night" (35–37).

There was no going back. One evening he and his brother Jesse sneaked out of the house after dark to meet the neighbors' son, an older boy, in a secluded field. There they were entertained with shocking, erotic stories. It seemed great fun, at first, to be disobedient, but on the way home Methodist guilt set in. Thunder rumbled in the distance, and a fearful Jesse began to cry. Swan suggested to his younger brother that they stop and pray to God to be forgiven for their vile sins. "So we knelt down in the moonlight, by the pond in the pasture, and asked humbly that these stories be erased from our minds. We soon arose feeling better, and ran full speed the remaining way home, as if to prevent the heavy-loaded confession from overtaking us" (57). But the naughty deliciousness of the tales often returned to conscious thought during safer daylight hours.

Not long after, Swan sneaked out alone into that same dark cornfield, where he shouted in the most manly voice he could muster, "Damn the Holy Ghost!"

He waited.

Nothing.

From that moment, he began a lifelong effort to be the maker of his own reality and the author of his own relationship with God. "It is too important to leave such matters to deputies," he later paraphrased William Blake to friends.

He began to take the Lord's name in vain more openly—an activity that drove his mother into earsplitting rage. At last he was having an effect on her. "Her blind earnestness, . . . her intolerance toward any interpretation of the Bible differing from her own, discolored an otherwise clear glass" (41–42). Swan thought his childhood had desensitized him to hurt and toughened him early for the hardships of life, but his memoir suggests that he was always sensitive and that old hurts remained raw. He never forgot and only partially forgave.

Although angry about his father's lack of support, he thought that Randolph Swan was essentially a good man who was overwhelmed and a little frightened by his wife's fundamentalism. Swan admired his father's sense of responsibility to keep his family fed and clothed, but his memoir, letters, and conversations with friends suggest that he sometimes deliberately crossed Randolph in order to get a response from him. Randolph, always searching for the least confrontational path, accepted that his eldest son was both troublesome and clever. He nicknamed him "Tackie" because of the child's precociousness. "Sharp, always a year older in the things you say than other children your age," he told him (17–18). But the relationship remained strained.

More by design than accident, Swan often embarrassed his father with odd behavior and strange dress. When it was his turn to help plow the fields, for instance, he covered his hands, face, and arms with burlap—even on the hottest summer days. Aware at an early age that he possessed unusual beauty, he hated the damaging bright sun and did all he could to avoid it. One day, a neighboring farmer could not contain his amazement any longer and in front of the fifteen-year-old asked, "What is wrong with your oldest boy, Ran?" The son noticed that his father did not answer but only shook his head and looked away in dismay. It was a moment that hardened Paul Swan, and he began to plot his escape.

5. *John Randolph Swan* by Paul Swan, 1925. Oil on canvas, 20 x 18 in. From the collection of Dallas Swan Jr. and Margaret Swan.

> What can I do with outsiders in my heart who cannot leave me and yet have no key to unlock the door behind which I live? **Paul Swan**, *Philosophical Musings*

3 Mentors and Lovers, 1897–1906

Flight from Crab Orchard

Uncompromising, fundamental, literal: a less powerful faith than Adah Swan's might have diminished Paul Swan's desire to escape Crab Orchard. When she placed God between herself and her eldest son, and made God the center of her universe, she marred her son and strengthened his resolve to remove himself, psychologically and physically, from further hurt. Adah's need to be devoted to God rather than to provide emotional safety for a complicated, unhappy, difficult little boy became paramount, at least in Swan's judgment. "If I put my art between me and God, as she said, she certainly put her Bible between herself and her children, even in her effort to guide their feet. She ignored the personal factor—the confidence which a child wishes to bestow upon an understanding parent" (DS 41–42). None of the other children left behind any record of serious conflict with either Randolph or Adah, but for her eldest son, her neglect was real.

His way to survive was to rebel, by skipping chores and refusing to go to church. What bothered him most was that she had misled him with her apocalyptic vision and had, at least for a time, arrested his own intellectual growth. He wrote in his memoir in the early 1930s:

The assurance that Christ will come to earth again in a cloud and pop down in front of my mother's window does not move me. There was a time when . . . I expected the "last day" to come every time I saw an especially beautiful bank of clouds at sunset, or every time the stormy nights rolled their fathomless echoes across zones of thunder. The blinding flashes of lightning were the voice of vengeance which struck so promiscuously, so incalculably. The moon rising like a red disc was the chariot wheel of Gabriel.

It is clear today; so have the veils blown from my eyes, that if the Last Day did come upon the earth some morning, it would not matter to me, as I am not in America, in Nebraska, more than I can help. (62)

Conflict between parent and child is not unusual, but in the case of Paul and Adah there were irresolvable issues. It is difficult to conceive positions more unrelenting and opposite than those held by this mother and child. For her part, Adah knew that God was on her side and that her son's opposition was proof that he was in Satan's power. She would not, could not, give an inch without risking her own damnation. Her son might have been inclined to compromise on some issues (he was, after all, the product of years of Adah's indoctrination), but her unwillingness to concede on any point made him more stubborn.

Adah wielded the power in the family, and whatever opinion Randolph had was clearly filtered through her. With no strong male model, and with a female that Swan both loved and despised, Jung's archetype of the terrible mother is implied. The parent who should be most nurturing, most accepting, instead rejected what Swan considered the very essence of his being. Modern opinion has it that homosexuality is not so much shaped by experience as it is inherent, but if there was ever a reason to turn away from the conventional and embrace the unusual, Adah provided it.

Tensions grew and wounds festered. Swan's misbehavior became more blatant. His father stepped in, finally, to try to control the situation. Randolph's patience had certainly been tested as he watched a rift grow between his son and just about everyone else. What entitlement allowed *him* to escape the hard work? Why should *he* get to languish in bed when the cows needed milking? Why should *he* challenge the Word of God and not be punished? Randolph had enough one summer night in 1898 and whipped his son. What initiated the event is not known, but Paul remembered the occasion with great clarity: "They preferred to make me feel in the wrong when they should have understood my sensitivity and championed it as a valuable asset" (86).

The "spasm of punishment" Swan received the night his father struck him cut deep: "What fanatics parents are, who can bring physical pain to their own flesh and blood—though years more tender—for some offense of mere disobedience of most fallible interpretation!" (86). He ran away, but only as far as the family's barn, where he spent a miserable night, tired and hungry, listening to rats scurry, waiting for his parents to come looking for him. The next morning he thought they must be frantic and so returned to the house. "I thought they would surely take me to their arms and promise never to whip me again. . . . [Instead] my father made a jesting comment on my absence and . . . my mother asked me to bring her a pail of water from the well" (87).

One Sunday in September, the day before school began, he decided to run again. He tied up some belongings in a knapsack and, like many a fractious young boy before him, set forth on an adventure. He wanted to go to school in Tecumseh, seven miles away, because he had finished at nearby Rose Hill. Quite reasonably, Randolph and Adah said no. Swan saw this as their retribution: they wanted to make him suffer by keeping him in Crab Orchard.

Later he understood better that "youth is blind, so that only the desired consummation appears to [one's] impetuous eye" (88), but at fifteen he saw only possibility:

> I wanted to be a "town boy" who wore his Sunday clothes every day and still kept clean. I wanted a white-pink face not burned brown by constant exposure to wind and sun. . . . I wanted to be far away from the smell of sweating horses, the smell of cows, and the smell of hogs, away from the smell of barn lots and pens. . . . The boys in our rural neighborhood seemed like colts with shaggy hair at the end of winter. . . . I wanted to be educated and cultured, and to possess graceful, polite ways. (88)

After the rest of the family had gone to church (Swan had refused), he left a note on the kitchen table and walked out the door. Twenty years later, on a rare visit home, he found the note tucked into a family Bible:

Parents:

Do not think hard of me. I could not help it. I will help you back sometime.

Do not tell everybody. If I cannot get a place soon I will come home.

I cannot think of school beginning without going. . . .

Perhaps I am doing wrong but maybe I am right. I would wait till you come home but it would be too late then. If you knew how my mind was upon it I think you would get along some way.

Perhaps you will think I am very wicked.

From your . . . . son.
Please forgive. Paul.

P.S. I will pay you back some day—I cannot help it. (91–92)

It was a "warm and summery" afternoon, with barely a hint of changing leaves or approaching harvest. He thought of Randolph and Adah returning home to find him gone. Would they come and get him before he reached Tecumseh? "I tried to remember they did not always suffer as I thought they should" (93).

Swan's memoir and letters are replete with examples of his often self-deprecating sense of humor. Although feelings of entitlement and solipsism dominate his writing, he also laughs at himself, ridicules his silly behavior, and hints at his immaturity. But often the humor has an edge: "I tried to remember they did not always suffer as I thought they should." As he told his story, he would say this with a smile on his face, brush in hand, while putting the finishing touches on a portrait. Someone who knew Swan well would know better than to ask, "Why *didn't* they come after you?"[1]

Randolph did, a week later. It was perhaps wise for parents to let their wandering Tom Sawyer have his adventure for awhile.

After a few miles on the road, Swan realized that his great escape was getting a bit unpleasant. His neck itched as his white starched shirt grew damp with sweat. He was getting hungry but thought he should save food for later in the day. He didn't care about discomfort. He was going in the right direction, away from Crab Orchard and toward "the hallowed domain of High School" (93).

The Apperson family of Tecumseh was at that hour out for a Sunday drive in their carriage. When they passed a tired-looking young man with a knapsack tied to a stick, slung over his shoulder, Anna Apperson leaned forward and tapped her husband's shoulder. "Stop here, and give that poor boy a ride." She and her children seemed so friendly during the journey that the teenager was happy to tell them of his dreams. "Then you will stay with us, and Mr. Apperson will take you to school tomorrow," Anna Apperson told him. Paul Swan's life would never be quite the same.

That night he found himself in a beautiful home where "no one became loud of voice or threatening of manner. No one sulked or scolded." Alone in a large bedroom, he suddenly missed his brother Jesse and his parents. "My heart ached for my father and mother. How could they ever forgive so wicked a son?" But then, when he awoke the next morning, "I thought of the milking which must be done, and I was glad I held fast to my purpose" (94). He was not late in rising that day. He was going to high school.

"How goes it, Paulie?" his father asked a week later in the Appersons' living room. His tired parents had decided to let him stay where he was, at least for the time being, and Randolph brought some new shirts that Adah had made. The Appersons assured Randolph that his son would earn his keep by helping with household chores—cooking, sweeping, and washing dishes. Satisfied that the situation was good for all (and perhaps a bit relieved), Randolph drove off in the wagon pulled by his two mules, Old Jack and Florrie. "I watched this good man in his shirt-sleeves drive toward home," Swan recalled. "I was strongly impelled to run after him and beg him to forgive me for wanting so much the things our home on the farm could never seem to give" (97).

Swan understood the goodness of his father's heart at that moment, and later wrote, "Parents rarely receive their full valuation until they are gone." But in a characteristically double-edged statement, he continued: "Parents should be used for the new generation and not vice versa.

The child owes the parent no thanks except for the love which cancels all debts. If the debts are not cancelled by love, then they deserve the ingratitude they often find. This seems to be the living scar in my inner heart, the sense of something unforgiven; a faint shadow of unfairness; an unresolved difference like a fissure in a wall suggesting division instead of union" (97).

Swan was intending to write what he called "a psychological memoir" when he penned these words, so it was natural for him to consider all the sources of his feelings. Several publishers rejected the book, perhaps because by page 100 the sometimes turgid prose and self-absorbed tone convinced them to stop reading. Nor was his vanity confined to publication attempts. In letters he wrote to friends like Jeanne Foster or French courtesan Fernande Lara Cabanel (see chapter 6), or to family members when he asked for money, the theme is the same: Paul Swan and his needs are paramount. Yet it is this self-absorption, this sense of entitlement, this perfect egoism that—when combined with his humor, insecurity, and compassion—made him the complex man he was.

Swan's insecurity during high school years is illustrated in a relationship with a fellow student named Raymond Albertson. Decades later, after Swan had the experience of living with his partner Fred Bates in Paris, he understood that his sexual urges were inexorably intertwined with his artistic impulses. But when he was only fifteen and straight off the farm, Swan saw Raymond as an idealized David and himself as David's Jonathan. His impulses were confusing and no doubt frightening: "A sexual urge . . . it may have been. . . . I realized, during this spell of enchantment, only the religious phase of a poetic worship" (99).

A public declaration (it is unclear exactly how Swan announced his love) only humiliated him when a no doubt confused and apprehensive Raymond "turned upon me the insults and ridicule of his true nature. Many other students were present at this tragic moment and I never forgot that the fair can be most unmerciful. I had then no philosophy to meet this turn of the wheel" (98–99). There were many other incidents in his life when Swan, who certainly included himself among "the fair," was equally unmerciful to those who courted him. Just as Groucho Marx would not join a club that would have him for a member, Swan often distrusted those who professed to love him, particularly at the height of his fame.

After the fiasco with Raymond, Swan turned to Flossie Whittaker. What motivated him to choose the teenage daughter of a Methodist minister? Was it a move to supplicate or please his mother, or a way to get revenge? Could Flossie have in some way represented Adah? According to Swan, Flossie made the first move, determined to make a conquest of the handsome teenager. "I took my cue and blushed girlishly," and before long the crush "ripened into bloom—a most roseate affair" (102). But Swan saw the relationship more as a chance to act the puppeteer, pulling strings to see how he could make Flossie jump.

He wasn't completely insincere: "I loved her, or more accurately . . . her professed emotions." His was a passionate, sexual, youthful adoration. At this time in his young life, Swan fell in love with girls as easily as he did with young men. He was just beginning to realize his sexuality, and being attracted to a female was certainly easier to profess publicly. He may have been what Marjorie Garber in *Vice Versa* calls a sequential bisexual, a man who once loved both men and women and, finally, by the end of his life, was exclusively homosexual (129). In any case, after several weeks, Flossie sent him a note confessing that she had a new beau. "I was humiliated," Swan wrote in his memoir.

It was a brief liaison, but Swan's recollections expose a peculiar meanness of nature. Did Flossie's rejection merit an attack on her character forty years later? He intended his injurious words for publication, knowing full well that Flossie, or at least some of her family, would likely still be living: "I never forgave her . . . until the years had buried her under a thousand others who likewise served me. . . . I [was] condemned to see her accompanying many young men of most inartistic flavor, into dark alleys and parks where passers-by were scarce, where the actual and carnal she sought in me could be realized with these male elements who never bored her with verses on the moon. This long story symbolizes my affairs with Alice, Maude, Myrtle, Bertha, Jane, and Betty" (104–5). A silly (his adjective) story about himself that he could at first "hardly remember" transforms to symbolize his treatment of many other women. Like Swan's own mother, Flossie had rejected him; he would get even.

Mrs. Apperson was his best friend during all of these dramas, letting him know that she believed in his integrity through all of his learning experiences. However much she may have liked her young boarder, she had the advantage of not being a worried parent.

Swan returned home during the next two summers to help his family with the farm. Randolph insisted that he sign a contract regarding his duties, but it didn't do much good. He had become too used to Tecumseh and the Apperson home to keep his end of the bargain. At the beginning of the second summer, when he was seventeen (1900), he flatly refused to help in the fields: "Never again," he declared (105).

Understandably, Randolph told him to leave. From the perspective of twenty-first-century child care philosophy, he may seem unduly harsh. Certainly the cognitive powers of a seventeen-year-old are not developed enough to prepare him for all that he might encounter. But Paul was a disruption in the family. How long would it have been before his brothers, who were already complaining about Paul's special treatment, decided that they might try taking unscheduled holidays from their farm duties? Randolph was confronted with choices that he did not want to make, but what was one to do with such a son?

With a little money and a head filled with dreams, Paul left for Lincoln, some sixty miles from Crab Orchard, where he found employment as an assistant window trimmer in Herpolsheimer's department store, with a weekly salary of five dollars. At first the Lincoln years (from ages seventeen to nineteen, 1900–1902) seemed filled with failure and disillusion, but the experiences there made Swan confront more seriously who he was and what he was to become. From his earliest visits to theaters, to a sexual solicitation from an older man, he discovered that he was someone very much alone in a world he found dull, if not despicable.

Big-City Life

The first professional dramatic production Swan saw was *Corianton*, starring Joseph Haworth.[2] It was an epiphany for him. He felt a rush of joy, of energy that "fired me with longing to appear on stage" (106). He decided to organize his own troupe of Herpolsheimer employees to produce Sir Edward Bulwer-Lytton's *The Lady of Lyons, or Love and Pride*, with himself as the leading character, Claude Melnotte. Claude, the foppish young man who goes off to war and returns a conquering hero, particularly appealed to Swan. Unfortunately, most of the other employees at Herpolsheimer's found their daily routines enough to keep them entertained, and though some expressed interest, and even practiced with him a bit, the troupe never materialized. "Being a 'beautiful youth' was not enough to inspire adherents in Herpolsheimer's" (106). But the dream at least had been dreamt.

By this time, Swan was a handsome, facile seventeen-year-old with little understanding of how to handle his feelings. No longer just a pretty little boy, he was attractive to a more adult population in Lincoln. For the first time he faced a darker, more frightening element of humanity.

One of Herpolsheimer's more distinguished customers, a gentleman of some standing in the local area, became friendly with the young clerk and asked him to his apartment. Swan had few friends in the city and was happy to have the invitation. Why he decided to create an oriental garb from discarded store window material and go to the man's apartment dressed as "a veiled daughter of the desert" is unknown. Although he attributes this to "a silly caprice" (107), could he have at some level been presenting himself to this customer as a possibility? He would have denied it, but it was at the very least an unusual fashion choice for the occasion. When he arrived, the landlord mistook him for a woman and refused to admit him. The confusion was soon cleared up when Swan spoke and showed his full face—although the landlord was no doubt perplexed by the entire production. In any case, his newfound friend received Swan, and the evening's dalliance began.

It was a pleasant few hours, and Swan agreed, when asked, to spend the night. His less attractive and lonely room did not appeal to him. He had been used to sharing a bed with his brother Jesse at home, but one wonders if he could have been so innocent as to think the older man had nothing else in mind. And yet, for a lonely teenager in 1900, perhaps a distinguished customer seemed quite safe: "When we were in bed and the lights were out, he began to narrate to me his indulgences in the unsanctified pleasures of man or woman. The calculated effects upon my idealistic mind revolted me with his obscenity. This situation alarmed me beyond speech. So my loneliness had led me to his bed, as he had planned. I got up, put on my absurd costume, and stole along the silent street to my home, disgusted but wiser" (107).

Whether this experience had anything to do with Swan's changing behavior is not clear, but shortly thereafter he took to dressing like a young woman to join his landlady's daughter and her friends on various expeditions around Lincoln. He enjoyed fooling people and was surprised and intrigued to draw more glances from men than from women.

Cross-dressing soon became unpleasant for him. It didn't adequately satisfy his dramatic impulse or need for attention. There were, perhaps, not enough people looking at him, and the fun became boring. Later in life he abhorred female impersonators as dramatic performers, thinking it a "ridiculous travesty of a man underneath the woman's costumes by adding breasts and diminishing in other ways the appearance of masculinity, such as the use of a falsetto voice and mincing gestures, frizzy wigs, and *precieuse* expressions of the painted face. These *grotesques* excite the curiosity of the mob, but repel a sensitive artist" (108). Like Yukio Mishima decades later, whose book *Sun and Steel* advocates rigorous exercise as a tribute to the body, Swan always felt that one should engage in physical training and make the body, male or female, a thing to admire.

This dedication to natural form is also what finally made him more comfortable with his sexual appetites than one would expect from someone who lived when bisexuality was shameful and illegal. At least by age twenty, Swan had begun to think that he belonged philosophically and emotionally to another age, a Hellenic one where bisexuality did not suffer the consequences found in twentieth-century America, where art was, at least in Swan's view, the culture and life and the air that was breathed. He began to form a definition of himself, connecting his own ideas to the aesthetic movement of the late nineteenth century.

Two years of window dressing wore him out, physically and mentally, and he quit. He missed his family, but he dared not return home, because nothing had changed; he still was not going to muck stalls or plow the fields. He had another home once, near Ashland, Illinois, and so he headed northeast toward his earliest memories.

His mother's Aunt Leah and Uncle Rodman took him in, perhaps because one simply didn't leave the eldest son of a favorite niece adrift.

With them, Swan found almost as many rules as at his own mother's home, and all equally centered around a cold Methodism he refused to recognize. They clucked and frowned and no doubt wondered how good Adah Corson could raise such a heretic. They would have none of his misguided behavior and at one point demanded that he participate with them in a ten-day Methodist camp meeting in Springfield. He had no choice if he wanted to stay. He had little money, didn't want to return to Nebraska, and wanted a rest from the drudgery of a working-class existence. In any event, Springfield might prove interesting.

If there was a trace of devotion left in him for his mother's faith, it was extinguished by that trip. His relatives did not make much effort to hide their dislike of him, nor he of them. When he saw his aunt "groveling in the straw and clasping the mourners' bench, as if it were the Rock of Ages," he could only laugh, he said, and think her completely absurd (112). She, in the meantime, observed him lingering outside the preaching tent, charming young women, young men, and even a preacher or two with his boyish good looks and articulate, engaging conversation.

In his memoir, Swan acknowledges that Methodist guilt damaged him and contributed, by contrast, to his bohemian lifestyle. The arts—dancing, painting, sculpting, acting—all provided an avenue for him to express urges that fundamentalist Methodism had taught him were foul and evil. His anger toward those who were duped by what he considered silly and destructive teachings led him to embrace the opposite.

Aunt Leah, Uncle Rodman, and Paul lived an uneasy existence after their return from Springfield, and he knew his days in that household were numbered. Still he lingered on, reading his uncle's library, including favorite stories by Ella Wheeler Wilcox, Anthony Hope, and Richard Harding Davis. He particularly liked Davis's tales, which were illustrated with drawings by Charles Dana Gibson of "Gibson Girl" fame. Little did he know that he would become good friends with Wilcox, or that another future friend, Jeanne Foster, was already modeling in New York City for Gibson and Gibson's competitor, Harrison Fisher.

Fear provided Swan with the impetus to quit Ashland late in the summer of 1902. One Sunday, still under the household laws of his relatives, he attended church in nearby Bethel: "I beheld a pale face which I loved and ached to possess in embrace. Strange to say, this was . . . where my father looked for the first time upon my mother, 'the blue-eyed Corson girl' " (114). He saw before him the life his mother and father had made: ten children and grueling work, hard land and tired minds, and sublimation of artistic impulse. He left Ashland and the "pale face which I loved," almost immediately, for Chicago.

Although Swan had not thought of freeloading as a career choice, these early adventures led him from one relative to another, until he was made too uncomfortable to stay, or was simply asked to leave outright. Such was the case in Chicago. The trial of getting there on a hog train warned him that his dreams of fame might have a more earthy outcome, but he was determined to dream. Sometimes he was mean-spirited; sometimes his sense of entitlement irritated friends and family; but often the world could be falling apart around him and he would still believe in the beauty of shape and color, and in life itself. When the stench of the farm bothered him most, he saw perfection in the muscular form of a sweaty workhorse. Years later in Paris, as Nazi shadows seemed everywhere, he created some of his best artwork, almost as if the fear and loathing that worked against beauty helped him to define it.

In Chicago, Swan arrived at his mother's cousin's home quite un-expectedly. Hattie greeted him warmly, anyway. Adah was beloved by her relatives, and everyone embraced her son.

For a time.

He may have lingered too long abed in the mornings, or he may have been too comfortable to consider joining the working class he had grown tired of in Lincoln. He might have acted kind and polite and helpful, but he simply wore out his welcome. He was no doubt somewhat vague when Hattie asked him how long, exactly, he planned to remain with her family: "I thought a relative, no matter how much removed, was naturally a friend, but after two weeks I was told . . . that they needed my room to dry their annually washed lace curtains" (117).

After he left Hattie's, he tutored a young woman whom he consid-ered "a dolt." The family required that he live in their home, and even though one might wonder why they would invite a handsome young man to occupy the room next door to their teenage daughter, Swan saw it as an opportunity to stay longer in Chicago. He soon decided that his student "needed tutoring in a way no human could compass," and apparently verbalized the fact: "The father told the mother to tell the daughter to tell me that my intellectual services were no longer required" (118).

His job as a housecleaner for an aristocratic family named Harmon was also doomed before it began. They didn't mind, they told him, that he was artistic, as long as he was a hard worker. "There was not really an understanding member of the household," Swan remembered. "I was told . . . that with all my rug-beating, bathroom cleaning and dishwashing, I did not nearly earn my place" (119). Considering his aversion to such tasks, one might wonder how many rugs he actually beat.

Bedbugs literally drove him from his next position, serving as tutor for a young man on North Dearborn Street. (Swan often slept in the bathtub to escape the insects.) He described his charge as "a sickly hunchback, who had been, since birth, a spoiled, precocious invalid, disagreeable, uncanny, intuitive, contrary, and completely unlovable." And, most unforgivable, "his mother spoke of opera singers as great artists . . . and shaved the moustache from her upper lip and chin every morning" (120). That Swan remembered such details thirty or forty years later is curious. Sadly, he did not see an opportunity to instill in his young charge a sense of the beauty that was such a part of his own life. His harsh words seem incongruous with later stories his friends tell of his generosity to a nearly deaf boy and several elderly indigents whom he befriended in the 1960s.[3]

When Swan saw an advertisement for a Chicago theater group, he tried out for a role in *Carmen*. As an extra in the mob scene, he experienced the thrill of audience and met fellow actors. One such introduction resulted in his first commissioned painting, that of well-known actress Grace Reals, who played the lead.

But one commission did not pay the rent. He answered an advertisement that sounded hopeful, "artist wanted," and began a short employment of creating small oil paintings on frames. The room where he worked was cold and damp. Poor eating habits, little money, and seedy lodgings contributed to a bout of inflammatory rheumatism. A doctor feared tuberculosis. The train that had taken him so full of hope to Chicago, to dreams of the Art Institute, now took him back to Crab Orchard. He was twenty years old and sick.

Adah and Randolph greeted their son with concern and open arms. He made it clear that he intended to leave as soon as he was well, and so there were no efforts to lure him back behind a plow. In such a crisis, they didn't seem to care. First priority for Adah was nursing her son back to good health. Other problems paled for the moment.

When he did return to Chicago several months later, in 1903 (there was, after all, no tuberculosis), Swan was hired to pose for drawing classes at the Art Institute. The instructors soon discovered that their model could draw at least as well as their students and arranged for him to be admitted. He paid for his tuition by continuing to model and by taking charge of a large costume room where instructors kept props for period paintings.

John H. Vanderpoel and Lorado Taft quickly became interested in their new pupil.[4] Swan always credited Vanderpoel for training in drawing figures, and Taft for teaching him to create the sense of texture (particularly in clothing) with both oils and clay. Decades later, when Swan won a medal for a sculpture at the Paris Salon, he paid tribute to these two men who had spent so much time with "the farm boy."[5]

Unfortunately, he continued to have difficulty in personal relationships; he thought other students at the institute were jealous. One day, a group staged a hazing. Several held Swan by the arms and legs while two others cut his unconventionally long locks. A few students came to his aid, and a big enough fray resulted that reports of it were published in the *Chicago Tribune*. Although Swan was grateful enough to treat his rescuers to an evening out (to see Julia Marlowe's *Fools of Nature*), he was wounded that peers disliked him so much. All of his life he would accuse people of jealousy, but a close examination of his letters, his memoir, and conversations with friends reveals a man who searched for love and affection at every turn. When he did not find it, he became the victim (at least in his opinion) of envious hearts.

Swan left the school after a few months. He attributed his departure to destitution: he didn't earn enough money to feed himself or purchase warm clothing. He often changed rooming establishments when he was temporarily broke, and during one difficult period he lived in the costume room at the Art Institute, unbeknownst to the administration.

But other factors may have figured in as well. Swan met "someone who seemed a vision of ideal beauty" and fell in love. He "worshipped indiscreetly" and was "consumed by this nameless torment" who finally "ridiculed, scorned, even insulted me. I was wounded time after time, but persistently I followed my Uranian star into the black valley of despair."[6] *Uranian* was a term first used by German writer Karl Ulrichs to characterize an "inverted man," or one who has a "woman's spirit in a man's body" (Chauncey 49). Swan accepted this as his nature and considered his ability to see the essence of beauty in both female and male forms as, simply, part of being the complete artist.

In this case the beauty was female, a young woman named Ella House from Lewiston, Nebraska, not far from Crab Orchard. Swan probably met her in 1903 when he returned home during his illness. Now back in Chicago, he missed Ella intensely. He abruptly decided to change schools and dreams, from the institute for artists to the state normal school in Peru, Nebraska. He would be a teacher and prepare himself for a life that might be better suited to supporting a young wife.

Home, Again

Swan seemed born with a sense of isolation that he carried with him to Lincoln and Chicago. Nothing changed in Peru. He was an unhappy and dull student who often had his nose in an unassigned book of verse instead of the required algebra or grammar text. His favorite poet was Byron, who made him dream of far-off places and romantic adventures. "When April's blooms unfurl again, / 'Tis then I'll think of you"—an example of Swan's own attempts at this time—shows him to be a conventional poet at best, but filled with a yearning he could not satisfy. Somehow he received his certificate before any major catastrophe befell him, and he took the teachers' examination in August 1904.

When Flora B. Quick hired him to teach at a school in Red Willow County, she thought she was hiring someone with more experience. Swan embellished his résumé with false credentials, but no one checked, and he was hired. He began his career in September in District no. 4, in the far southwest corner of Nebraska, bordering the Kansas state line.

Before he left, he spent time with Ella. He sculpted a primitive bust of her, perhaps one of his earliest attempts—a roughly shaped head that does not capture the beauty of his dark-eyed friend. Ella's family still owns the bust, along with photographs of the two young lovers and one letter that Paul wrote on 17 September 1904, a few days before he left Crab Orchard to begin his teaching career:

> I have been thinking so much about you and how much I love you and how much you are to me and how long it will be before we meet again. . . . Oh, Ella how I do love you, you know I do, don't you dearest. . . .
>
> To me you are the most beautiful, pure and good of any one in this whole world and I love you more every day. . . .
>
> I know you love me and would trust you to the end of the world.

What ended the romance is not clear, but Swan wrote in his memoir that they stayed in touch until 1911, when all contact was severed. "But my heart had broken first. . . . I had learned to say: 'I love you, but what is that to you?' " (123).

Swan's own behavior may well have convinced Ella to end the affair. His good standing with colleagues and students in Red Willow County did not last long. He became strongly attached to one of his pupils, a "full-grown youth of eighteen" named Forest Weaver. Nowhere does Swan admit a sexual relationship, but at the very least he acted unprofessionally. He and Forest began "rehearsing" scoldings and punishments that Swan would give Forest in front of other students so they wouldn't think he was such a pet. When Swan decided to take a room near Forest's own home, he was fired. He blamed the dismissal on the school director's wife, claiming that she made up stories about his being tardy to work too often—which may have been true. No matter, he was glad to leave at the end of his first year (June 1905) and immediately found his way back to Chicago, hoping to find that the art world was finally ready to embrace him.

He got employment as a photographic colorist and, for once, liked his employer (some vestiges of this job can be discerned in later life, when Swan would improve his own publicity shots by inking in—or out—parts of his physique). But some customers complained that the work was "too artistic"—he added his own flair to escape boredom—and although the shopkeeper tried to sell the pieces as "art," he had no choice but to fire Swan, who said that he could not become less artistic. By this time his former student Forest had joined him, and although Swan had little money, at least he was not alone.

He auditioned for the William Owen Theater Company, not really expecting to get a position. They hired him immediately to begin a season's tour in St. Charles, Illinois, for a weekly salary of twenty dollars. It was a good position but had its price. He was away from Chicago for a number of weeks, and Forest felt lonely. He finally packed his bags and wrote to Swan that he was going back to Nebraska. They did not meet again until 1913, when Swan appeared at the Odeon Theater in St. Louis as a celebrity. Forest had become a streetcar conductor by then. It was a brief meeting of two friends who had found far different worlds.[7]

Late that autumn of 1905, Swan was cut from the William Owen Company when it came under new management. He returned to Chicago, taking what must have been for him a humiliating position at Mandel Brothers department store to make fashion drawings and decorative paintings for window displays, for a weekly salary of fifteen dollars. This was not the art world of which he had dreamed, and he grew despondent. Professor Vanderpoel, still his friend and adviser, encouraged him to keep trying. Although Vanderpoel's words carried weight, Swan was tired, "wretched," unable to operate in a "time-punched existence" (126). In the spring of 1906, with nowhere else to go, he headed again to Crab Orchard. He took employment as a teacher for the local school, where four of his brothers and two sisters were among his students. One can only imagine the problems that arose from such a situation. To complicate matters, Swan lived at home. There he was merely the older sibling, required to share household duties. It was a tinderbox waiting for a spark.

Anna Apperson, who nine years earlier had rescued him from his first runaway attempt, remained Swan's close friend, and he was a frequent

6. Paul Swan, about 1905. Photograph from Swan's scrapbooks courtesy of the collection of The John and Mable Ringling Museum of Art, the State Art Museum of Florida.

visitor to her home. Mrs. Apperson saw before her a handsome young protégé whose dreams she enjoyed encouraging. They shared tea as he delighted her with stories of his theater experiences. On the opposite end of the spectrum were his parents, who did not understand or approve of their errant son. One day, Adah Swan felt obliged to call on Mrs. Apperson to ask that she stop filling her son's head with silly dreams. Chicago, Adah informed her, made Paul forget God. Whether Mrs. Apperson was angry over Adah's interference (Swan was, after all, now twenty-three years old) or simply felt it best to be honest with Paul about his mother's visit, the result was yet another explosion in the Swan household: "This was the last straw! When I recalled how I had nearly starved; how I had struggled with stupid, visionless people; how I had endured those who thought they were generous. . . . All this travail I had passed through in order to go forward even so slightly toward the realization of a career!" (127).

It is of course impossible to reconstruct the scene between the two women, but it's likely that Adah's concern for her son's soul was tinged with jealousy. It was enough that Paul look for a mother figure elsewhere, but it must have been particularly galling that he chose a woman so steeped in worldliness as Anna Apperson.

So Adah Swan watched her firstborn leave home once more. All she had ever wanted was to raise her children and make them productive, God-fearing members of society. But Paul was beyond understanding. His only thought was to get away from her: "I say again I never forgave my misguided mother for trying to cut off from me my only real friend . . . who believed in my budding gifts" (127).

It was with overwhelming sadness, no doubt tinged with a sense of regret, that Randolph again said farewell to his eldest son. He would always love "Tackie," but he had to send him on his way, knowing that Paul jeopardized family unity.

This time the young artist would cast the net farther afield. In three days he would be in New York City.

> . . . to burn always with this hard gem-like flame
> . . . poetic passion, the desire of beauty, the love
> of art for art's sake.
>
> **Walter Pater**, *Studies in the History of the*
> *Renaissance*

4 Apprentice to Adonis, 1906–1911

Meeting Helen

Taken aback by the intensity of Adah Swan's religious fervor, Anna Apperson decided to provide Paul with a means of escape. After purchasing his train ticket to New York City, she stood on the platform, waving good-bye to her young friend: "Her constant belief strengthened my wavering, quixotic nature," Swan recalled in his memoir. "Her vision of me made it impossible to fail. . . . She condoned my natural egotism. . . . She condemned to the deepest limbo anyone who dared to detract from my worth. She taught me I was unique, in gifts, in person and in charm" (DS 128).

It was a long ride through that night, another day, and another night before Swan reached "some place in New Jersey" on 14 May 1906 and was ferried across the Hudson to New York City. As he settled into his room at the Bartholdi Hotel, he felt a happiness that even his first arrival in Chicago could not match. He arose the next morning, confident that his talent would be quickly recognized. When he left the hotel after breakfast, he carried a few drawings under his arm and twenty dollars in his pocket.[1]

New York City was filled with life and energy, and he was sure he belonged at the center of that vitality. He stopped to watch a police parade, pushing through the crowd for a glimpse of the bluecoats. Later he made his way, portfolio in hand, to *McClure's* magazine. After a brief, unsuccessful interview, he was on the street again, not in the least daunted. No one knew his name, yet; but certainly some discerning editor would give him a chance.

When he stopped for lunch at Childs' Restaurant on Twenty-third Street, a noted gathering place for gays, he struck up a conversation with a Dr. Rosenberg about the menu. When that gentleman heard that Swan was an artist, he mentioned that his wife was a fashion artist at Butterick and Company and that his good friend Mr. Rebele worked on the staff of the company magazine, the *Delineator*. He asked Swan to meet him there, at Spring and MacDougal streets, the next Monday afternoon for an introduction.

Mr. Rebele greeted him a bit brusquely: "Can you do good heads and hats? We're looking for a good head man." Swan set to work, all day, drawing heads decorated with various styles of hats. When the editor saw the results, he only said, "How much do you want?" Swan had no idea, asked for thirty dollars a week (a fortune to him), and was hired (132). New York was surely the land of milk and honey.

Swan found more permanent lodgings for eight dollars a week at an establishment run by a middle-age French landlady "with ugly lips and queer blotchy skin" (134). He said little to her when he discovered her in his apartment a few weeks later kissing a nude painting he had done of himself. She fled from the room, never giving him cause for concern again. Of course he could not fault her taste, even if demonstrated in such an unusual way. Life was good. He rented a piano, bought silk sofa pillows, and for the first time felt some control over his destiny.

Mr. Rebele and Swan worked well together. On several occasions, Swan accompanied him home to meet the rest of the family. They were friendly, but as on so many occasions in his life, he grew bored with them and was disappointed that Mr. Rebele's favorite topic of conversation was favorably comparing his possessions to those of his neighbors.

At the *Delineator*, Swan punched a timecard every morning, sat at his desk, and drew his daily allotment of heads with hats. It was good pay for such work, but after nearly a year of repetition he found it to be another dead-end job. "It irked me to punch the time clock like these other mortals" (134). And once again, "slanderous references" about him cropped up, made by one of his colleagues, a "well dressed but ugly woman from Brooklyn" (135). No dismissal resulted; in fact, Mr. Rebele offered him the position of the staff's top artist. One of Swan's greatest fears, though, was that he would settle for a dull, comfortable life away from art. On the other hand, when life was difficult, when he was out of work and hungry, he painted. Like many other artists, he chose to give himself trouble in order to stimulate his muse. Accordingly, he quit the *Delineator* in the spring of 1907.

Swan always had the advantage of his appearance, which more than once saved him from destitution. Perhaps because of his beauty, which often made people tolerate him when they might have demanded better behavior from someone else, he didn't become socialized in the way that the more ordinary among us must. It was not for want of intelligence. He recognized his solipsism. That insight, though, did not keep him from impatience with those who refused to put his needs above their own.

He rarely took blame for disagreements or failed relationships, preferring to cast the other person as insensitive or brutal. On the very night he left the Butterick building for the last time, he decided to have an elegant meal on Fifty-sixth Street with most of the money he had left. There he struck up a conversation with two gentleman whom he had heard discussing a recent art exhibition. One of them was George L. Turner, a pianist who was then director of a girls' finishing school. The other man was Turner's companion, who lived with him at Carnegie Hall, the residence of a number of artists, musicians, and dancers. The men invited Swan to accompany them to the theater that evening to see Tyrone Power Sr., Edith Wynne Matthison, and Walter Hampden in *A Servant in the House*. When the performance ended, Swan accepted Turner's invitation to spend the night at Carnegie Hall.

Turner then invited Swan to his summer home in Vermont. Wishing to avoid paying more rent to the French landlady, he accepted immediately, leaving the piano and silk sofa pillows behind, spending the night with several homeless men under a stairway on Broadway near Forty-seventh Street, using newspapers for a blanket. The next day, Swan received his train ticket from Turner and left for Vermont.

He was later embarrassed by his own behavior during his visit. He acted "tyrannical," inconsiderate, and moody (138). The more he behaved like a spoiled child, the more they tried to please him. Turner and his friends had recognized an unusual talent and were willing to put up with bad behavior for longer than Swan deserved. His saving grace was that he loved to paint and draw, and so between tantrums he captured all of the residents on canvas. His pictures soon filled the cottage.

Even among this group of musicians, actors, and followers of the arts, Swan felt like an outsider. No doubt his tantrums demonstrated his desire to belong, without knowing how to accommodate himself to others. Some flaw in their own characters must be to blame: "The consideration of the established meant too much to them," he wrote in his memoir, "and the disguising of real reactions annoyed my honest soul" (138). Swan could often defend his hurtful remarks as "honesty," although he seemed always sensitive himself to negative criticism.

To be an established artist, recognized and lauded, was what he dreamed of. To be a great artist, one must have an audience; he knew that. The point was simply that this particular audience did not seem to love him quite enough to make him one of them. Finally, they grew tired of him and introduced him to other friends who were visiting, a couple with a young son who needed tutoring. In September, Swan departed with the Hiltzes for their apartment on West Seventieth Street in New York. His life-size portrait of the boy had delighted the parents and secured his position.

Swan left one of his earliest large murals in Vermont, hanging on the wall in the Methodist church in the town where Turner's cottage was located. This genre of painting began largely as the result of early influence from John Vanderpoel, his teacher at the Chicago Art Institute. Similarities in style can been seen in Vanderpoel's eight-section ceiling mural at De Paul University's College Theatre, Lincoln Park Campus, and several of Swan's murals painted in New York and Paris during the 1920s and 1930s.[2]

Swan's Vermont mural depicted three angels descending from the sky, "with a golden sun behind the head of the central figure, throwing out, like spokes in a wheel, great shafts of light toward the margin of the picture" (139). He often mentioned this "first big work" to friends—not superlative art, he said, but grand considering the unnamed hamlet that surrounded it.

Impropriety ended Swan's employment with the Hiltzes in December 1907. Mr. Hiltze was a gifted pianist but a drinker who was subject to great mood swings. Still, Swan liked him, tolerated the son, and respected the wife. He acted as a sympathetic buffer between her and her sometimes abusive husband. But in early December, a friend of Mrs. Hiltze's informed her that Swan had made an indiscreet remark about the family, that he "could get along with Mr. Hiltze as long as you praised everything he did" (140). Swan couldn't deny the remark. His habit of gossip had gotten him in trouble before and would again. He packed his suitcase and left, with nowhere to go.

A friend he knew from his months at the *Delineator*, Ethel Traphagen, helped him find a place to stay. He had not, however, learned tact from his misadventures with the Hiltzes. In fact, while visiting Traphagen and some of her friends a few days later, he informed the guests: "You are stars—you merely twinkle. Miss Traphagen and I are comets—we shall leave a path in the sky" (141). Traphagen later founded the Traphagen School of Fashion in New York and wrote extensively for *Fashion Digest*.

But for every instance of egotism, there was with Paul Swan a predictable and equal episode of uncertainty, depression, and even despair. A friend of Traphagen's introduced him to Ralph Delmar, an assistant Methodist minister. Delmar provided Swan with an attic room in the parish house at Sixty-first Street, and the two developed a friendship that lasted nearly a year.

What happened the next December (1908) is not completely clear. Swan said the minister controlled him, Svengali-like: "I followed my lonely star into a morass of violent confusion. . . . He made evil out of my innocent ideality" (143). Delmar may have replaced Adah Swan as Paul's Jeremiah; or Swan may have made a confession of love that was not welcome. In any case, he felt rejected and immoral when Delmar rebuffed him.

Sleeping pills were easy enough to acquire. He poured a glass of milk and swallowed a handful. When he awoke (he never mentioned who found him), he was in the hospital. Other than nurses and doctors, no one visited him. For someone used to attention, it was a sobering experience.

While Swan was still recovering, his first paid published work of art appeared on the cover of *Putnam's Magazine* (December 1908). One would think that such success might overcome almost any other disappointment. Instead he sank deeper into a quagmire, unable to feel anything but his own despair. A lifetime of need overwhelmed him. He wanted to be coddled, but no mother appeared.

Why he continued to have contact with Delmar, one can only guess. Perhaps he simply had no other place to go. One day when Swan arrived at the parish district office, Delmar was on his way out and passed Swan off to a secretary, Helen Gavit. His life changed instantly, forever. He wrote in his memoir in 1943:

> I remember to this day the poised, refined expression of her sweet face as she turned from the bookshelf to greet me. After a frank conversation concerning my recent disillusioning experience, she invited me to her home, which she shared with a Miss Harding, with whom she had lived for seven years.
>
> That evening [in early 1909] I went to her apartment to supper and before many hours had passed I knew I had found a lifelong friend; also I became a lifelong rival of Miss Harding. (144)

What that frank discussion was Swan does not reveal, but if he told Helen Gavit of past indiscretions, she was not deterred, and in fact found him interesting enough to continue the friendship. A gifted pianist, Helen played works of MacDowell and Chopin for Swan as he fell in love with "the back of her head, the curls on her neck, and the thick knot of hair" (145). From the beginning these two sensed a symbiotic attraction. At thirty-four (b. 1875), Helen had no marriage prospects on the horizon. She had been living with Allie Harding in a "Boston marriage," a turn-of-the century term that described a partnership (often but not always romantic) among women.[3] Examples of their contemporaries who had such relationships include writer Sarah Orne Jewett and Annie Adams Fields; and William Morris's daughter, May, who found her soul mate in Mary Lobb. But Helen wanted children. Paul Swan, not Allie Harding, provided the means to that end.

Swan did not like Allie. Tensions between them would increase in the next several years, but during the early weeks and months of his friendship with Helen, Swan didn't care what Allie thought. Helen was one of the few women with whom he was ever smitten. She was bright, beautiful, and affluent. He also knew that she was the granddaughter of Erastus Dow Palmer (1817–1904), one of America's premier sculptors. She could understand Swan's temperament; art was her heritage.

Encouraged by his friend, who supported him in his dreams more than anyone since Anna Apperson, Swan found new vitality. No matter how unconventional their relationship might be viewed by others as years wore on, he had found his anima. "How exalting it was that someone so respectable thought I had a right to be *me*! To Helen spirit and motive were all that mattered in this tangled life" (144). It is notable that Swan was attracted to Helen's respectability and status after having vehemently denied interest in such qualities for most of his young life.

Armed with new determination, he began to work on an original entertainment called *Peter Pan and the Pied Piper* to present to theater directors. Sometime in early 1909, funded by Helen and her mother, he hired several actors and a stagehand and presented his program to the managers at Proctor's Fifth Avenue Theatre at Twenty-ninth Street. Helen supplied the piano accompaniment.

Unfortunately, the stagehand was not able to manipulate the full-size rat puppets correctly across the stage. At the same moment that their strings got tangled into a chaotic dance, the large canvas backdrops that Swan had painted broke from their supports and crashed to the floor.

The managers were kind, and somewhat intrigued. "Throw away all this claptrap of stuffed rats," one mustached gentleman told him, "and go on and do the sketches [on cloth backdrops]; then we'll book you at once." It was the best professional theatrical encouragement Swan had received. If he worked more on the story and simplified the set, perhaps he could be on the stage in New York, in his own production.

He visited the booking office the next day with some revisions and waited to meet with the managers. Panic set in as he paced the floor. He left before they arrived, went back to his room, got in bed, and

7. *Erastus Dow Palmer* by Paul Swan. Oil on canvas, not dated, 19½ x 15½ in. From the collection of Margaret Russell.

stayed there for a week—refusing to answer the door, even when Helen knocked. He never went back to Proctor's. *Peter Pan and the Pied Piper* never saw the footlights.[4]

The episode was definitional. Not performing, not seeing the production through to its conclusion, not letting an audience judge his work—all contrived to shield him from failure. If *Peter Pan* had been successful, what might be expected of him in the future? For the moment, hiding under covers seemed the best option, until he could blame someone else for doing him wrong or for being too jealous to give him a chance.

Swan began to spend more and more time in Albany with Helen, where the Gavit family was well known. There he felt at peace for the first time in his life. Mrs. Gavit, who was charmed by her daughter's handsome and clever beau, introduced him to society. He began to earn money by painting and drawing her friends. Life was easy, and his reputation as a portrait artist was improving with each commission.

Alla Nazimova

When the famous Russian actress Alla Nazimova played the lead in an Albany production of *The Passion Flower*, the city was abuzz. She had been away from the stage for two years and had chosen this play, written by her lover, Brandon Tynan, for her return.[5] It was an artistic failure. Her producer, Lee Shubert, closed the production after two weeks in Albany and a month in Washington and Philadelphia. But on opening night, 29 November 1909, Paul Swan and Helen Gavit (and most likely Mrs. Gavit and Allie Harding) were in attendance. Nazimova's performance was magnificent, Swan thought—in fact, it was a defining moment in his life: "I was so excited by this artistic event that I could not sleep that night. I cannot describe the exhilaration that her acting, her movements, her accent, her face, brought into my days. She seemed to reveal to me a potentiality, a possibility I had felt, in solitude, must be somewhere in the world. . . . I must know her! What could life not become with personal counsel from such a great person?" (148).[6]

As often as he was the source of his own disasters, Swan also created his own good luck. He wrote to Nazimova, asking to draw her portrait. He was effusive, telling her that there have been "only two great N's in the world and that one of them had won his fame in battle" (qtd. in Vickerman 2). She did not respond. When he returned to New York City he purchased several photographs of her in costume and painted a life-size portrait. Using all the cash he had on hand, he had the painting framed, boxed, and shipped to Nazimova's Thirty-ninth Street theater as a gift. She was playing there in Ibsen's *Little Eywolf*, which had opened on 18 April 1910 (Lambert 150).

One can only imagine what Nazimova must have thought when a huge wooden crate almost too large to get through the theater door arrived. There must have been a flurry of activity among her assistants, searching for crowbars to pry open the box, and stepping away with startled looks when the painting finally was unveiled. Nazimova stared at an exact image of herself magnificently costumed, wondering what sort of artist would do this fine work for no recompense.

Two days later, Swan visited the theater himself, hoping to gain an audience. When he told the doorman that he was the artist who had sent the painting, he was immediately ushered into Nazimova's dressing room. She rose and signaled to him with a theatrical wave, making him feel he was in the presence of royalty. She did not say she liked the painting. She did not thank him for it. She looked at him regally, arching her eyebrow as if she were considering what his motives were, what his character might be. Then, with a deep Russian accent, she said, "Would you consider painting me in my Ibsen roles this summer?" (DS 149).

Swan was too awed to do more than nod agreement. Arrangements were quickly negotiated with Nazimova's secretary, and within days he was on a train bound for her residence in Port Chester. Brandon Tynan met him at the station. Swan thought him a snob, but others who knew him considered him good-natured, modest, and humorous. Swan may have misunderstood some reserve on Tynan's part during the short ride to Nazimova's magnificent home. Tynan's love affair was in the first stages of decline, and secret demons were haunting him. Tynan was Catholic, with a consumptive wife, and so felt doubly guilty about his adultery.

Swan must have smiled at his good luck when Tynan turned in to Nazimova's estate, Who-Torok ("little farm" in Russian). Labeled "Madame Nazimova's American Doll's House" by *Theatre Magazine*, it

8. *Alla Nazimova* by Paul Swan, 1910. Oil on canvas. Location and size not known. Photograph courtesy of Dallas Swan Jr.

was an eighteenth-century home with a covered veranda and porticoed entrance. It was filled with Russian antiques that might give one the sense of a country house in a Chekhov play, an estate that included an apple orchard, a rose garden, two black thoroughbred horses, a blue parakeet, and three carriages (Lambert 147). The farm boy from Nebraska had stepped into a dream.

Swan began his series of portraits almost immediately. This was his great chance, he knew, to win a reputation as an artist. Nazimova was charmed by his youthful good looks and told him, "You are a Dorian Gray before he knew sin. You are too old to adopt, but not old enough for a lover. You are young and natural now, but when you become sophisticated you will become impossible" (DS 151). It was a comment that made Swan smile, because he was at that time a follower of Oscar Wilde and embraced the aestheticism that Dorian exemplified. Swan would not have approved of Dorian's behavior, but he would have granted that the pursuit of beauty, of art, is outside normal moral restraints. In the preface to *The Picture of Dorian Gray*, Wilde states:

> The artist is the creator of beautiful things . . . The only excuse for making a useless thing is that one admires it intensely . . . All art is quite useless. (*Artist Critic* 236)

Art was, for art's sake, the taproot of life. Wilde's view emphasized that art's great value is its lack of practical application. Art exists for its own sake and is separate from politics, government, economics, "the age." It is not a guide to moral conduct. It simply *is*. An age does not shape it; it shapes the age.[7]

Swan would revise his own definition of aestheticism often in the years ahead, selecting appropriate passages from Wilde that suited his needs but rejecting much that did not fit his own career choices. His was a theory that needed constant amendment. Perhaps more tellingly than he knew, Swan used to joke with friends later in his life: "People always compared me to Oscar Wilde. I've always thought myself more like Sarah Bernhardt."[8]

Alla Nazimova was younger than Helen Gavit and only four years older than Swan. He lied to her that he was twenty-three, when he was actually twenty-six in 1909.[9] At first, actress and painter charmed one another. Nazimova loved Swan's work and delighted in the vision he captured on canvas, and she encouraged him to pursue his study of all classical arts. As time wore on, though, Swan began to feel that he was little more than a court painter, "administering to her self-appreciation." That summer at Who-Torok a larger ego than his own kept him in check. One might expect Swan to have ruined this employment opportunity as he had so many others, but he did not leave; he did not complain. He was too awed by his subject, he was at least painting, and the money was the best he had made in his life. When Nazimova treated him like a petulant child, he continued to work. When she ignored his attempts at friendship and conversation, he felt reprimanded but continued to work. When he finished the portraits, was paid, and left, he was sure that she was delighted with the results but was just as happy to see him go.

After that summer of 1910, they never met again. Swan watched her onstage as often as he could, but there were no replies to his letters. He always seemed grateful to her for giving him his first big commission and for displaying his portraits in her theater.[10] He reproduced a couple of the portraits he did of her during the summer, later exhibiting them at M. Knoedler's Gallery and the Albert Roullier Galleries in Chicago in 1929. The reviewer for the *Chicago Evening Post Magazine of the Art World* called one portrait "vivid and sensitive . . . done with an artistry that adds the inner personality of the sitter to a definite pictorial likeness" (SB).

Egypt and Greece

If Swan had wanted to build his reputation as an artist in New York, he probably should have stayed to cash in on the publicity he received from the Nazimova portraits. Instead, he sailed for Italy in the fall of 1910. He wanted to immerse himself in a culture he had only been able to dream of as a youth. At age twenty-seven, finally, he could. If he ran out of funds, surely he could find people who would want their portraits painted. Not wanting to leave Helen but determined to see the world, he sailed on the *Princess Irene*, an ill-fated ship that later was sunk during World War I.

Things did not go quite as planned. When he arrived in Naples, the city was under quarantine because of an outbreak of yellow fever.

The ship was diverted and finally docked at Genoa. He had only a few days to spend there and was disappointed with what he saw. Genoa's "tawdry symbols of banal emotions," sculpture created by artists who "were dominated by the patrons of their art" (DS 152), did not appeal, and very shortly he left for Egypt. On shipboard he met a physician and his wife, Dr. and Mrs. Henry, who persuaded him to visit Cairo, where the doctor would arrange several commissions.

Swan was enchanted: "Egypt—the clear, blue, unclouded sky. All nature breathes forth a mystic spell" (153). During the several months he was there, he painted portraits and landscapes. Three of his favorites were *The Secret of the Sphinx*, *The Pyramids in the Light of Afterglow*, and *The Reflection of the Nile*. A reporter in Cairo for the *Eastern and Western Review* (Boston) commented on Swan's work: "Whether it be the swift flowing Nile with its sandy banks, or green oases of waving palm trees; whether it be some brown-skinned Arab leaning against a background of white lotus blossoms, there is always the fresh colored East before us with its blaze of pulsating light that lives on the canvases of Mr. Swan" (DS 164).

Dr. Henry was true to his word and arranged several lucrative portrait commissions, including ones of Sir Eldon Gorst, the English governor of Egypt; Mrs. Hylda Hunter of Castle Combe, Gorst's sister; and Gorst's young daughter, Kitty. Swan's studio method worked particularly well for his younger clients. He always encouraged his sitters to talk and to move about the room whenever they wished. He wanted to get an idea of their personalities and their physical presence. His portraits were often composites of impressions from everything he absorbed.

Ronald Storrs, Gorst's assistant, was so pleased with his portrait that he arranged for Swan to paint a wealthy sheik. The sheik arrived with his Bedouin daughter, garbed in lavish Parisian clothing and Arabic jewelry. He wanted his portrait painted on the same canvas as his daughter's but only wanted to pay the price of one portrait, as only one canvas was being used. Swan refused, his pockets full at the time. "Think what would happen," he tried to explain, "if on the Day of Judgment I should be required to supply two souls for the price of one!" (155). The sheik was not amused, and the commission was canceled. Many other Egyptians he painted for no charge—natives who seemed to embody Swan's requirements for beauty. His favorite among these was a Coptic student named Zackie Salami.

Mrs. Henry posed for Swan's rendition of a Pre-Raphaelite-styled *Ophelia*. The painting, a large oil on burlap, was his tribute to Dante Gabriel Rossetti. A photograph of it appeared in a Greek newspaper in 1911, but it vanished after that. None of the photos of Swan's studios show it hanging on the walls. In 1972, John Swan (Swan's nephew) located it in a private collection in Virginia. That owner died, and the painting disappeared again until a physician from Ohio saw it in an antique shop in Kentucky in 1999. He purchased it, and it remains today in his collection.

When Dr. Henry chose to return to the United States, Swan decided it was time for him to leave Egypt as well. He bought a railway ticket to Alexandria and sailed for Athens. He had grown disillusioned with Egypt, depressed by the enormous poverty, and found himself "disgusted at such depravity": "How ugly is life devoid of ideals! It is just as well that one half of the world does not know how the other half lives" (159).

In Greece he felt he had finally found his home: "I was awakened to the insistent impression that I had seen it all before, centuries ago, when the neglected road of today was paved in marble, and a chariot was my carriage. . . . This was indeed a homecoming to me such as I had never felt anywhere else" (160). The problem was that the homeland he had dreamed of was a land buried beneath the detritus of many centuries. Athens had lost its golden tradition. The beautiful Greeks of old were now "only mixtures of many alien races; black-bearded minions touched with Turkish blood, and peasant strains from the neighboring states" (161).

On the second day of a planned three-day stay in Athens, Swan visited an area of the city where a number of artists had studios. He entered the first door he saw open—the studio of Thomas Thomopoulos, a well-known Greek sculptor. Not blind to Swan's handsome figure, Thomopoulos asked him to pose, and Swan did so on numerous occasions over a period of weeks. When he showed Thomopoulos some of his own work, the Greek decided to teach the young American his own style of sculpture. They talked and worked, sharing ideas about art and beauty, refining their works, painting and sculpting one another.

9. *Ophelia* by Paul Swan, 1911. Oil on burlap, 80 x 47 in. Private collection, Ohio.

One day a dark-haired gentleman stopped by to visit Thomopoulos. He had heard about the handsome American and wanted to see for himself. He, too, was immediately taken with Swan's appearance and with the bust Swan had done of his teacher. "I am Jeremiah Vocas," he announced. Swan knew he was the editor of the popular Athens art magazine *Kaletexne*, a man who could as easily destroy or create the career of an artist in Greece. In the case of Swan, Vocas chose the latter and wrote in the next issue: "When Thomas Thomopoulos saw the young artist, M. Swan, enter his atelier one morning, he thought he was dreaming of an ancient Greek youth. His dream was realized in the bust he has just finished. M. Swan is a mystic of the beautiful, as his work clearly shows. He is a realist like the ancient Greek sculptors, who portrayed in their works the ideal types of their epoch" (SB; DS 170).

Word spread that Hermes had reappeared in Athens. Exhibitions of Swan's work were arranged, and Athens came calling. Other journals and papers picked up the story:[11]

The last few days we have had the honor of visiting M. Swan, the young American artist, who has extraordinary talent for an artist of our times. I was amazed to find in his works a truly Grecian spirit—the expression of a truly great artist. (*People and Things*)

What he has in his soul is not merely the understanding of art, but the feeling, and this he portrays by vigorous colors on his canvases. The Greek artists who have seen his works were amazed at his ability. (*The Day's News*)

We need many columns to say what we have to say about this young American artist who recently came to Athens. . . . We found ourselves before the vision of an artist. (*Neon Astay*)

In order that one may give a clear conception of M. Swan's works of art, one may require much time and space, but since we have neither available we may express it in two words: truly beautiful.
From his smallest sketch to his largest portrait . . . his work is beautiful, great, profound and expressive. M. Swan is not only

an artist with a soul, but a psychologist who presents people and things as living. (Irene Nicolaides, *Woman's Magazine*)

He represents himself in his works. He cannot escape it. Byron also could not liberate himself from his works, but he was of the few whom Destiny favored. This is necessary that creation may exist in Art. . . . No foreigner since Lord Byron has ever received such public acclaim. (*Patrie*) [12]

One newspaper reported that in Athens "a crowd followed him to his hotel when he first set foot in Athens and kept at his heels for the rest of his stay there. . . . 'See him and then see our marbles!' said the superstitious. 'Is he not the Hermes of Praxiteles come to life again? Or is he Antinous?' " (qtd. in "Hailed in Greece" 6).

Were it not for these records from different newspapers and journals, one could be forgiven for thinking that Swan might be boasting when he writes of the furor he caused, but in fact he was received as a kind of avatar of Hermes, an example of live ideal statuary. He was not averse to such praise, extravagant as it may have been, for his own estimation of his beauty was essentially in agreement with that of Athenian admirers. Who can blame him? For most of his young life men and women had been dazzled by or envious of his form and face, and now the birthplace of classical refinement hailed him as the reincarnation of the Greek standard.

In his letters and diaries, Swan writes of his devotion to the ideal form exemplified in Greek statuary and of the power of this ideal to move us. Greek art, unlike Roman, was not intended to be a likeness of the human form but rather its perfection. W. B. Yeats speaks of the capacity of such a form to arouse real people in his poem "The Statues." According to Yeats, "boys and girls pale from imagined love" would steal from their beds to press "at midnight in some public place / Live lips upon a plummet-measured face" (Yeats 336). Swan believed with Yeats that the deepest emotion was engendered by ideal forms rather than particularized, realistic execution. It seems an appropriate analogy, particularly considering the friendship Swan would later have with W. B. Yeats's philosopher-father, portrait artist John Butler Yeats.

So it was that, surrounded by Greek culture, Swan allied himself even further with Wilde—and with Pater and Ruskin—who argued against the utility of art in order that it serve a higher purpose. "Art for art's sake" has been interpreted many ways, but the most direct application of the phrase is an understanding that if art is subsumed to another end, whether it be religious, political, or commercial, then the art is vitiated to the degree that it serves that end. In order to achieve what Wordsworth called "thoughts that do often lie too deep for tears," art must have no agenda other than its own existence. Only then, paradoxically, does the art work upon us to improve our lives.

Swan was still primarily a painter of faces, but he often gave these faces features that reflected the ideal rather than the real. A decade later he told Jeanne Robert Foster that during his time in Greece he began to limit his portrait choices, selecting the more beautiful clients for his subjects. Perhaps his most acclaimed painting of this period was one of his friend G. X. Konstantinos Theotokis, a writer. Euphrosyne C. Kephala of the *Eastern and Western Review* chose it as her favorite work. [13]

Swan began to experiment with portrait form, slightly elongating necks and fingers and correcting flaws in facial symmetry in order to approximate his vision of the Greek ideal in his subjects. In one instance he accepted a commission from a "young man with a face which at once suggested the long pale ovals of Vandyke's portraits. . . . Everyone praised [the result], proving that art done *con amore* is the only art really worthy of the name" (DS 178). But, like the repugnance he felt a few years earlier toward his erstwhile deformed student in the house of bedbugs (Chicago, 1902), Swan's physical repulsion toward six members of the Greek man's family made the execution of those portraits (which he was hired to do before he had seen their faces) unusually difficult. "A fat, common, wholesale-grower, a wizened grandmother, three dumpy children, and the sister. . . . But I painted them all. . . . They were flattered by my ability to disregard unpictorial defects" (173). He rarely stooped to capture the character of the non-beautiful, of the wizened peasant's face. One might quarrel with Swan's unwavering devotion to his definition of the beautiful, but he was not alone in his passion.

Because of the public praise he had received and the increasing interest in his art, cognoscenti invited him to give a lecture at Athena Hall. There he so captivated his critics that the entire lecture was published in Jeremiah Vocas's magazine, in an issue devoted almost entirely to Swan's work. One reporter, Caliguropolis, wrote in *Neon Astay*: "As if he were proud of the rare gift of beauty he himself has received at nature's hand, he does not hesitate to paint himself in his pictures. . . . His portraits are excellent. Without idealizing the face he has the ability to please his subject while making small concessions to artistic standards. Mr. Swan's studio has become the centre of interest and is visited daily by the cultured and fashionable to an extent most flattering to the young artist from over the sea" (SB). How much better could life get for a lad from Nebraska?

In Greece, Swan also learned to be more at ease with his sexual desires. He may well have read John Addington Symonds's work on Greece as an ancient model where "homosexuality could be noble and dignified when valued by society rather than repressed." He was in accord with contemporary work by Edward Carpenter, who claimed that "homosexuals tended to have exceptional mental and spiritual abilities that made them superior" (Greenberg 4).

Swan resisted defining himself. When he used Karl Ulrichs's term *Uranian*, he came closest. Sex was more a joining of two beautiful forms, and whether those forms were male or female didn't matter. Beauty was the motivating force. In most instances, though, he found the ideal male figure, the Greek model, the most exquisite.

In Athens, Swan met Kostas Dimitriades, "a beautiful youth with a rarely pure soul. . . . There was little about him which was not spirit. I consider the best work I did in Athens was the painting and drawing of his refined, geometrically perfect face" (DS 173). Swan saw himself as Socrates to the beloved Alcibiades. He taught art to his companion, who also aspired to be a great painter. "I liked him because he spoke to me as a brother, not as one speaks to a feted celebrity. He advised me whom to accept and whom to reject of the multitudes who flocked to my presence. He served me when I was 'off parade'; when I was disillusioned or discouraged; . . . when fanfaring admirers proved themselves undependable friends" (175).

Little more is known. Swan told friends that Kostas was "my true brother" and that their friendship endured for many years, though they rarely exchanged letters. Whether or not they had ever been physical lovers, his friendship with Kostas was one of many half-developed relationships. Swan seemed always to leave before any permanent commitment was made.

He was not reticent about discussing the affairs he had with the women of Athens. Some of his later revelations to Jeanne Robert Foster amused her at first, but as her own life came under more scrutiny by biographers years later, she said she wished she had been better able to advise her complex friend. After she read Swan's unpublished memoir in the early 1960s, she felt that the book would not serve him well, commercially or personally. Did he think he was making himself attractive? Was he looking for sympathy as a victim? Was he playing the role of "bad boy" that some people found intriguing? Did he think the narratives were comic?[14]

One story at least partially explains Swan's motivation to include tales of his skill with women. He knew that Julia Dragoumis, an Athenian socialite, was a great fan and decided one day to accept her invitation to lunch. She and her daughter had been at a reception in his honor two days earlier, and she told him, when she greeted him at her door, that she had not been able to sleep since:

> After a short luncheon was finished . . . she conducted me by the hand to her bedroom with the pretense still of showing me the house. . . . She began to undress me. Poor Adonis! She got under the bed covers, and with a jerk or two disrobed. . . .
>
> "Oh, if the world could see you now; you are Hermes! It's a shame you must wear clothes . . ."
>
> Her fierce passion . . . shocked me. Her abandonment toward her momentary objective produced the opposite emotion in me. I was cooled to trembling. And in this momentary lull flashed too many persistent images: her grown son and daughter; a divorced poet-husband; the functions of motherhood, child-bearing, nursing, caressings; ugly natural acts—all this made my fertile brain sick. . . .
>
> I was rendered ridiculous as a lover. Yet since I had been so caught in the current of her fierce desire, I was calm enough

to see the absurdity of failing in this normal function. Finally, visualizing someone else, whom I did care for, I acquitted myself with laurels. . . . Surely, epidermal friction is not all there is to sexual experience. . . . I was weary with hate for women who crave a man's body, any man's body, in spite of his aloofly scorning soul. . . . Yet had I not acquiesced, the fictitious story would have been invented of my nature's abnormality. This is the female's most subtle blackmail. (176–78)

In spite of his preferences, Swan loathed the term *effeminate* and was fearful of being viewed as anything other than manly. In his opinion, masculinity had nothing to do with sexual predilection, but he understood that if he was to have a career that was based in part on his good looks, he must be able to prove himself to women when called upon. Several descriptions of other encounters during his stay in Athens (e.g., "Mme. Potaufeu wallowed on the coverlets like a obsessed cat, and was quite as disgusting" [175]) anticipate James Baldwin's *Giovanni's Room*, in which David, a bisexual, thinks that he has done something awful to his lover, Sue, and that it is a matter of his honor not to let her know.

Swan's feelings for these women were not born of the same youthful passion he had felt for Ella House or the deep friendship he shared with Helen Gavit. Simply put, by the time he reached Athens, he knew that young men were more likely than young women to fit his conception of ideal beauty. It followed naturally that he would be attracted to men on more than just the artistic level. But he wanted no one to doubt that he could perform whenever asked.

The stress of living a double life began to show. Swan alienated those who had been his staunchest supporters, repeating the problems he had had with previous admirers or employers: "Thomopoulos had fallen away because of envy and jealousy. Vocas had been pushed out of my door as a persistent bore, taking with him a flock of envious detractors. Factions grew up, debates took place. . . . Evil carnal seekers came to visit me, entirely misconstruing my ideals, physical charm having to them only a base usage" (174). Whether or not these were real or imagined afflictions, they validated his own opinion: If others are jealous of my art and my person, then I must be a good artist, and I must be beautiful.

By the time he left Greece, there was no evidence of a public shift in its admiration. The Athenian newspapers of the day still touted him as Hermes, and his fans loved him long after he had gone, no matter what internal demons he might be fighting.

What Swan took away from Athens was international reputation and extensive training in sculpting. The ideas of his old teacher from Chicago, Lorado Taft—and even the modeling practices of his grandfather Swan—blended perfectly with the philosophy of Thomopoulos. Swan used all three to create his own style, something very Greek, usually robed (Taft's influence), with a tilt or turn of the head that gave the sculpture a sense of movement, another dimension.

It is also appropriate that Swan's romance with dance began during this period. For a painter such as Swan, the step from the two-dimensional canvas to the figures carved in space by his body was a natural progression. It is as if speech, in its inadequacy, moves to gesture, and we employ our hands to make a point; and then gesture evolves to dance to make clear with our bodies what language cannot express.

The night before he left, Swan climbed the Acropolis to the Parthenon to make his own farewell to Greece. He wondered how he could absorb all he had learned and give the world a new art. Athens had been the seat of so many "great truths, great tragedies, great joys," and he wondered how he could express this tradition in his art. When he looked at the carved marble figures dancing along the frieze opposite where he sat, he had an epiphany:

Though I had never studied dancing in the academic ballet sense, I realized it sculpturally; pose and line and expression of hands and face I had long practiced. Could I not learn the dynamic passages, the transitions from pose to pose? Was not dancing fluid sculpture? Was not sculpture such as I had seen on this visit, every day, the rendering of static life? . . .

As I arose from that meditation . . . my career as a dancer began. I was there consecrated to that art expression which has brought me most of the sorrow yet most of the joy which has since filled my life. (179)

The next morning, in a soaking rain, Swan's closest friends saw him off to the town of Piraeus, where he would catch a ship for the final leg of his European trip before returning to the United States. G. X. Konstantinos Theotokis was among the group of well-wishers, which also included art critic Irene Nicolaides, the ever-faithful Kostas Dimitriades, and even the revolting Madame Dragoumis and her daughter.

Swan . . . the most beautiful man in the world . . . danced at the Plaza Hotel today for hundreds of enraptured women and a handful of disgruntled men. **Washington Post**, 21 April 1915

5 "America's Premier Dancer," 1911–1921

Getting Married

After a stop in Taormina, Sicily, Paul Swan visited Rome.[1] While he was attending an art exhibit, he noticed someone staring at him: "He began by winking his light-blue eyes at me" (DS 167). The gentleman was Sir Alexander Nelson Hood, also known as the Duca di Bronte. A noted sponsor of young artists and musicians, he was attracted to Swan's exceptional good looks. Hood paid Swan in advance for a portrait to be painted later in England. The exact amount isn't known, but Swan was suddenly affluent again and rescheduled his trip accordingly.

New friends came calling almost as soon as the artist-turned-dancer had engaged a room at Albergo Fisher's Park.[2] It was a glorious, festive few weeks. He spent money as soon as it touched his hands because, he said, he had to keep up the image of the worldly artist. It was all part of the mystique he was attempting to create.

Before Hood returned to London, he introduced Swan to Robert Hichens, author of several popular novels, including *The Green Carnation*. This book chronicles a connection between aestheticism and bisexual-homosexual passions. Although Hichens's book is an attack on the aesthetic movement and even on Oscar Wilde himself, it is a good-natured parody, perhaps due in part to Hichens's bisexuality. He was an important contact as Swan developed his own ideas about art and sexuality.

Hichens was in the midst of writing *The Fruitful Vine* at the time. Swan captured him on a canvas that is lost today, but he described him in his memoir as "oblique of eyes, with curly, short-cropped hair. He was silent, watchful, like a creature of the woods. He carried a Pan-pipe with him, and he played it wistfully like the goatherd he resembled. . . . He was, I'm sure, a faun" (DS 185).

In Rome, at the Salone Margherita, Swan finally saw his original artistic icon, Cléo de Mérode, perform.[3] He sat spellbound in the audience as she danced three different numbers. Her pale, oval face, with a garland of pearls in her hair, was the same image he had drawn twenty years before. He also saw Vaslav Nijinsky dance with Tamara Karsavina in *Spectre de la Rose* and immediately recognized a great talent: "that flying elastic figure bounding in and out of the scene to the music of Weber was an ecstasy never before experienced. . . . How could one be a mere everyday mortal after witnessing such poetic beauty, grace, movement, color, music, harmony? This was what life should be. This was the dream in my soul which no one had ever before awakened. And the corn fields in Nebraska! And the stockyards in Chicago! And the unbelievers everywhere!" (187–88)

It is a remarkable contrast to juxtapose the young Swan — staggering behind a plow horse, and swathed in burlap to keep his skin from the sun's harmful rays — against the beautiful man poised at the beginning of a career that would consolidate all of his aesthetic aspirations. Nijinsky's performance convinced Swan of the sculptural quality of dance and motivated him to work on several performance pieces of his own.

In the midst of this challenge to Swan's aesthetic senses, Danish painter Baron Arild Rosenkrantz visited his atelier. Rosenkrantz was exactly the mentor Swan needed at the time, for not only was he the man to advance Swan's technique, but he would also introduce him intimately to the world of dance. A noted portrait painter, Rosenkrantz was taken with Swan's beauty and hired him to pose for several pictures. One of these survives in Denmark in the private collection of Bente Rosenkrantz Arendrup, the artist's grandniece. Known today as the "painter of the invisible," Rosenkrantz often told family members that

10. *Paul Swan* by Baron Arild Rosenkrantz, 1912. Oil on canvas, 19½ x 16 in. From the collection of Bente Rosenkrantz Arendrup.

he could not talk seriously about the arts to people who did not have a deep understanding of the Greek tradition. In Swan he seemed to have found a living model for his ideas.[4]

In the springtime of 1911, the two were suddenly off to visit Paris. Swan found the trip frightening, overwhelmed by the city he would cherish in the decades ahead (189). Art bombarded him from all sides; he felt exhausted, inferior, and incompetent when he looked at his surroundings. The two stayed in the rue Cambon, painted and sketched together, visited the Louvre and the salon of the Société des Artistes Français at the Grand Palais. In an interview for *New York World* four years later, Swan reported that the Salon accepted one of his paintings at this time. If so, Baron Rosenkrantz surely used his influence on behalf of his friend, or at least introduced Swan to the right people. What is certain is Swan's encounter with a Hungarian laborer, whose classical features arrested him. "I think I can make something out of you," he told the man, and arranged to sculpt him. The result was *L'Opprimé* (The Oppressed), which years later won a medal at the seventh Exposition des beaux-arts et arts décoratifs (1937).[5]

Almost as suddenly as they arrived, Swan and Rosenkrantz left for London, where Swan took a room at the Arundel Hotel, off the Strand. Rosenkrantz was a frequent visitor, and the two enjoyed exchanging ideas about art. Between 1911 and 1913 the work of both artists reflected classical traditions, as exemplified in Rosenkrantz's *Portrait of a Young Boy* (1912) and Swan's *Portrait of a Greek Poet* (1911).[6]

But Rosenkrantz had also started to explore new artistic ideas. He had become interested in anthroposophy and the writings of its leading proponent, Rudolf Steiner, whose work he had been reading for several years.[7] When he finally met Steiner in 1913, Rosenkrantz showed him one of his large oils, *The Omnipresent*. Steiner suggested that Rosenkrantz could progress further: "Now you should paint the answer from the spiritual world; such a picture can be developed out of yellow, red, and orange."[8] It was an important moment for both Rosenkrantz and his American pupil. As their friendship progressed over several decades, Swan's work became richer in color, as demonstrated in *Self-Portrait in Egyptian Dress* and *Jeanne d'Arc*, both painted in the mid-1920s. From 1915 until the end of Swan's life, red tones dominated the majority of his work, very likely inspired by Rosenkrantz, who was now applying Goethe's theory of color to his work.

Swan's stay in London was brief. No doubt he executed the promised portrait of Sir Alexander Nelson Hood, the money for it long ago spent. By May 1911 he was running out of funds. He often visited the Tate and National galleries, where he chose several painters to study, including Frank Dixie, Richard Jack, Lawrence Alma-Tadema, Edward Burne-Jones, Dante Gabriel Rossetti, and James MacNeil Whistler.

11. Paul Swan in his Paris studio about 1935. Several sculptures of note are *L'Opprimé* (front, center), *Guy Holt* (left of *L'Opprimé*), and *Raquel Meller* (above *Guy Holt*). Swan is shown working on *The Serenity of Fred. Madame Dao* is to his left, above an unnamed sculpture of a young man. Photograph courtesy of Dallas Swan Jr.

John Singer Sargent's portraits were his favorites. He copied in pencil one or two from memory as soon as he returned to his hotel room, experimenting with his technique by intentionally elongating the neck and fingers in his own versions, as he had occasionally done in Egypt and Greece. He concluded that this method added elegance even to Sargent's figures.

Then, for no other reason except to return to Helen as he had originally planned, Swan quietly left his London apartment one day in June, bill unpaid, and set sail for home. On 27 June the *New York Herald* announced the arrival in New York of the White Star Line's *Baltic*, carrying the United States' newest celebrity. Swan's earlier decision to leave the city following his summer with Alla Nazimova had seemed impulsive. Ultimately, it turned out well. He left an aspiring artist with a few respectable notices; he returned a budding star. Now, back in the United States, he would try to capitalize on his European success.

Helen met him at the ship. Except for two telegrams about his expected arrival, she hadn't heard from him in nine months. In his absence she had decided to marry him, much to the delight of her mother. As a sculptor's daughter, Mrs. Gavit liked the idea of having another artist in the family. Swan seemed the perfect match for Helen, who was now in her thirties and had spent the last decade in a relationship with another woman. Perhaps Helen and Paul were not in love in the traditional romantic sense, but they found qualities in each other that compensated for any lack of passion. He cared for her more than he would for any other woman, and, as Helen told him in a curious yet revelatory declaration of her feelings, "I married the only man I could endure" (DS 193). It's only too easy to look askance at such a match, but every report testifies to the durability and depth of their marriage. In 1932, Swan wrote more about their union: "The impression that I married for money and had thus tumbled into the lap of luxury was an enormous misinformation. But it is true that my family's comfortable and inherited income [which Helen received upon the death of her mother] has kept them independent of my own ups and downs and comings and goings. Certainly the freedom I have had to follow the caprice of my creative work has been part of the silver lining of my frequent clouds" (233).

They were married in New York City on 29 June 1911 at the Church of the Transfiguration, also known as the Little Church around the Corner, on East Twenty-ninth Street, between Fifth and Madison avenues.[9] Mrs. Gavit, beaming with approval, served as their witness. After a celebratory dinner, Helen, who still worked in New York, saw her new husband and mother climb aboard a train for the Gavit home on Lafayette Street in Albany. She did not see Swan again until August. For the time being, everyone decided to keep news of the marriage to a minimum. It's difficult to understand why such secrecy would benefit Swan's wife or his mother-in-law, but there is little doubt that a married "Hermes" might not be as marketable as an eligible bachelor.

A month after Swan's arrival, marriage, and departure to Albany with Mrs. Gavit, Helen arrived with her friend Allie Harding for a summer stay at Helen's own Skiwaukee Farm near the southern Adirondack village of Stony Creek. Swan and Mrs. Gavit joined them, and husband and wife were finally under the same roof. The contrast between the bustling capitals of Europe and the sleepy northwoods town could not have been more marked, and Swan may have appreciated the peace and quiet. All was not bliss, however, for Allie and Paul vied for Helen's attention. The new husband watched with both pleasure and anxiety as Helen pushed her friend away with seeming indifference. He wanted to replace Allie in Helen's affections, but he also appreciated that the relationship between the two women allowed him a certain freedom. His wife had a new plan, though, and Swan was a necessity to its implementation. At thirty-six, she decided that she wanted to be a mother. Allie Harding's importance in Helen's life would never be the same.

There was nevertheless an appropriate use for Allie in Paul Swan's life. One day, after he finished a portrait of her in a canoe, Allie said something a little more cutting than usual to him about his portrayal of her. With an exhibition of his work on the horizon and Helen ever willing to support his artistic vision, Swan had a more secure sense of himself. He quietly revised the portrait with a few brush strokes, idealizing Allie's strong but not pretty face "until it was past all recognition." Like someone who sees a touched-up photograph, Allie recognized herself in this more attractive girl.

When Swan sold the work (*Girl in a Canoe with Lily Pad*) to the Delaware and Lackawanna Railroad Company for the cover of a travel booklet, several men in the railroad's office asked where they might meet this wonderful woman. "This my poor metamorphosed Allie!" wrote Swan in his memoir. It had been great fun for him to immortalize her, and he took perverse delight in knowing that her beauty was his creation. What did he care, so long as the painting sold?[10]

The Artist-god

Among the visitors to Skiwaukee during the summer of 1911 was naturalist John Burroughs, a friend of the Gavit family. Swan found him "without imagination or whimsy," too scientific and not at all poetic: "He looked at birds and stones and trees without becoming of them" (195). Art collector John Quinn, who had once lunched with Burroughs and Irish portrait artist J. B. Yeats, commented that Burroughs "looked at old man Yeats, like one fox looking at another" (*PFR* 330). It was exactly the way Swan saw him. He distrusted him. "He was chockful of facts," Swan said, "but facts are not always truths" (DS 195). Still, Burroughs had an interesting face, and he sat for several drawings and an oil portrait.

However he might have failed to impress Burroughs, Swan did charm two other Adirondack summer residents, Reverend and Mrs. Charles Albertson, who were so taken with his portraits that they arranged his first solo exhibition in their hometown of Rochester, New York, at the Powers Hotel.

Now Swan had patrons who got him "American" press. Although hardly the center for art that New York City was, Rochester provided him with lucrative commission work, including a portrait of Mrs. Junius Royal Judson, wife of the inventor of the steam governor. "Young Artist Guest in City: Has Striking Personality"; "Success of Young Artist: Swan Here from Italy, Greece and Egypt"; and "Marked Success for Artist: Favored among Mortals" were clippings Swan chose to preserve in his scrapbooks. Praise from a 29 September 1911 article in the *Rochester Post Express* must have thrilled him. The reviewer's comment describes Swan's unusual use of color: "Transparency in oil colors is a 'trick of the trade,' to give to a work in heavy oils the appearance of a work in lighter and more luminous watercolor. There is that in Mr. Swan's work—and something more. Especially notable in two of his pictures—not portraits, but figures—is this exceptional quality. It is

12. Naturalist John Burroughs (1837–1921) at Skiwaukee, Helen Gavit Swan's summer home near Stony Creek, New York, about 1914. Photograph courtesy of William and Caryl Hutchens.

translucency rather than transparency. If light does not shine through these colors, it appears to shine *from* them" (SB). In the *Rochester Herald* on 21 September 1911, a reporter wrote:

> His paintings belong to the idealist school and as a consequence possess much that reminds the beholder of the old masters. . . . Each one possesses a certain charm, distinctive and appealing, yet leaving much to the imagination of the onlooker to bring out hidden characteristics and meaning. . . . His pictures fulfill the mission of the idealist which transcends the creeds and reaches

the observer by the effect of the beauty which is reflected in his materials.

. . . [Swan] pointed out that the idealist must be an idealist of color, an idealist of form and an idealist of subject. An idealist of color is one who exaggerates certain effects for their results. An idealist of form is a painter who regards grace of line prerequisite, sublime, and the idealist of subject brings out the beautiful for beauty's sake. (SB)

Success in Rochester may only have served to feed the turmoil in an already troubled soul. As Swan's popularity grew and his reputation began to spread to New York City, he bragged of his success to his Nebraska family. He hinted for financial assistance, but he did not feel properly appreciated by any attention or money he received from them. Misunderstanding on both sides marks the history of his relations with them. For his part, he found it difficult to comprehend why they did not support the artist in their clan more generously. He had, after all, painted some very important people in Europe during the previous year; he had been called the new Byron in Greece, "a Greek God Reincarnated."[11] They in turn had problems comprehending why they should underwrite his career, especially because he seemed to be working steadily. Throughout his life Swan appeared to distinguish funds earned by his art from money required for necessities. The former were his to dispense as he pleased, whereas family or friends should supply the latter.

Trouble in Swan's life may have come from another source as well. He was a bisexual married man in the United States, a difficult place for him to explore his unconventional—and illegal—desires. His heart yearned to return to the more bohemian circles that European cities could offer. He therefore did not stay long with Helen. His first extended absence after marriage began in December 1911, when he left on the *Cameronia* for Great Britain.

In the diary he kept during this voyage, Swan records his love for an unnamed man. His affection for his wife was never diminished by such passions; he appeared to have no difficulty keeping his heart compartmentalized. While comparing himself to a butterfly, he reflected: "There is a face I love beside me; there is youth and beauty smiling as he holds his yellow-winged capture. There are no lowering clouds, no monotonous voyages, no strange faces—just love and beauty, and memories of a last kiss." He also wrote of Helen, of waving good-bye to her at the pier, and of "terrible feelings of loneliness." He added, almost hopefully, "What I now leave behind will some day be all the dearer for the leaving."[12]

Swan arrived in Glasgow on Christmas Eve 1911, made his way to London, and soon took a studio at 45 Roland Gardens in South Kensington. With the help of Baron Rosenkrantz, he acquired immediate commissions. One was to paint the portraits of Lady Ian Hamilton and opera singers Louise Dale and Ada Crossley. Lady Hamilton would sit for John Singer Sargent in 1915, but now her artist of choice was Paul Swan. She also purchased Swan's bust of a Greek youth, the first sculpture he ever sold.

As word of the handsome young American circulated around London, his studio became a gathering place. People of note sat for him: the Duchess de Seville (Doña Enriqueta de Borbon y Parade, cousin of the king of Spain); the Marquise of Dufferin and Ava, Lady St. John; Baron Rosenkrantz and his wife, Tessa (whom Swan particularly liked); the singer Zelie de Lussan; Duchess de Lousada; and the Marquise Dusmet de Smours (former lady-in-waiting to Empress Eugenie of Russia). Perhaps his favorite subject was American poet Ella Wheeler Wilcox, who told him when she met him at a society gala, "I don't know who you are, but I'm sure you're *somebody*." "I'm nobody," he told her, "but I will be." She became a fan of his; he always considered her "human, so romantic, and lovable" (DS 207). They remained in touch long after both had returned to the United States.

Rosenkrantz introduced his protégé to dancer Andreas Pavley, who became Swan's immediate, if transitory, friend. A complicated, disturbed man, Pavley had talent and youth and an ego at least as large as Swan's. Even though Swan was jealous, he admired Pavley's physical abilities and boyish good looks; for a time, Swan promoted him in spite of envy. With assistance from Rosenkrantz, he arranged a special performance for Pavley one evening at his studio at Roland Gardens. Pavley and his partner Vallya Lodowska performed an interpretation of Schubert's "Death and the Maiden." "With his long hair and well-made-up face, he created . . . a striking appearance," wrote Swan. "I made many drawings of him. He was very 'spoiled' and condescending in his attitude toward me. He thought I would never become a dancer, as I was not tall enough. He said, 'Your face isn't bad, Pigeon, but your legs are too short.' He spent much time inventing costumes after the drawings I had made." Rosenkrantz also made costume drawings and wrote scene descriptions for a Pavley-Lodowska performance called *The Gate of Life*, produced in July 1912 and performed to music by Beethoven.[13]

Swan practiced dance with Pavley, who helped him refine movement, particularly leaping. "We did not remain friendly, for he assumed a patronizing air toward everything I did which did not revolve about himself." Nine years older than Pavley, Swan was becoming aware of the relentlessness of aging. One day when Pavley stopped by the studio, Swan did not open his door. Had jealousy finally won? Swan only said that it was the end of their "maladjusted friendship" (208). Pavley committed suicide in Chicago nineteen years later, at age thirty-nine. Curiously, Swan, who was nearly fifty at the time, was still attracting audiences, enjoying seeing his name in lights in cities in the United States as well as London, Paris, Berlin, and as far south as Santiago and Buenos Aires. It would not be the first time that his persistence and determination would overcome a rival.

While in London with Rosenkrantz, Swan also took instruction from Russian dancer Mikhail Mordkin, preferring Mordkin's athleticism to Pavley's more balletic style. Swan believed that dancing was as masculine as any sport, and Mordkin, more of a Gene Kelly than a Fred Astaire, was one of his models.

The night before his departure from London in March 1912, Swan accompanied Rosenkrantz to a huge masque—the coronation ball of King George and Queen Mary at the Coliseum Theatre. He donned classical Greek costume, assuming the character of Hermes. Although he thought he might be able to offer an impromptu dance to the masquers, his costume and his bare legs raised eyebrows; he spent most of the night standing behind chairs, avoiding sharp glances and wry smiles, listening to the musical compositions of Edward Elgar. It's easy to imagine the scene straight from a Charlie Chaplin movie, with the inappropriately dressed Swan tugging at his costume as he endured the stares of the British upper crust. The next day, undoubtedly still red-faced, he sent a telegram to Helen to say he was coming home. He left that afternoon from Liverpool for New York.

The couple returned to London together the following September. Helen's several weeks with him were by all accounts pleasurable, two great friends enjoying each other's intimate company. She pretended to be only a friend, agreeing with Swan (if not contriving the idea herself) to dupe the public into thinking he was a single man. "An individualized artist is worth twice as much for success as the settled air of a snugly married one" (208). The ruse worked well enough until the birth of their first child, Paula, in February 1914.

After Helen left London in October 1912, Swan felt a great void in his life and began to think of returning home. Success, as always, made him nervous: the old insecurities began to mount; he thought that too many people were becoming envious and would destroy him; it was time to flee. Because of a recommendation from Rosenkrantz, he received a large commission from Major Dupre of Taplow (Rosenkrantz had designed stained-glass windows for the church in Taplow) to paint a life-size portrait from a photograph of Dupre's dead son. The parents were overcome by the results and paid Swan several hundred pounds. He bought his ticket for the *Baltic* and packed, secretly, for New York. [14] Once again he escaped payment to a landlord, this time by sleeping in the basement of a friend's home for his last few days in London.

When Swan arrived in New York City around Thanksgiving he took a separate residence from Helen on 18 West Thirty-seventh Street in order to preserve his bachelor reputation. He shared the studio with an Englishman named Quinn, with whom he had a brief but close friendship. Quinn desperately missed his fiancée in England, lost his job in New York after a few months, was forsaken by his bride-to-be, left for South Africa where he contracted syphilis, subsequently recovered, enlisted in the English army, and was killed in his first month of service at the front. Such was the brief "résumé of a friend who was too good to have been wasted . . . too much the dreamer for the life of every day" (211–12). Quinn became the inspiration for one of Swan's wartime portraits, *There Are No Dead*, which depicts a bloodied soldier lying in a trench. [15]

One of the women Swan had painted in Cairo in 1910, Maude Bigelow, had returned to New York and in late 1912 introduced Swan to a small-time promoter, Francis Milland, who was immediately attracted to the artist. The friendship with Milland ended later that same year. As a person who doubted his own worth, Swan distrusted Milland, who doted on him. The excuse Swan gave for ending the relationship was that Milland did not hold a compatible artistic vision. It was as if Swan could not respect such a person for his devotion and finally became contemptuous of someone who thought him handsome and talented but was not interested in sharing Swan's ideas of aestheticism. In their last encounter, Swan wrote, "I insulted [Milland], hurt him, even struck him, so hovering about like a humid day he seemed to me. So on this combustive occasion, he gathered up a few of the most costly presents and called a cab to throw them into. . . . I see now he never understood me, or rightfully interpreted me, so much could I do no wrong. . . . I am not a type. I may be a universal composite type, outside of ordinary cataloguing" (214). Milland had worshipped him, recommended him, and waited upon him. When it became apparent that there would be no reciprocity in the friendship, the fights began.

Early in their association, however, Milland arranged for Swan to be one of the performers at an annual gala ball at the Waldorf Hotel. It changed Swan's life, giving him an audience for his aesthetic dances. Swan was granted a solo at the end of the program. The spectators were simply told that "a mysterious and extraordinary manifestation is about to occur." Then wild leaps across the stage, as Swan played imaginary Pan-pipes, disappearing, returning to leap and play again: he had become "Iolaus, the dancer." A few days later, on 17 December 1912, the *New York World* published a two-page article on him, with a photograph of his profile next to a reproduction of the statue of Antinous. "Hailed in Greece as a Greek God Reincarnated," the headline claimed.[16]

An extraordinary career was born. In the same month Swan was the featured dancer at the reception for President William Howard Taft at the Bellevue-Stratford Hotel, New York, where he performed *The Dance of the Winds* and *The Bacchanal*. On 4 February 1913 he shared the stage with dancers Ruth St. Denis and Pedro de Cordoba at the famous Louis Comfort Tiffany fete.[17] Seven days later, distinguished dancer Violet Romer presented him as "Iolaus" at the Lyceum Theater. He performed *The Dance of the Winds*, *Andante Cantabile*, and *Hu-*

moresque, following Romer's *The Sphinx*, a dance Swan quickly adapted for his own repertoire. [18]

Public and Private Wars

Demand for Swan's various talents continued unabated. On 7 March 1913 his portrait of playwright Ada Patterson appeared in the *New York Star*. [19] About the same time, his drawing of Wallace Stevens's friend Laura Sherry Dexter was published in the *New York Sunday Sentinel*. [20]

Swan next danced throughout the Midwest and eastern seaboard, painting and drawing portraits at each stop. Before spending time in North Carolina in May at the invitation of Swedish American literary critic Edwin Bjorkman (1866–1951), he performed on 29 April at the Odeon Theater in St. Louis, winning critical acclaim but beginning to suffer from the stage fright that would plague him for the rest of his career. [21] Bjorkman first saw Swan that night, and a St. Louis paper later quoted him as saying, "In one year, if nothing halts his progress, Swan will be the greatest dancer the world knows" (*Reedy's Mirror of St. Louis*, sb).

Another admirer in the audience that evening was Swan's former companion, Forest Weaver. They had not seen each other since they had been together in Chicago a decade earlier. It was a sad meeting, punctuating the end of an old friendship. Forest had become a streetcar conductor in Arkansas and was worn down by a hard life. Once he had wanted to be like his teacher; now he barely scraped out a living. "This is, I suppose, a 'so long,'" he told Swan. "You're the only real friend I ever had. I have these women friends, of course, but only for one thing. They are not my friends. Hell no!" In the 1930s, Swan wrote in his memoir, "I always expected the impossible; he expected nothing" (222).

By 16 May 1913, Swan was performing at the Modern Dancing Carnival at the Mechanics Building in Boston. His innovative style was creating positive attention everywhere. In June a two-page article entitled "Swan: An American Who Revives the Greek Ideal" appeared in *Theatre Magazine*: "He is the first of our countrymen brave and bold enough to champion the dance, and to claim for it a place high among the arts and professions of men whole and entire," the author wrote. "Although he . . . is an artist, he dares to be a dancer; and though he

13. Paul Swan performing *The Sphinx* (photo not dated), a dance he first presented in 1913. Photograph from authors' collection.

is a dancer, he dares to be a man. Such is his temerity, and when you consider that the world still suspects artists of being only half-men (the other half may be goblin, woman, divinity or devil), it is indeed temerity" (SB).

Not to be outdone in advertising this new heartthrob, *Vanity Fair* published a photograph of Swan dancing. Reporter Janet Vale's article, "From Plowboy to Greek God," appeared in the *Morning Telegraph*. In yet another journal, Arthur Row (an actor who served as press manager for Sarah Bernhardt's American tour) wrote: "I would like to call him a genius, and have done with it, were it not that that word is worked to death and no longer means anything; besides, this would confuse him with a lot of rather ordinary people" (SB).

Swan's final engagement for the season was at Governor's Island for the "Farewell of General Thomas H. Barry," who was retiring after being presented the Medal of Cuban Pacification by Theodore Roosevelt. It was a grand festival, and Swan was the only performer for the occasion. A few days later he left with his mother-in-law, his pregnant wife, and a cache of paints and canvases for the Adirondacks and Skiwaukee. Because of Helen's pregnancy, they didn't return to New York City but spent the winter in Albany with Mrs. Gavit. When baby Paula made her appearance on 10 February 1914, no one was happier than her father.

Swan danced *A Greek Phantasy* at Frazee's Longacre Theater on Forty-eighth Street on 3 March 1914 and was in St. Louis in April dancing again at the Odeon. On 21 April, Macbeth Gallery's exhibition "A Group of Selected Paintings by American Artists" opened. Swan's *Pavlowa* hung next to Robert Henri's *Bridget*, Maurice Prendergast's *The Sea Shore*, and Charles W. Hawthorne's *Twilight* (Macbeth Gallery brochure, SB).

By now Swan had come to the attention of Loney Haskell, who managed Arthur Hammerstein's Victoria Theater on Forty-second Street and Broadway in New York. Haskell was looking for a starring act for the theater's jubilee week in October and was attracted to Swan's theatricality. He contacted Swan's agent, and the dancer was hired.

Swan was shocked when he walked into the theater to see his name blazoned everywhere: "Swan pronounced the Most Beautiful Man in the World, A Reincarnated Greek God." He was tagged for life. "What do you care, as long as you get the money?" Haskell asked him. Swan threatened to withdraw, upset at the "circus advertisement." But he did not. On 27 October the *New York Evening Journal* ran an article entitled "The Prettiest Male in Captivity," which did not calm Swan's distress: his aesthetic dance program was being turned into a vaudeville act. By the time opening afternoon arrived on 6 November, his stage fright began to surface. Short of breath before the first dance was over, he fell down. Papers reported that one man in the chorus fainted as well and that "wild excitement" ran through the audience. Swan recovered, apologized to the audience, and continued (SB).

The after-dinner show was even more difficult. Swan was the first solo male dancer ever to perform in such a theater setting in the United States, and the vaudeville audience didn't know how to react. There was laughter and bewilderment. On the second night he was fed up, stopped the program midway, and left the stage. Hammerstein rushed into the dressing room, furious. He had a boisterous audience demanding to be entertained. Swan returned to the stage but did not continue his dance. Instead, with an innate grasp of the situation, he gave a short lecture: "Ladies and gentlemen, my act is not supposed to be amusing, and if you find it laughable, I cannot proceed. I am not a vaudeville performer. I hope I am an artist. . . . Shall I go on with the dance?" (DS 230). The audience responded positively. Hammerstein held him over for a total of twenty-eight performances because, as one paper reported, there was "insistent public demand" (SB). The money allowed Swan, Helen, and baby Paula to move into a more elegant studio on West Eighty-sixth Street.

Demand for his portraits, his dance, and his lectures on art and aesthetics continued throughout the decade. In 1915, shortly after his return to New York from a tour in the mid-Atlantic states, Swan was sent to lecture and give several dance performances in Louisville, Kentucky, by invitation from writer Eleanor Mercein Kelly and the Louisville Woman's Club.[22] What especially pleased Swan at this time was that shortly after he left Louisville, Diaghilev's Ballets Russes arrived in town and drew much smaller crowds.[23] One newspaper headline read "Swan delights Hundreds," and the reporter wrote that he "realized himself in the presence of a master artist." About this time, the *New York Herald* called him "America's Premier Dancer" (SB).

14. *The Artist's Wife and Child* by Paul Swan, 1916. Oil on canvas. Location and size of original not known. Photograph from authors' collection.

In Louisville, Swan developed a new program based on a Negro spiritual, "The Downward Road Is Crowded with Unbelieving Souls." He created the dance extempore, hoping that the spontaneity would contribute to the effect of primitiveness. The patrons were delighted. The challenge of facing spectators with only a framework of choreography appealed to Swan, as it seemed to impart a vitality to his performance that more formal dances lacked. It was not the first time, and it would not be the last, that he counted on fear and inspiration to give birth to a new dance.

What happened later that night was known only to Swan and a

mysterious paramour, clearly not his wife: "This began for me a seven-year tragedy," he wrote in his memoir. An effusion of poems followed, from "Transmutation" ("A gentle tap at the door- / And Heaven's glory reigns!") to "July 24th 1918" ("I have come these thousand miles. . . . / Yet as I knock upon your door / . . . Unbearable eternity seems to yawn / In this suspense!") to "Now" (" . . . the lagging postman / Is no longer the messenger of Destiny— / Now, when my boughs are bare and numb / And winter-stilled" [DS 242–45]). *Southern Woman's Magazine* later published one of the group, "Parting." Four other poems by Swan appeared in the same issue, along with two photos of him and one of his oil painting *Refugees* (SB).

Refugees represented a major change. By the time Swan painted it, Europe was at war. It was as if the age, confronted with the horrors of the first modern conflict, was reacting against aestheticism. The painting, inspired by the devastation resulting from the Battle of Flanders (11 November 1914), shows a donkey laden with bits of their life salvaged by a displaced family. A mother holds a baby as two other children stand, worn and thin, beside her. A dog follows alongside and, farther behind, an old woman clutches her coat. The war seemed to have modified Swan's preoccupation with physical perfection and inspired, at least in this instance, a more realistic depiction.

A later issue of *Southern Woman's Magazine* published yet another of Swan's war paintings, *Unheeded*, in which "soldiers [dressed like World War I combatants] surge past the crucifixion, unheeding the sacrifice of Christ." A photograph of it also appeared in a January 1917 edition of the *Louisville Evening Post*.[24] Of course, Swan was not the only artist changed by war. Even John Singer Sargent, whose paintings Swan had long admired, created such works as *Gassed* and *The Interior of a Hospital Tent*.

What set Swan apart from other artists of this period was that his view of war was reflected not only in his paintings but also in his sculpture, dance, and poetry. *Petit Soldat Inconnu* and *Lest We Forget* are two examples of his best war-period sculpture, and they show the influence of his former mentor Lorado Taft. The first depicts the embattled soldier, an ideal Greek youth with a shawl wrapped around his neck. Unfortunately, soon after it was shown at the Paris Salon in 1939,

15. Detail from Paul Swan's *Refugees*, about 1915. Oil on canvas. Location and size not known. Photograph courtesy of Dallas Swan Jr.

Swan had to leave the country and entrusted the work and dozens of other paintings, sculptures, and drawings to an Italian insurance company (the owner of the building where he lived). None of the artwork was ever returned to him after the war. *Lest We Forget*, one of two sculptures that made the trip back to the United States with Swan in 1939, was pictured in the *Los Angeles Sunday Times* in 1923 and is seen in a photograph of Swan's Carnegie Hall studio in the 1950s, but its location today is not known.[25]

Swan cut his performance fee or danced for free for benefits to raise money to help those directly affected by the war. He had friends from England fighting, and he was worried about them. In his poem "War

Proclaimed," he lamented that young men not much more than children "have learned to hate, and blindly wield the tools of retribution" (DS 256).

As early as 1914, Swan began to develop a series of dances to honor soldiers. One of his most famous, last performed in Andy Warhol's 1965 movie *Paul Swan*, was *To Heroes Slain*—a tribute to those who "lie / In Flanders fields."[26] According to the *Washington Herald*, in May 1915 Swan drew huge crowds at a benefit for the French Ambulance Fund when he performed for several nights in one of Mrs. Christian Hemmick's plays, *The Opium Pipe*, at the Belasco Theater in Washington DC (SB). In fact, a letter from one of the promoters (A. R. Elmore) later informed him that "300 people were turned away" on one occasion (SB). *To Heroes Slain*, performed within the framework of the play, was an immediate hit.

Rumors now surfaced of Swan's marriage to dancer Ruth St. Denis. Several newspapers confirmed the story. "How could it be me?" he asked reporters, informing them of his wife and baby daughter. Finally the confusion was straightened out and the papers corrected their error: St. Denis had married someone named Theodore Shawn (SB). Shawn became a noted dancer himself, copying several of Swan's early creations.

A few weeks after his performances at the Belasco Theater, Swan was on his way to England again, "not realizing the depth into which England had been plunged by war" (DS 249). Sir Philip Ben Greet, the director of Aldwych Theater, near Covent Garden, arranged for a series of performances. Swan was also eager for another opportunity to work with Rosenkrantz, who by then spent most of his time in the anthroposophical community in Dornach, Switzerland, but occasionally had commissions in London.

London was not as he had left it three years before. The signs of war were everywhere: "The suspense and anguish of the women's faces as the wounded soldiers arrived at Charring Cross or Victoria Station, maimed, mutilated, blind, made me ill with inexpressible helplessness" (251). When he returned to the United States later in the summer, Swan painted battle victims and war scenes exclusively for more than a month. He said that if he did not "paint out the war" he would go mad, and he called the months that followed "the first winter of the shadows" (251). He became two separate people, he said: the one who danced, entertained, and painted society folk, and the one who knew that *To Heroes Slain* was an image of bloody truth. He did what little he could for the cause of peace. On 18 May 1916, for example, he performed *The Faun* and *The Moonlight Sonata* at the New York Biltmore Hotel's benefit for the Allies Hospitals Relief Commission (SB).

In June 1918, Swan danced for the National League for Woman's Service benefit for France at the Orpheum Theater in Lincoln, Nebraska. He performed two of his standard dances, *The Sphinx* and *Narcissus*, which fans familiar with his earlier work would have expected. But after the United States entered World War I on 6 April 1917 and American soldiers started dying, audiences demanded *To Heroes Slain*. Had he thought to omit it, it would have been as if Kate Smith declined to sing "God Bless America" at a concert.

Swan found the last few years of the war a particularly difficult time. While between engagements in early 1918, he was summoned for his draft interview but given a family exemption. His second daughter, Flora, had been born the year before (5 June), and Paula was only four.

When Flora was an adult, she told a cousin that she had been conceived at Skiwaukee Farm out of disappointment. Swan had been neglected by a boyfriend (the cause of his "seven-year tragedy," no doubt) and so made love to his wife to exact some odd sort of revenge. Whether or not the story was true, why either Helen or Paul would tell this to their daughter boggles the mind. Did Flora misunderstand something she heard, or could her parents have thought that she might appreciate the drama of the story? She did not.

In any case, in 1918 Swan joined the Seventh Regiment of Home Guards and trained soldiers to march every Friday and Monday night at the Sixty-ninth Regiment Armory in New York. "I now teach men the way to march / Through rage, through pain, / To Death's annihilation. / . . . I who know the spirit's sovereignty," he wrote in "In Camp," one of his poems from that year (256). The images that this training elicits have little to do with military formations, but perhaps Swan subdued his choreography for anxious soldiers.

The disastrous secret love affair was still upsetting his equilibrium. "This was the period of my life's highest exaltation and darkest despair; I lived as one in a whirling dream, with the anguish of the untellable as my daily bread" (255). Fortunately, he had met a friend a few years earlier who would see him through good times and bad without being judgmental. American poet Jeanne Robert Foster, who had been proclaimed "the loveliest woman in the world" by *Vanity Fair* in 1903 and whom Swan sculpted in 1917 when she was thirty-eight, was now often by his side. Her apartment on West Forty-ninth Street was within walking distance of his own, and he found solace in their companionship (*DY* 168–72). Both of them appreciated the magnificence of human form, and if neither was quite in the prime of beauty, they had an understanding of what had been. They were friends for as long as they lived and shared a dedication to fighting for the oppressed.

One such fight involved a woman's right to vote, and it became Swan's primary cause on the home front. Between 1913 and 1920 he gave numerous benefit performances in support of the suffrage movement, often in conjunction with playwright Mrs. Christian Hemmick, a friend of Swan's who allowed her house at 1626 Rhode Island Avenue in Washington DC to be used as headquarters for the National American Woman Suffrage Association. On February 17 and 18, 1913, he acted in the Women's Political Union production of *Lysistrata* at the Maxine Elliot Theatre in New York. "He personally trained the dancers for this production," one article stated.[27] "Also, he himself led the legions of the light fantastic dressed (some might say undressed) as a shepherd" (SB). "Suffragettes Gasp as Iolaus Prances," announced a headline in the *New York Herald* (SB). The *New York Evening Journal* ("Suffragists Seek an Adonis," 12 April 1913) published a photo of Swan with Inez Milholland. Whenever these brave friends called on him, Swan happily gave his time, with no expectation of recompense.

After Milholland died in Los Angeles in 1916, Swan memorialized her in a life-size sculpture. Pictured in both the *New York Times* and the *Brooklyn Eagle*, it shows Inez in flowing gown, reaching outward and upward with one hand, as if trying to grasp the tenuous spirit of equality.[28] First displayed at the Metropolitan Museum of Art, the

16. *Jeanne Robert Foster* by Paul Swan, 1917. Plaster. Location and size not known. Photograph from authors' collection.

sculpture was later moved to the Milholland family estate (Meadow Mount) near Elizabethtown, New York, in the Adirondacks. Inez's father was John E. Milholland, a friend of Swan's and an editor for the *New York Herald*; her mother was journalist Jean Torry Milholland (DY 220–22). After the Milhollands died and their Adirondack home was sold, the statue disappeared.

When Swan was spending occasional summers at Skiwaukee in Stony Creek during the late 1910s and early 1920s, he may well have taken the train thirty miles north to see his sculpture of Inez guarding the entrance to Meadow Mount. Between 1913 and 1921 he spent most of every July and August in northern New York. With Helen's encouragement, Swan invited friends, artists, and philosophers to join them at Skiwaukee. He wanted to establish a community where young artists could find instruction, audience, and appreciation. "We especially discourage the commercial craftsmen who work only for money," he said in an interview with the *New York Sun* published on 10 May 1914. Like William Morris, Swan longed to make artistic creation available to ordinary people. "The type of worker whom we aim to interest in our colony," he said, "is the honest laborer in the realm of the ideal who has something to express and is brave enough to express that something, even at pecuniary loss and in the face of ridicule." He explained his different feelings for his own work: "I paint to get it out of my system, and I dance to express those subtle emotions and hidden meanings which help us to feel that life is somehow good and beautiful—and pass the news along." How successful Swan's Adirondack community became is unclear. One participant was John Burroughs, perhaps because he was interested in the venture, or because he was an old friend of the Gavit family. Skiwaukee still stands today, but only in the minds of the oldest residents of Stony Creek are there vague memories of the handsome artist who tried to create a new golden age in the mountains.

There were some glorious, carefree moments during the war years when Swan reveled in his celebrity and could, for at least a short time, be light of heart. When Lillian Russell came to see his artwork at the Gamut Club portrait exhibition in May 1916, she told him, "I know who *you* are, the most beautiful man in the world!" (DS 246). On 24 April 1917 he found himself on the same program as Russell, performing

17. A page from Paul Swan's scrapbook at The John and Mable Ringling Museum of Art. Shown are Swan's sculpture of Inez Milholland, Swan with his daughter Paula, and his sketch of musician Evelyn Starr. Photograph courtesy of the collection of The John and Mable Ringling Museum of Art, the State Art Museum of Florida.

for the Professional Woman's League at the Criterion Theater in New York City.

Swan shared wall space at the Gamut Club exhibition with only three other artists—John Butler Yeats, Lillian T. Schmidt, and Charles W. Hawthorne. Yeats and Swan were well acquainted by now. Each was an admirer of Jeanne Robert Foster, and both had known John Burroughs for nearly a decade. At the Gamut Club show, Swan's portraits took up most of the space, with *Nijinski, Mme. Nazimova, Mrs. Swan and Daughter, Miss Bertha Galland,* and *Mrs. Winnifred Harper Cooley.* Yeats's works were *Mrs. Franz Bellinger* and *Mr. Guy Holt.*

Performers began to imitate Swan's dances, some as comedy. Who could resist spoofing "the most beautiful man in the world"? In 1916, two young performers named Fred and Adele Astaire used Swan's name in one of their dance routines when Adele would exclaim, "Don't think *you* look like Paul Swan!" (DS 247; SB). Ten years later, Ira Gershwin used the line in the lyrics of a song in his brother's musical *Funny Face.*

On 21 May 1916 an article in the *New York Herald* titled "The Art of the Mural Painter, the Portrait Painter, the Sculptor, and the Caricaturist, Paul Swan" publicized the June release of *Diana the Huntress,* one of the first color movies. Swan watched himself on the big screen at the Strand Theater in New York playing two roles, Pan and Apollo. He drove wild horses hitched to a chariot and rode over clouds of smoke to create, as he called it, a "celestial" effect. Bray Studios made several "shorts" of him as various Greek mythic figures. A photo still exists of him in *Narcissus.* Swan (as Narcissus) reposes in a pond in Central Park, no doubt enticed into the water by the beauty of his figure. The photo doesn't show the blood that was oozing at that moment from a large gash in his foot, caused by broken glass in the pond. After stitches and an uncomfortable night, he was ready the next day to film *Orpheus* for the same company (DS 253–54; SB). The pond scene in *Narcissus* was ultimately used in *Diana the Huntress.*

Helen's labeling of Swan as "the good-bye-saying husband" was certainly appropriate as the third decade of the twentieth century approached. In 1918 and 1919 he rarely saw his wife and daughters except for part of each summer in Stony Creek. By 1920 he was still touring and spending a great deal of time painting and dancing, this time primarily in New Orleans. At Christmastime he was back in New York to dance for an event at the Dewitt Clinton Hotel. After the holidays he left again for New Orleans to finish a lucrative commission for Louis Grunewald: murals for the lobby of Grunewald's famous six-story hotel on Baronne Street, near the French Quarter. On this trip he met Bernard J. Callaway, a young man who would play an important role a decade later in the story of *Self-Portrait in Egyptian Dress*, one of Swan's most famous paintings.

Shortly after his return to New York in late January 1921, Swan waved good-bye again to his family as they stood on the dock, watching his ship set sail for France. Success in New Orleans "enabled me to be free in my own Paris studio" (259). Two little girls and a wife weren't going to deter him.

Swan's actions may seem less than admirable to those not privy to the dynamics of this strange family, and in fact for the next ten pages of his autobiography Swan doesn't mention Helen, Paula, or Flora. When he does, he speaks of his "two sweet downy cygnets in the nest whom I long with all my heart to see." He was willing to admit that he was an inadequate parent: "Can an ambitious artist really be a good father?" (270). But he had a wife who was "a perfect mother" to take care of them. The pleasures of Paris awaited.[29]

6 All the World's a Stage, 1921–1925

Paris, New York, and Nebraska

Isadora Duncan (1878–1927) called to the attractive man making his way to the dance floor. "O, beautiful youth, come here to me! Where have you come from? Arcady? Who are you? Why haven't I seen you before?"

"I'm Paul Swan," he told her as she caught his hand.

"Oh well, that explains you; you *are* from Arcady, from my beloved Greece. I've read often about you."

Swan felt awkward when she pulled him closer in their dance, feeling people's eyes on them. "What do we care?" she whispered to him. "We don't see them. That's the point. We don't see them."

Then she was gone, called to the table for a toast in her honor.

It was a brief encounter on the night of the Bal Noir et Blanc given at the Théâtre des Champs-Élysées in 1921. Swan and Duncan became neither romantic companions nor long-term dance partners, but for a short time they shared a friendship and visits to each other's studios (Swan's was at 49 boulevard Berthier). At Duncan's studio in the rue de la Pompe, Swan and two of Duncan's friends—Samuel Small Russel and Mary Desti—spent Duncan's last evening (2 April) in Paris with her before her departure to Russia, via London.[1] She was everything Swan had fantasized her to be, possessing "an elegance of nature which, no matter what she might do, on or off the stage, could never permit her to descend into the realm of the common or coarse. . . . Isadora was authentic, fundamental, primitive. . . . She felt what she did; she did what she felt: a perfect résumé for her heroic art" (DS 263).[2] It isn't remarkable that he felt a kinship with the bohemian Duncan. Her capacity to live life on her own terms appealed to Swan, for no matter how much he wanted to be free of bourgeois restraint, there was always enough of Crab Orchard in him to make him care what others said.

Buoyed by a letter from his wife, who told him that three of his poems had just been published in *American Poetry Magazine*, Swan felt excited to see how Paris would receive his painting.[3] He began immediately. At least partly because of his famous friends, portrait commissions were easy to obtain, but he also experimented with new techniques in murals and landscapes. One of his acquaintances, Aimée Crocker (an American friend of occultist Aleister Crowley and future wife [1925] of Prince Mstislav Aleksandrovitch Galitzine of Kiev), introduced him to Polish artist Boleslas Biegas, whose studio was in the Latin Quarter. In Biegas's atelier, Swan was surrounded by stylized heroic figures in plaster, many in grotesque poses illuminated "by weird half-lights, and [sounds of] faint music from a harmonium accompanied the smoke of incense" (265). One evening the cognoscenti who had gathered at the studio asked Swan to dance, and one lady suggested, perhaps on a whim, that the dancer should fit the setting. He disrobed and for the first time in public danced nude, moving among the white, contorted statuary. According to Swan the audience loved it, and after that he performed there regularly *au naturel*. The press subsequently noticed him. *Le Théâtre et Comoedia Illustré* printed photographs of him (in costume), praised his genius in several articles, and chose him for the cover of the February issue. On 23 July 1921 the Paris edition of the *New York Herald Tribune* reported that he was dancing at Le Pré-Catelan Hotel in Juans Les Pins, near Cannes, by invitation of actor and choreographer Harry Pilcer.[4]

Swan was drawn to Biegas's work, which created in him a near-hypnotic state as he danced among the strange forms. Inevitably, some Biegas motifs crept into his own art. Swan's description of two of his paintings of the period suggests not only his continued dedication to Rosenkrantz (as in Rosenkrantz's *Death*)[5] but Biegas's influence with respect to negative space and gray coloring: "One was a gray *Nocturne*, with faint stylized trees in front of a lake with high horizon line faintly discernible. The other, tall trees silhouetted against the sun-path of a lake. In the foreground Orpheus stood with his lyre. This was called *Vers le Soleil*" (263).[6]

A year later, both of Swan's paintings were accepted by the Salon d'Automne, held in the Grand Palais on the Champs-Élysées (November–December 1922). Unfortunately, both disappeared from Paris during World War II and remain lost to this day. But several extant canvases by Swan, including *Fête Romantique* (1951), with its fine, tall poplars framing and dwarfing the festive human figures, are testimonies to Biegas's influence.[7]

The famous courtesan Fernande Lara Cabanel visited Biegas's studios one evening sometime in 1921 during Swan's performance. The "sumptuous" actress (as Swan called her), with diamond dust sparkling from her eyelashes and lips, aroused him. He wanted to make love to her, and until he did he thought of little else. It was an unusual passion for him. He had known many beautiful women to whom he had been attracted aesthetically, but there was something about Cabanel that made him want her in the most literal way. Cabanel, called "Paris's lioness" by Princess Georges Ghika, was trouble.[8] An opium addict (Swan avoided all drugs, including caffeine), Cabanel was the seductive "bad girl" who had sex appeal, notoriety, money, and "Frenchness." And, to complete her allure, she bought Swan's art. Her first purchase was the sculpture *Douleur* (also known by its Americanized spelling, *Dolor*), which was later shown at exhibitions in both North and South America, including the National Academy of Design in New York and Gallerias de Los Amigos del Artes in Buenos Aires.

Trying to hold himself "aloof from the temptation of [Cabanel's] opium" and "the promiscuity of sex acts," Swan fled in November 1921 to the United States, into the arms of Helen and his two daughters. His previous trysts had been almost exclusively with men, and he did not consider his homosexual relationships adulterous in the same way that he did his few sexual encounters with women.[9] An idiosyncratic and personal definition of adultery is of course not unique to Swan.

Straying spouses have often decided for themselves what did or did not constitute disloyalty, running the gamut from oral sex to whatever sex act they decide is outside the purview of fidelity.

But Swan desired Cabanel and so needed to get a measure of Helen to sober him. "Whether I was gleaning information for use in my after computations of human values, or whether I was merely looking for adventures . . . remains a question for some clearer judgment than mine" (269). Although some may argue that the true bisexual is relatively rare, Paul Swan at this stage in his life seems to be the kind of person for whom Freud employed the term "polymorphously perverse" (Freud 664).

Returning to Helen felt like making "a pilgrimage to the feet of my Taj Mahal, for counsel and revaluation," Swan wrote. "This lady gives me a crystal glass wherein I may see my complicated, many-faceted life in clear perspective." His choice of a beautiful tomb as an epithet for his wife was appropriate. He speaks of Helen as an art object, and that function may be more important to him than her physical presence. Helen belonged to "reason, philosophy, inner growth, and the silent places of the soul" (270).

Cabanel, on the other hand, represented "the senses, the arts, achievement, worldly glamour" (270). If Helen attracted Swan's Apollonian sensibility, it was not for long, for after three weeks of comfort and good sense he returned to the Dionysus, Paris, and Cabanel. In this day of easy transatlantic air travel, a hurried trip such as this seems of little consequence, but one must consider that the ocean voyages alone would have taken as much time as Swan spent with his family. Whether running toward or away from temptation, Swan rarely considered the logistics of his decisions.

Together in her apartment, they lay on Cabanel's lush black-and-white velour divan, "contemplating the physical beauty of our persons." This was his justification. Shouldn't they consummate the affair as an artistic, orgasmic, and, according to his account, athletic tribute to their perfect, "beautiful" union? "There is much I would like to tell to convey the splendor, the sensuousness, and the pagan naturalness of our *amour*, which became, in that opium-scented room with the rose lights, the drawn curtains, the sultry tropical temperature, contrasting the icy snow of February outside, a passionate physical union, for its own sake indulged, because two beautiful bodies were drunk with the sumptuous feeling of health and vitality" (271).

The reader of Swan's unpublished memoir, "The Distorted Shadow," is witness to cinematic voyeurism that begins on a genuinely erotic note but modulates into the comic, or even camp, principally because of the narcissism of the author. It is as if the artist must cease copulation in mid-stroke and divert his energy to paint a voluptuous scene. Adulterous sex can be justified if it makes a beautiful picture. Swan explained his behavior by once again rejecting the "Puritan . . . cold, depleted, ugly-faced suppressors" that Adah Swan had wished her son to emulate. He refused to "castrate natural impulses." The affair was a "sacrament of the body" as "a ritual service to the glory of self." Whether he ever confessed the indiscretion to Helen is not known, but as she was the occasional typist for his memoir, it is likely that there were few secrets between them. She had married her artist, had borne two lovely children, and seemed content. Their friendship never wavered.

Cabanel knew the power brokers of Paris. When Swan gave a public performance in her Babylonian-styled ballroom (she kept several rooms in a hotel on rue Raffet) he won instant fame, and Paris journals, the tabloids of their day, were happy to chronicle the activity. On 15 February 1922, for instance, *Dansons!* gave him front-page praise: "Une Révélation: Paul Swan." A *Comoedia* article, "Mlle Fernande Cabanel présente le danseur Paul Swan," mentioned that Raymond Duncan, Isadora's brother and the dancer's friend, was in attendance (SB).

By then, Swan had recognized that he and Cabanel were both "self-centered beings, each more in love with selfhood than otherwise" (DS 271). Inevitably, a passionate fight ensued between the two egos, with at least one antique urn reduced to shards. Few other details are known. Cabanel canceled her ex-lover's already-scheduled shows. He was banned from her presence before the *Dansons!* review appeared in print. Had he not paid proper homage? He may have realized that he didn't need her anymore; he may have decided he was no longer one of her "Pomeranians," a term used in the French press for her lovers.

The management at Théâtre de la Potinière (rue Louis le Grand) heard that the dancer was suddenly available and hired him for seventeen performances. There he danced "nude except for the most in-

18. *Fernande Lara Cabanel* by Paul Swan, 1922. Graphite on paper. Location and size not known. Photograph courtesy of Dallas Swan Jr.

significant of draperies."[10] One reviewer glorified him in no uncertain terms: "Even if there were no music, no costumes and no dances, and he should stand alone upon the stage, no doubt Paris audiences would gather to admire him, for a figure like his has not been seen in Europe since Apollo Belvedere's model went home to sit near the Gods" (sb).[11]

Praise from noted Parisian critic Guillot de Saix of *Le Petit Bleu*, who called Swan "a priest of rhythm," established the man from Nebraska as "one of the biggest hits of all the dancers" (sb). One can only wonder if Swan's brothers and sisters in Crab Orchard frowned or smiled when they read the *World Traveler*'s interview with their brother after his debut: "I am a farmer's son. When I was back home I ploughed the straightest furrows in the county." A background that he once wished to minimize had become an asset, for it suggested his rising Antaeus-like, from the earth itself. How many furrows he actually plowed he neglected to say.

Reports of his breakup with Cabanel reached the American press. On 23 April the *Pittsburgh Dispatch* published photos of him onstage at La Potinière and of his painting depicting a voluptuous Cabanel. The paper noted that after Swan's performance at Cabanel's studio, she was furious and wrote him a nasty letter (why she was angry is not stated). Swan is quoted: "Had I received the letter she wrote me immediately after the performance I should have committed suicide. . . . But it's all over now and I feel I have triumphed in spite of [her]!"[12]

Despite his success at La Potinière, Swan decided to leave for New York shortly after his obligation to the theater had ended. If his 1910 departure from New York, or from Athens in 1911, seemed ill advised, his return to the United States at the time when his star was on the rise in Paris seems reckless. Why he did not stay to reap rewards from his efforts? Did he miss his family so much that he had to leave the city he loved at the moment of acclaim? His name was everywhere. His work was exhibited in the Salon. People clamored for him to paint their portraits. Young men in reviews were even stripping to dance nude "like Swan." (Of course, Swan knew they were only poor copies: "Not possessing the Greek spirit, they had no sense of the sanctity of beauty. They simply succeeded in being naked" [ds 273].) Nudity became the rage, and Paul Swan was the paragon of nudity.

"I was glad as always to be near my family again," Swan wrote after his return to New York (274). He had brought back from Paris several paintings, including the stunning *Jeanne d'Arc*, which would later draw attention in an exhibition in New York. He had three portrait commissions waiting for him to execute in Greenwich, Connecticut, and dance performances at the Edgewood Inn. It was as if a pitcher for the New York Yankees had decided in the midst of the World Series to go semi-pro. Despite aching for bohemian Paris, he did not return. His spirits rose in September when the magazine *Shadowland* ran a long article with photos: "Paul Swan, Artist."[13] In the same month, his own article, "On with the Dance," appeared in *Gargoyle*.

Swan's home state of Nebraska acknowledged him, too. He was invited to the Second Annual Nebraska Artists Exhibition from 6 to 29 October 1922 and received more attention than any other artist. On 19 November the *Sunday Magazine* of the *Omaha Daily News* ran flattering photos of him in "The Perfect Man." Cabanel, who had decided that Swan was someone too important to ignore and so made gestures of reconciliation, was no doubt pleased when he wrote to her that *Douleur* was featured in the news story.

Hollywood, Paris, and New York

Thinking he might now build upon his earlier success in films, Swan moved to the center of the industry. With Helen's approval, the family packed their bags and headed west, renting for a time in the Laguna Beach area. He won instant attention. *Laguna Life* ran numerous articles about him, replete with photographs of him and his artwork in several editions.[14]

After Swan made the obligatory rounds at casting offices in Hollywood, an agent spotted him in a dance performance and arranged a meeting with Cecil B. DeMille. They liked each other immediately. DeMille, who said that Swan reminded him of actor Wallace Reid (the matinee idol who would die in January 1923 at the age of thirty), saw a star in the making. A contract was quickly signed for Swan to play the Captain of the Pharaoh's Guard in *The Ten Commandments*, with the stage name of John Randolph. During the first day of filming the court scene in the Pharaoh's throne room, as the man from Crab Orchard knelt before his new king, he thought that he was on his way, finally, to "universal glory" (DS 275).

19. Paul Swan (kneeling) in *The Ten Commandments*, 1923. Photograph courtesy of Dallas Swan Jr.

After a brief honeymoon period, during which DeMille was intrigued by Swan's classic good looks and engaging personality, disagreements ensued over the function of dance in *The Ten Commandments*. Swan had been directed to train four actors who played the part of slaves. "I rehearsed the clumsy Negroes . . . but it seemed that, from their comic awkwardness, they could not learn the mastery of their undisciplined bodies sufficiently to perform this simple piece of stage business" (276). He insisted that they be dismissed and more professional dancers employed. He had been expected to train these neophytes in a few days, and after one or two vain attempts he said he would no longer waste his time. Not surprisingly, DeMille didn't appreciate the challenge to his directorial authority and, according to Swan, kicked him off the set after four days of filming. In a gesture of ill-thought defiance, Swan refused his salary.

The DeMille experience was not entirely a waste of time. Swan's part did not end up on the cutting-room floor, and for a few days he had lived in an Egyptian milieu. Inspired by the movie and by *The Sphinx* dance from his usual repertoire, he painted one of the central portraits of his career. *Self-Portrait in Egyptian Dress* seems flat at first glance, especially when compared to other Swan self-portraits, such as one of him seated at a piano.[15] Usually he lavished loving detail upon his own image, but in this case there is little in the rigid pose to suggest the vitality of the subject. Of course there was from the turn of the century a Western interest in orientalism, reinvigorated in the early 1920s by the discovery of Tutankhamen's tomb.[16] But in the case of this painting, there is more than homage to the current trend. Why not reference the sources of his inspiration with a more carefully delineated face and figure?

If one examines the picture, however, one finds that it follows the principles of Egyptian painting, especially that of frontalism, in which the head of the character is always drawn in profile, while the body is viewed from the front. It may be that Swan, in his attempt to be recognized as the subject, incorporated elements of Amarna, the style instituted by Akhenaton, the pharaoh who introduced monotheism to Egypt. Akhenaton decreed that his likeness be naturalistic and not ignore his thick lips and ample belly. The Amarna style did not survive Akhenaton's son-in-law, Tutankhamen, and subsequent rulers chose to be shown in more abstract poses.

Swan, with his love for Grecian abstraction, would of course be sympathetic to the idealized Egyptian forms as long as they dealt with the perfection of the body. But he did consider his own body to be such an exemplar, so it is understandable that his face is clearly Paul Swan, matching photographs of him in the same pose.

Swan stayed in Hollywood for a while to see if another film opportunity might turn up. On 27 January 1923 the *Los Angeles Evening Express* reported that he was "the sensation of the evening" at the California Arts Club benefit at the Philharmonic Auditorium the previous evening. He was still on the West Coast in late spring, when the *San Diego Union* ran a long article with pictures, "Famous as Painter, Sculptor, Dancer, Paul Swan Called Incarnation of Art" (6 May).

After showing several works at the Los Angeles Museum's Fourth Exhibition of Painters and Sculptors of Southern California (4 May–4 June) and the Exhibition of American Sculptors (14 April–1 August),

Swan grew tired of the United States. On 6 July 1923 his photograph appeared on the cover of *Holly Leaves*, a Hollywood weekly, but he no longer seemed to care if directors noticed him.

Settled again in Paris in the summer of 1923, Swan stayed at a studio on the rue Delambre, behind Hotel Namur, for more than a year, resuming the life he had left behind after his split with Cabanel. They reconciled and became good friends, although there were no more documented sexual encounters.[17] One of his sculptures of this period was accepted into the Salon des Artistes Français. *L'Opprimé* would become important again in Swan's life a decade later. He also painted a sensitive portrait of young Joaquin Nin, brother of Anaïs, sitting at a piano.

In May 1924 Swan danced at the Olympia in Paris, under the auspices of Paul Franck, but not long after his December performances at Le Théatre Ésotérique in Paris (4, Square Rapp) with noted dancer Nadja (Beatrice Wanger) he returned to California. Ostensibly, it was to see his family, but actually he was trying to break into the movie business again. He wanted to be Valentino, but the best he could manage was the job of an extra in J. J. Cohn's 1925 *Ben Hur*.[18] Hollywood was not buying Swan's stubborn brand of theatricality. He was used to the larger-than-life persona that he projected onstage, as opposed to the close-ups that were an essential part of the vocabulary of film. It was not that he did not love close-ups but rather that he tended to exaggerate (even more than film actors of the day) for the theatergoer in the last row.

Swan was in good company on the set of *Ben Hur*; other extras included future superstars Myrna Loy and Clark Gable. But they were young and appealed to the director's vision; Swan was forty-two. He began to lie more often about his age, sometimes subtracting as much as two decades.

By April 1925 he was once again working in his New York City studio, electing not to return to Paris. The *New York Times* ran an article on him on 25 May, with photographs of him sculpting Cabanel. During the summer he traveled back and forth from New York City to the Adirondacks, where he still maintained his barn studio at Skiwaukee and where Helen and the girls were visiting. He didn't see them often. His studio at 139 West Fifty-sixth Street became a center for dancing, dramatic expression, and stage deportment. Before he knew it, his family was gone again, finally settling in Van Nuys in the San Fernando Valley, less than two hours from Laguna Beach. Swan was not callous; it was always heart-wrenching for him to say good-bye, but he also chose not to return to California, and more specifically, Hollywood, a place that failed to appreciate his aesthetic.

A *New York Times* story on 23 August and a *New York World* article on 6 September (both running several photos of Swan leaping through the air) announced that millionaire Frank Vanderlip had hired "the most beautiful man in the world" to perform a ballet at a grand fete on the Vanderlip estate in Scarborough on 13 September. Society was abuzz. Called *Narcissus and Echo*, the ballet was Swan's own creation. Swan played Narcissus; a dance student, Josephine France, played Echo. It was reported as one of the finest society events of the year.

Mitchell Kennerley, the master of Anderson Galleries (Fifty-ninth Street and Park Avenue), proposed a December 1925 Swan exhibition with paintings, murals, and sculptures. He had been a fan of Swan's work since he first met the artist on shipboard in 1911, hiring him at that time to draw portraits of both his sons. The *New York Times* ran a long article with photographs on Sunday, 27 December, titled "Noted in the Art Galleries, Symbolism Enriching Design." "Symbolism is a dangerous tool," the critic explains. "Paul Swan, however, has used symbolism so that it enriches design instead of interfering with it. [In one mural] Three faceless angels hang in the air, tread on the air rather, with the assurances of support. They are designed so as to make three mathematical crosses, one higher than the next. The idea is held symbolically and the design decoratively by three great golden curves that follow one another in parallels across the composition" (SB).[19]

Time magazine wrote about the exhibition in its 4 January 1926 issue; by then New Yorkers had already crowded the showroom:

An urbane and well slicked Manhattan mob twittered about the famed Anderson Galleries last week and endeavored to understand the mystic symbolism hidden in the 21 large mural paintings and eight pieces of sculpture there on show. Strange forms of a significance remindful of the tortuous ideas in novelist James Branch Cabell's *Jurgen* revealed themselves. Famed etcher Joseph Pennell was loud in his praise of their originality.[20] Much interest centered about a bust of the famed Spanish singer Raquel Meller.

The mention of these "strange forms" and "tortuous ideas" is intriguing. Were there experiments that, as in the case above, elicited approbation from a New York audience? We have hints of Swan's attempts described in similar reviews in several countries, but little evidence remains in his extant work. There are, however, photographs of his Carnegie Hall studio in 1955 in which paintings hanging in the background show his work in different styles, from surrealism to abstraction.

The event was a huge success, and Kennerley was pleased. He liked the idea that some of the work in the Anderson exhibition had won previous acclaim, including *Vers le Soleil* and *Nocturne* from the 1921 Paris Salon, three murals and a sculpture from the Architectural and Allied Arts Exposition (April 1925), a painting from the 100th Annual Exhibition of the National Academy of Design (April 1925), and two sculptures from the National Sculptors Society's 1923 show (SB).[21] Shortly after the exhibition closed, Swan was touted in the *New York World* (24 January 1926) as the founder of the School of the Aesthetic Ideal. As indeterminate as that designation is, there is no question that whatever Swan wished to call his style, the public and the critics loved both him and his work.

How could an artist be displeased at such success? Yet Swan carried a "heavy, disastrous weight . . . that has burdened and handicapped me, [and] has rested on me like a blight in the eyes of the world." Was he a dancer who could paint, or a painter who could dance? He understood that critically his identity as either must suffer. Does a modern-day collector, for example, buy the paintings of Dennis Hopper because Hopper is a fine artist, or because he is a famous actor who can paint well? " 'The curse' was on me, and it weighed me down at every step," Swan said in a *New York World* article.[22]

One of the reasons he was so depressed at this time was because of a rare artistic failure, blamed partly on an act of God. Financier Otto Kahn decided that he would back a Swan production at the Three Arts Theater in New York in January 1926, a few weeks after the Anderson show closed. Nothing worked right. Winter rain poured down on the city, people in low-lying dwellings got flooded out, and even the theater suffered damage. Some of the production materials got soaked and were rendered useless. Negative reviews trickled out after a few sparsely attended performances. "It was like being buried alive," Swan wrote later. "Everyone who did not know personally what I had accomplished abroad since the early days when I was so widely acclaimed, imagined that my public career was finished" (DS 301). Swan was right that he had an established reputation on which to draw. The rainy failure at Three Arts Theater would soon be forgotten by a mercurial public, and, as he had done so many other times in his life, Paul Swan would simply reinvent himself.

At times Swan's reputation as a talent divided by his interests in painting and dance undoubtedly hurt him, but no matter how much this bothered him he felt strongly that his study of dance stimulated his work on canvas. There is, of course, validity in his position. Dance, the most ephemeral of the arts, has in its very transience the essence of all arts. If art is made by "dying generations," as W. B. Yeats suggests in "Sailing to Byzantium," it can be argued that what is most beautiful is most fleeting. Who better to understand and interpret this position than a painter-dancer?

His own best agent, Swan parlayed "the curse" of many talents into more success. He played the victim so well in the press that instead of losing commissions, he profited from publicity and curiosity. The editor of the *New York World*, Joseph Pulitzer II, frequently saw Swan's exploits as newsworthy and set aside a great deal of space for articles and photographs. In one such feature, Swan complained about being called "beautiful," saying that he only wanted to be a humble and dedicated artist: "Again and again I have had experiences of which the following is a kind. It was announced that I would be one of the artists represented in an exhibition of pictures [Macbeth Gallery, 1914]. One line of newspaper comment stung me. 'It will be interesting to ask what kind of painting can be expected from the most beautiful man in the world'" (SB).

The *World* article led with a large photograph of Swan dancing a ballet with Sari Karenyi and included a photo of his bust of Raquel Meller. The coverage successfully promoted both careers. By the spring of 1926, people who had means knew that it was fashionable to be painted by Paul Swan and to be seen at his performances.

The purpose of the Anderson exhibition was to advertise Swan's seriousness as an artist, and with good press from the *New York Times* and the *World*, it worked. If he had stayed in New York, Swan could have been kept as busy as he wished with exhibitions and commissions. But fate intervened three months after the show's closing. Adah Swan sent her son a telegram, asking her eldest child to return to Crab Orchard. Randolph Swan was dying.

Needn't tell me that I'm not so pretty, dear,
When my looking glass and I agree,
In the contest at Atlantic City, dear,
Miss America I'd never be,
Truth to tell, though, you're not such a bad lot yourself,
As a Paul Swan, you are not so hot yourself.
And yet.

Funny Face, 1927

7 Death and the Celebrity, 1926–1929

Nebraska

Swan had been home on several occasions over the years, but never for more than two or three days. Usually he would cut the trip short because issues with his mother would resurface. He often spoke about his hasty departures, watching his parents diminishing in the doorway of the old farmhouse as the car headed down the road. He always felt a mixture of guilt and relief as he left them, realizing that differences would never be resolved, wounds would never be healed.

On this visit, however, Swan accepted his duty as eldest son, staying in Crab Orchard for two months and spending most of the last five weeks of his stay next to the bedside of Randolph, who was dying of congestive heart failure. In early April, Governor Adam McMullen heard of the arrival of Nebraska's most famous artist and convinced Swan to give an exhibition in Lincoln at the governor's suite in the state capitol building. No doubt grateful for an excuse ("a duty to Nebraska," he told his family) to escape the gloom of Crab Orchard for a few days, Swan agreed. The 13 April 1926 issue of the *Omaha World Herald* publicized the event in two multiple-page articles. One ("Like an Alger Hero, Nebraska Artist Rose") included photographs of Swan's portraits of Maurice Block (director of the Omaha Society of Fine Arts) and Governor McMullen himself (SB).

Back at the homestead, Swan found Randolph even more frail. The family constantly whispered in hushed tones, as if speaking in normal voice would somehow hasten the death of the old man. Swan was disturbed by the atmosphere but felt a new love for his father during those final weeks. Drifting in and out of consciousness, Randolph once asked, "Fan me, Paul, fan me," and then, "Take me to the green alfalfa field, Paulie."[1] In that moment the years melted away and a connection formed between parent and child. Randolph was too ill for his final request to be fulfilled, but Swan never forgot that his father turned to him in at least one brief moment before death.

Randolph lingered, slowly drowning from his disease, and Adah began to irritate her artist-son with religious visions of his father's ascent into heaven, each version more elaborate than the last. Swan was determined, on this one occasion, not to rise to her bait, not to give her the opportunity to turn a father's dying into another polemic on a son's loss of faith.

As a way to bear the long hours, each member of the family needed to find something to do to pass the time. Swan began to observe, almost as if he were an invisible guest, the scenes around the deathbed. He found comfort in sketching the activity. Only one sketch survives, a sensitive drawing of Randolph Swan hours before he died. The portrait shows a strong face of a handsome laborer. There is no sense of death, no gloom. The subject's eyes are closed in a peaceful repose, looking as if he might rise at any moment for another day's work. One of the more admired drawings at the Macbeth Gallery's Swan exhibition in 1929, the piece was titled *Mr. J. R. Randolph* to disguise the family connection.[2]

Is it possible that in the moments before his father's death, Swan the artist saw in this subject a model for the aesthetic beauty he always sought? There is something repulsive and irresistible about death, and this sensation is intensified when the subject is beloved. Perhaps Swan felt no such dramatic conflict when he drew the final portrait of his father, but there is a fascination with the moment that illuminates this work, and his artistic impulse was to be the explicator, through his art,

A. *The Three Graces*, Swan's portrait of Beatrice Wielich and her daughters, Carmen (dark hair), and Dorothy, 1927. Oil on canvas, 69 x 101 in. From the collection of James Kieley.

B. *Jeanne d'Arc* by Paul Swan, 1922. Oil on canvas, 40 x 28 in. Private collection, Italy.

C. *Primitive Melodies* by Paul Swan, 1931. Oil on canvas, 30 x 24 in. Private collection, Florida.

D. *Bacchanal of the Sahara Desert* by Robert Barnes, 1958. Pastel on heavyweight cotton Fabriano paper, 19¼ x 25¼ in. Courtesy of Robert Barnes.

Paul Swan — 1926 —

20. *Mr. J. R. Randolph*, Paul Swan's portrait of his father, sketched a few hours before Randolph Swan's death, 1926. Graphite on paper on board, 8 x 10 in. Collection of The John and Mable Ringling Museum of Art, the State Art Museum of Florida. Gift of Helen and John Swan. Photograph courtesy of Helen and John Swan.

for that moment. If art is a way in which we can escape mortality, what better and more paradoxical subject than death?

Swan paraphrased Ralph Waldo Emerson when he wrote, "Art is Nature poured through the mind of the artist. If the artist is a true spokesman, he will always answer in some form our human longings. He is necessary" (DS 6–7).[3] Art also, necessarily, detached Swan, rescued him from too close encounters with emotions, and channeled the most alarming emotions of life into "inexpressible ecstasy." "The torturous days are done. . . . / And the hush of Death's gray wings / Is everywhere," Swan wrote in a published poem, "Tribute to J.R.S., June 8, 1926" (SB). He felt "a shivering grief" as he returned to the farmhouse after the funeral. Adah's ten children waited, allowing their mother to be the first to enter. The moment captured "the most woeful of all grief," Swan wrote in his memoir, "expressed in the cry of desolation my mother uttered" (307).

Swan's younger brother Dallas had paid for Swan's trip to Nebraska, and Swan expected the same free ticket back. After all, his brother had a steady income and plenty of money. Those who worked in a more mundane universe were obligated to support art. Whether the fight was about that or other family issues, Dallas and Paul had strong words for each other in the days that followed their father's death. "Damn him, let him walk back to New York. I'll not pay his way back!" a friend later remembered Dallas complaining.[4] Probably Dallas gave in. He usually did. What else was he to do with this sort of brother?

Adding to the complicated relationship, Dallas had married Olivia Buranelli on 29 September 1924. Olivia was one of the few women (including his sister Harriet and his own wife and daughters) whom Paul Swan truly loved. A gentle nature and a Mona Lisa smile endeared Olivia to him for the rest of their lives, and she became his favorite model. She appeared everywhere in his work. She was the noble beauty in several life-size oils; the angel who protected soldiers in his war drawings; and the pensive, slightly sad older woman who graced the work of his late career.

Swan also liked Olivia's brother Prosper (1890–1960), who was known for his intelligence and quick wit. For instance, one weekend, on a bet, Prosper and his friend John Chipman Farrar decided to write a publishable book together. The result, a mystery called *The Gold-Killer* (Doran, 1922), sold well under the name John Prosper.[5] Swan always applauded such spontaneity in artistic production. During the 1920s, Prosper served as music editor at the *New York World* and so was well aware of Swan's career. He never hesitated to praise him in public. They remained mutual admirers and continued to see each other when both lived in New York City in the 1950s. The friendship ended suddenly when Prosper died in his sleep one night while visiting Lowell Thomas's home.[6]

Swan was grateful to his younger brother for bringing the Buranellis into his own life, but why did such good luck always befall Dallas? It was not that Swan wanted to claim the beautiful Olivia for himself, but he couldn't shake the feeling that the gods of good fortune had again slighted him and, for whatever inexplicable reasons, smiled instead upon his materialistic brother.

New York, New Orleans, and South America
After his father's funeral, Swan was relieved to leave Nebraska and "too much family." He had delayed work on a commissioned bust of American poet Robert Underwood Johnson, once editor of *Century Magazine* and former ambassador to Italy. In an interview with the *Lincoln State Journal,* Johnson said of Swan's sculptures, "St. Gaudens would have been proud to have them compared to his work, as in my mind they are" (SB). The bust of Underwood, titled *The Singer of Odes,* was a great success. Photographs of it with Swan and Underwood appeared in several New York newspapers, and it was placed at New York University's Hall of Fame. It was also displayed at the Exhibition of Independent Artists held at the Waldorf in October 1927.

In early February 1927, the Edgewater Gulf Hotel in Biloxi, Mississippi, had held an exhibition of Swan's portraits, murals, and "impressionistic works."[7] The artist also executed several commissioned portraits. Two that drew particular praise in newspapers of the period were those of matinee idol Richard Bennett and his new wife, Aimee Raisch Hastings.[8] Bennett was so delighted with the portraits that he wrote to Swan on 18 February 1927, "Tonight I said you were a genius. Now I have the pleasure to put it over my signature" (SB).

Life continued busily for the next several months, with Swan making his usual trips around the country for dancing engagements and portrait work. When the Waldorf exhibition opened in October, his 1922 portrait *Jeanne d'Arc* created the biggest stir (see figure B). Caroline Beauchamp, reviewer for the *New York Times,* said that this oil "was considered by many of the intelligentsia as the best of this display" (SB).[9] One of the twelve thousand visitors to the exhibition, art collector Albert Wielich, admired Swan's work so much that he hired him on the spot to paint a portrait of his family for a thousand dollars.

Swan designed a pastoral scene with Wielich's wife, Beatrice, and two daughters, Carmen and Dorothy, as subjects on a large canvas of heavy Belgian linen. One of his most successful works, *The Three Graces* (see figure A) is in keeping with other murals of the time. Shortly after World War I, portraitists in America began painting finely dressed women and children in outdoor settings. Wanting to make the Wielich family part of this tradition, Swan succeeded in rendering the various textures of velvet, crepe, and leather, as he contrasted these with the vibrant flesh tones in his subjects. His training as a fashion illustrator two decades earlier enabled him to translate beautifully the sense of the clothed form onto canvas.

In general, Swan did not rely on piled pigment or impastos, a method that was commonly employed by portrait painters of the era. Instead, the drawing technique is somewhat linear, especially noticeable in the rich colors and textures of the mother's clothing. Swan agreed with William Hogarth's idea that variation of lines and curves (especially precise serpentine lines) is the key to pictorial beauty.[10] Time and again one sees this in Swan's best large canvases.

The sources of the painting are eclectic. The composition echoes Gainsborough's *Robert Andrews and His Wife Frances* (about 1748–50) and *Thomas Gainsborough, with His Wife and Elder Daughter, Mary* (about 1751–52).[11] The eerie, graceful branches of the white birches, reminiscent again of Boleslas Biegas's work, have overtones of the French fauves. Although the painting owes a debt to both English and French sources, it is truly an American production by a painter who is genuinely creative and at the height of his power. The picture is held together by excellent draftsmanship and a seductive juxtaposition of colors. Blues, oranges, vermilions, and yellows, so characteristic of Swan's work, add great vibrancy. Here, Swan's subjects are connected with nature, not just placed into a setting. *The Three Graces* is perhaps the one surviving large canvas that shows Swan's superb command of figure study and color. The name itself raises his subjects to the status of goddesses: *The Three Graces*—Thalia (Fruitfulness), Aglaia (Radiance), and Euphrosyne (Joy).[12]

Although the mural was a great success, October 1927 carried sadness with it. Swan received news that Isadora Duncan had been killed in a bizarre automobile accident. Distraught over her death, he organized a grand memorial service for her in New York City at St. Mark's-in-the-Bouwerie Church on 16 October. Besides his own tribute to the "sublime genius," he arranged for other friends to give eulogies, including author John Cowper Powys and actors Charles Coburn and Eva Le Gallienne. In the end, the event more closely resembled a

Swan production than a religious service. Group chants, his own dance creation, and a letter he read from Isadora's brother, Raymond, were all part of the drama.[13]

Swan was on the road two weeks later to fulfill exhibition and portrait commitments in the mid-Atlantic states. He stayed in Richmond and Charlottesville, Virginia, in November for two shows of his work and to complete two commissions—those of Virginia notables Dr. Stuart Michaux and Dr. A. L. Statford.[14] The *Richmond Times Dispatch* reported on 11 November 1927 that Swan was "a modern who does nothing not in keeping with old standards. The result is a freshness of expression without the bizarre."

As always, Swan kept moving. He participated in the Fifth Annual Nebraska Artists' Exhibition (Art Institute of Omaha, Aquila Court) in Omaha in early December, stopping briefly in Crab Orchard to see his mother.[15] According to the *New Orleans Morning Tribune* (1 February 1928), Swan was in that city by late January for a solo exhibition. The St. Charles Theater Players also hired him to play the role of Eugene Marchbanks in Shaw's *Candida*.

A review of Swan's performance as Marchbanks published in the *New Orleans States* on 19 March 1928 is one of the few ever written that offered anything other than effusive praise for his ability to master any artistic form:

> Leaving for the last Paul Swan is to deal with a newcomer to the ranks of the St. Charles Players, a guest artist as it were. Mr. Swan has acquired from the dancing for which he is well known, an easy stage presence and a perfect knowledge of posture; from his artistic work, for he is an artist, a temperament that can understand the character of Eugene Marchbanks and deal with it accordingly, but a lack of close touch with active stage work, has handicapped him as to his delivery of lines. Nevertheless he has created quite a character in his representation of Eugene Marchbanks that is unique.

It's not difficult to imagine Swan onstage in a production that required him to play the artist. It seems, at first, the perfect role, and in some ways it may have been. But the challenge would be to enter the part as actor rather than simply to play himself. Whether or not he was

21. Paul Swan as Eugene Marchbanks. St. Charles Theater Players' production of George Bernard Shaw's *Candida*, New Orleans, 1928. Photograph from authors' collection.

successful cannot be determined from this review, but it does consider the dilemma. Perhaps what the critic saw was the same thing that put off Hollywood directors.

Another reviewer liked him better in the role and wrote that Swan, who "is well known in every corner of the globe for his artistry in portrait painting . . . is the ideal type for the part, that of a poetic youth, struggling with emotions brought to the surface by his mad infatuation. . . . Not only is he equipped with the histrionic ability to adequately play the part, but his physique and appearance are ideal" (SB).

Now a regular visitor to New Orleans, Swan also enjoyed seeing old friends. One was Bernard J. Callaway, a young man who would later gain some fame as a drag dancer at Club My-Oh-My in New Orleans. It was probably on this trip that Swan gave him the gift of a favorite painting, *Self-Portrait in Egyptian Dress*. When Callaway died in the late 1990s, his brother sent the colorful oil to Hampshire House, a noted art auction company in Louisiana, for sale. Purchased by a gallery in New Orleans, it was put up for sale on eBay and subsequently acquired by the authors. Dr. Aaron DeGroft, deputy director of The Ringling Museum, became interested when he saw the piece and asked about acquiring it for the museum. *Self-Portrait in Egyptian Dress*, with its rich history and connection to *The Ten Commandments*, is now housed with some of the greatest artwork in the world. Swan would think it only right.

Early in the summer of 1928, a commission from the American ambassador to Argentina, Robert Woods Bliss, convinced Swan to sail for South America. After a short visit with his family, he left for Buenos Aires. Along with Señora Carmen Sánchez Elia de Quintana and Señor Pagano of the newspaper *Los Tiempos*, Ambassador Bliss arranged a series of lectures and an exhibition at Gallerias de Los Amigos del Artes on Avenida Florida in June and July. In addition to portraits of Bliss, Quintana, and Pagano, Swan painted a number of society people and a series of landscapes.[16] His most acclaimed piece was an appealing drawing of Benito Quinquela Martín, one of Argentina's most respected artists, whose work is found in major museums in both Europe and the Americas.[17]

South American papers, including *La Nación*, *A Manhã*, the *Buenos*

Aires Herald, and *Los Tiempos*, were extravagant in their praise.[18] Swan was quickly signed to give a similar exhibition in August in Santiago and Valparaíso, Chile, where he received at least thirty commissions for portraits and performed a series of dances at Theatre Principal. *La Nación* hailed his exhibition as "the most important event of the year." Writer N. Yáñez Silva of *El Diario Illustrado* compared Swan's sensitivity in painting to that displayed by Oscar Wilde in writing, and he hired Swan to draw his portrait for the cover of his forthcoming play, *Esperate, Corazón*. Even the usually conservative *Chile: Boletín Consular del Ministerio de Relaciones Exteriores* ran an article about the American, calling him "Artista extraordinario." After one of Swan's dance performances, *El Mercurio* wrote that he was "Nijinsky's successor."

New York and Chicago

After two months in South America, Swan decided to go home. He later wrote in his memoir, "South America is an experience an artist does not often repeat" (312). To stay longer would be "repetitive," and he didn't want to miss a few days in the Adirondacks with his daughters before their return to California after the annual summer visit. He booked passage on the *Santa Teresa* for New York, painted landscapes of Lima and Havana (port stops), and earned money by drawing passengers' portraits. It seems incongruous after such a lucrative South American experience that Swan was picking up extra cash by being in effect a sidewalk sketch artist, but the fact is that enormous sums regularly passed through his hands. He loved to play Lord Bountiful. Friends still living today attest to this trait; however, he had no financial sense other than periodically to discover that his funds were gone. If he could paint his way out of his difficulty, fine; if not, it was clearly someone else's responsibility to replenish the Swan treasury.

One shipboard drawing was of a young Indian man whom Swan nicknamed "Mosito." His portrait in oil later appeared on the cover of the *New York World* (SB). As *Mr. Wu*, Mosito is dressed in richly colored robes and a large, ornate multicolored headdress. Promising the young man a place to live, Swan persuaded him to return with him to New York City instead of disembarking in Havana.

It was probably wise for Swan to leave South America; news of cultural events there were not quick to reach New York. The city once again was beginning to forget the painter who had exhibited with Henri, Prendergast, Yeats, and Hawthorne ten years earlier and had made splashes with his exhibitions at the Anderson and Macbeth galleries. But Swan's dance performances were still remembered, and so younger art critics who wrote about him considered that his paintings and drawings were the result of hobby rather than professional dedication. When he arrived in Hoboken in August 1928 to the hugs of Helen, Paula, and Flora, Swan felt "unmeasured joy" that soon turned to depression, "all tied around with a woolen string" as he announced his return to the public:

Even dancers . . . began to invent stories of my insincerity as an artist and my laziness as a technician, ignoring willfully the very spirit of my expressions. These self-styled rivals and detractors ridiculed my work as non-professional and as belonging to no accepted school. They pointed out that I danced successfully because of the beauty of my person; but I was a kind of mountebank, confusing art with the trick of personality. Certainly much printed proof of success was in these disclaimers ignored.

Also, when my paintings and sculptures were shown, the art critics and *poseurs* casually denounced these expressions as the work of an amateur or as the sporadic work of an erstwhile dancer. They assumed . . . that I had lately, to attract attention, "taken up an art, which for lack of time and experience is naturally merely experimental and childish."

These critics did not know that I had worked incessantly for many years with my drawings, paintings and sculpture, and that the substantial sums of money I had earned came from my portrait drawings and paintings, and not from my dancing. (DS 316)

Mosito moved into Swan's New York studio, but for how long is not clear. Swan didn't stay with him because he immediately left for Skiwaukee, where he lived with his family for the remainder of the summer of 1928. When Swan was invited to Chicago for an exhibition of his portraits, the move coincided with Mosito's disappearance from Swan's memoir. Feeling unappreciated in New York City, Swan hoped that a successful stay in the windy city might boost his artistic reputation again.

It did. Under the management of Rachel Kinsolving, his exhibition in the foyer of the Blackstone Hotel, a gathering place for artists and musicians, attracted positive attention. In fact, the exhibition soon moved to the Albert Roullier Galleries in the Fine Arts Building, and commissions came pouring in. Mrs. Francis Stuyvesant Peabody (wife of the coal baron), Mrs. Leeds Mitchell (Chicago-Nantucket millionaire), Chicago mayor William ("Big Bill") Hale Thompson, Edward J. Brundage (attorney general of Illinois, 1917–25), and the daughter of E. W. Scripps (*Chicago Tribune*) were among his subjects. The *Chicago Evening Post* published a long article on Swan, titled "Nazimova Launched Paul Swan's Career" (29 January 1929), which observed that some of his portraits "have been done with backgrounds and some stand sharply and clearly defined on light paper, but all are endowed with that bright vitality identified with all his work." Swan's drawing of Bertha Palmer, granddaughter of Chicago art collector Bertha Honoré Palmer, later appeared on the cover of the 1 December 1929 issue of *Spur* magazine.[19]

Swan did much more than paint portraits. Hearing he was in town, the *Chicago Evening Post* ran a large photograph of him leaping blithely among the willows in Lincoln Park on 21 March 1929 with the headline "He Heralds Spring." On the same day, the *Chicago Evening American* ran a photo and article titled "Paul Swan Weds Two Muses," the reporter hailing him as "a modern Leonardo da Vinci." On 24 March he performed a series of dances at the Goodman Theater (now Chicago's oldest and largest residential theater) on North Dearborn Street to standing-room-only crowds. *The Hour of Destiny*, Swan's own one-act drama about a Chinese dancer, was used as an encore after the main performance and starred well-known actress-dancer Bertha Oschsner.[20]

Swan had almost decided to give up dancing to concentrate solely on portraiture because, first, it paid handsomely, and, second, he was tired of some art critics calling him "a dancer who paints." But the reception in Chicago convinced him to carry on his secondary career. The *Chicago Daily News* reported on 25 March that Swan had "enraptured crowds . . . in rich abandon to moving loveliness and his radiant belief in expression through color . . . put new life into things theatrical. . . . Swan gave a varied and brilliant program . . . uplifting." Such praise was hard to ignore, no matter how some reviewers might carp about his divided interests.

The New York critics who had called Swan's art "the work of an amateur" were quickly silenced when word arrived that M. Knoedler Galleries had chosen Swan to be the first artist to have a solo exhibition in its new Chicago gallery at 622 South Michigan Avenue.[21] This honor established Swan's reputation in the Midwest, giving him the opportunity to parlay the event into greater and greater success. M. Knoedler, after all, had been (and would continue to be) a favorite source for many of the best collectors. *Chicago Herald and Examiner* critic Ernest Heitkamp liked what he saw at the show ("Swan Sets Example in Art," 23 June 1929), welcoming Swan's "easy, swift facility of means" through "splendid draughtsmanship and a facile pencil and brush."

New York

Once again Swan left the site of his success just as his star was rising. Although his return to New York may seem ill-advised in retrospect, he had received a public subscription commission of sixteen hundred dollars to paint a large memorial portrait of Kentucky millionaire Edward Van Camp. Perhaps he could have hired studio space in Chicago, but he wanted to be with Helen and his daughters. He spent the summer with them at Skiwaukee, the last time they would be together in the Adirondacks. As autumn approached, his thoughts began to turn again to Europe. He wanted his measure of family love and support, but wanderlust was growing stronger by the day.

In the comfort of his barn studio, he painted a mural of a youth kneeling on a hilltop, "visioning before him three attenuate angels in diaphanous colored draperies, all against an ultramarine blue sky, which cooled toward the horizon into a cold cerulean." Paula Swan was the subject of two portraits, one of her dressed in yellow, drenched in golden sunlight, and the other with her in a vermilion riding vest and khaki trousers: "The golden curls, the bare arms, the seated figure, with a blue bird in the wild grasses and flowering weeds of the background, made a striking picture" (DS 321). *Paula and the Blue Bird* appeared on the cover of *Literary Digest* a few months later, in January 1930.[22]

Aware of the renewed interest in Swan's work, the Macbeth Gallery in New York chose Swan as the artist to inaugurate its new fall season in 1929. Eighteen oils and fifteen drawings (all portraits) were gathered from private and public collections in the United States and France for a two-week solo exhibition (1–14 October). The *Chicago Evening Post* reviewed the show positively. A *New York Times* reporter was particularly pleased with the portraits of Raquel Meller, calling them "delightful": "One is struck first by the sensitivity of his drawings . . . and he has been astute enough to reproduce the mood."[23]

Swan included in his scrapbook several mildly negative reviews of the show, which suggests either that he did not particularly mind the criticism or that he found in it suggestions he could incorporate into his work. Safely surrounded by many positive, and often effusive, accounts, he might have been curious about remarks from those less enchanted with his work. Could these comments have provoked him enough to consider their merit?

> Mr. Paul Swan . . . is a disconcerting type. He has two strings to his bow, but on only one of them can he depend. When he works in black and white he knows his way about and conveys a delightful impression. When he turns to color he is dogged, turgid, a painter of nerveless draftsmanship and perfectly commonplace surfaces. In oils he seems to work by main strength, to be carefully accurate, but not in the least interesting. In his drawings he is a free man, working with ease and certainty, skillfully defining his forms and making portraits far above the average in merit. (SB)

One writer suggested that the influence of stage acting and dance might have induced a certain "too radiant" effect in Swan's work, as if some of his subjects were poeticized, appearing a bit like the Greek gods he depicted in his dances. Swan countered this criticism about his use of color by pasting in his scrapbook the view of another critic, who praised the "lush and colorful" portraits: "All the sitters emerge incredibly picturesque in a decorative flourish that is almost bewildering. In

Paula Swan . . . the details and color notes [are] subdued to a unity of impression" (SB).[24]

Regardless of Swan's reaction to being called dogged and turgid by one critic, his life in the fall of 1929 was, by his own accounts, filled with serenity and success. Money, fame, and family—everything he had wanted—were his. "A happy home is essential to the real expression of art," he had once told a reporter for *Time* (4 January 1926). Although his family had returned to California, they were still loyal to him, still *his* family. He liked having them available when he needed them. "An artist more than anyone else needs mothering. And I call home a hospital for broken wings."

His wings were apparently healed. Shortly after the Macbeth exhibition closed, Swan boarded the steamship *Olympic* for London, "to knock again at her glacial portals." When he wrote about his decision in his memoir thirteen years later, he concluded, "I should have known better" (324).

Making money is art and work is art and good
business is the best art.

Andy Warhol, *The Philodophy of Andy Warhol*

8 Ateliers, 1930–1933

From London to Paris

A few days after he disembarked from the *Olympic* in early December 1929, Swan received word from Helen that a large photograph of his memorial portrait of distinguished librarian Electra Doren had appeared in the 5 December *Dayton Daily News*. The portrait, commissioned by the board of trustees of the Dayton Public Library, still hangs in the library today. At the end of February 1930, Helen wrote again. Her husband's colorful portrait of singer Raquel Meller, attired in the costume of her native Catalan Province, graced the 23 February cover of *New York World*.

Good news from America did not make Swan happier in England. He did not find "one Englishman more tolerant or hospitable to new ideas of art or life," and he blamed it on the suffering exacted by World War I (DS 224). Except for the ministrations of a few good friends, especially Lady Ian Hamilton, he felt very much alone. He began work in his studio at 16 Kelso Place in Kensington, but there was little joy in his life. Even Baron Rosenkrantz did not seem as attentive. The baron wrote that he had gone so far into the study of eurhythmy that "mere Classic dancing" no longer moved him. Nothing he said could have wounded Swan more, and so he wrote back that he did not wish Rosenkrantz to visit him again—that he "could not endure . . . half playful and half earnest destructiveness" (338).

Rosenkrantz restored the friendship with another letter in which he drew a dancing Paul Swan on the page to seem in the act of kicking a caricature of Rosenkrantz himself, "kneeling with halo-crowned, bald head and with hands folded benignly across his breast, begging for forgiveness." He had written these words beneath: "Don't be a fool! When can I come see you?" Swan telephoned him. As soon as Rosenkrantz arrived, he lavished praise on his former pupil's latest creations. Swan forgave instantly (338–39).

When a Chinese dancer from Melbourne named Rose Quong entered Swan's life, his spirits improved. Swan recognized in Quong some of his own professional flaws, for her "comings and goings" were, like his own, "sudden; her path seemed to follow every star or even every glow-worm which crossed it" (333). She told him that she never suffered from the stage fright that always plagued him. How did she seem so nonchalant? Although he sought to embrace her Eastern philosophy, he never could detach himself enough from his desires and fears: "I have seen her working over a theme which did not especially interest her, and then en route in the taxi to deliver it, she would abandon it altogether and as she bowed to the greeting of the assemblage and grinned her wide Chinese grin, she would begin on a [new] subject" (334).

Quong's patron, Mrs. Victor Henderson Climas, was another in a long list of socialites charmed by Swan. With her husband listed as director of the affair, Mrs. Climas arranged for Swan to dance with Quong on 10 and 14 March 1930 in Rudolf Steiner Hall at 33 Park Road, Clarence Gate, London. The two practiced for weeks. Swan's own Chinese playlet, *The Hour of Destiny*, was to be the featured entertainment. The event grew in scope, and other dances and dancers were added. Swan convinced a friend, British actor Rupert Harvey, to play the lead in the drama. Harvey also read "In Flanders Field" as Swan performed his most famous dance, *To Heroes Slain* (DS 334–35).[1]

The audience was "un-English" in its response, with cheers and long applause. As Swan took his bows he looked out to see the gracious, proud face of Lady Hamilton in the first row. Critics were generally positive, especially about Quong's performance. The English still had some reservations about an aesthetic male dancer. One reviewer from the *London Era* (19 March 1930) was particularly displeased with a dance series called *Pour Le Sport*: "Dancing—as Mr. Swan afterwards showed us—is a fine art, but we venture to say that this number was at times almost a travesty. We doubt that any one—save Mr. Swan—could, without the aid of the programme, distinguish *Tennis Match* from *Prize Fight*." But when the same critic saw him dance *The Great God Ra*, he granted that "Mr. Swan's dancing was most moving."

Delighted with the success of her venture, Mrs. Henderson Climas next commissioned Swan to paint her portrait.[2] While he was working, he moved in with the Climases, where Quong was already living. For a few weeks he enjoyed being spoiled by their generosity.

Another commission from Lady Hamilton came almost immediately. She wanted him to sculpt Prime Minister James Ramsay MacDonald. Although MacDonald was involved in a naval conference at the time and unable to sit for Swan, Lady Hamilton provided the artist with photographs. All three—Lady Hamilton, Swan, and the prime minister—were pleased with the results. A number of papers ran photographs and stories, including the *London News*, *The Referee* (London), and *The Home* (Sydney, Australia). Lady Hamilton had the bust packed and shipped to the Royal Academy as a gift.[3]

Even this success did not make Swan feel more at ease in London. He began to think of home, of Helen and his daughters, and of his aging mother, now alone in the farmhouse in Crab Orchard. One morning he picked up the Bible she had given him and opened it at random to 1 Samuel 17:1: "the soul of Jonathan [Saul's son] was knit with the soul of David, and Jonathan loved him as his own soul." Adah Swan certainly would have approved his method of divination, if not its secular purpose. At any rate, Swan loved the story. In fact, he was so enchanted that the next glance he took out of his window at 10 Kelso Place revealed to him an incarnation of Jonathan (for Swan saw himself as David). Across the street stood a young man whose "eyes held a goodness and his face a fineness which gave his youth a kind of remote ideality. He was standing astride his bicycle. . . . His expression was serious, his smile sudden and transforming, and then the whole face seemed to light up with a twinkling gaiety. The line of his nose was perfect in proportion. His voice was deep and mellow, I later found, yet he seemed in body more fragile than strong. He was, however, muscular and poised in his movements" (346).

Swan called to the young man, inviting him into his studio "to look at art, if you like." The gentleman introduced himself as Frederick Eric Bates. "I wish I could learn to do this," Fred told him after seeing the drawings and paintings scattered about the room. "Why don't you?" Swan asked him. The young man shook his head: "I work. I don't have time."

When he discovered that Fred made only twenty-two shillings a week, Swan hired him for the same amount to be his secretary. "Besides, I'd like to begin a portrait of you right away," he told his new friend. Fred didn't think he was much of a subject, but he was thrilled. Several early portraits show why Swan was drawn to him. One sees in Fred Bates the reflection of a more youthful Paul Swan. Swan found not only a true friend but also one whose good looks and sweet personality attracted people to his studio.

In May 1930 they moved to Paris, where two men could live more easily together. Rose Quong, the Climases, and Fred's mother (who, according to Swan, adored her son's new friend) saw them off. One of Swan's admirers, a Mrs. Netherland, paid for their passage, asking for nothing in return but gladly giving because of her belief in Swan's work (348).

The studio they acquired in Auteuil, at 37 rue Boileau (ca. 1820), had a high-walled garden with a huge acacia tree in the back corner. The skylighted studio was detached from the house, and with a number of Swan's paintings and Fred's expertise as a carpenter, the place was soon turned into "a luxurious temple of beauty" (349). On 20 June 1930 the *Chicago Daily Tribune*'s Paris edition ran a long article titled "Paul Swan, Artist and Dancer, Back in Paris as a Success after Tours of Both Americas, Leases Old House to Prepare Autobiography." Swan summarized his triumphs of the previous decade, recalled that he "was a great disappointment to my mother," and mentioned that he hoped his wife and two daughters would be joining him in the fall. There was no mention of Fred Bates. Immediately, photographs of Swan and his work and articles about the gathering of artists and musicians at his studio appeared in Paris papers (SB).

22. *Frederick Eric Bates*, one of Paul Swan's earliest sketches of his companion, 1930. Location and size not known. Photograph courtesy of the collection of The John and Mable Ringling Museum of Art, the State Art Museum of Florida.

Mrs. Netherland appeared again and invited Swan and his assistant to vacation with her in Zurich. During the trip, Swan enjoyed watching Fred delight in places he had never dreamed of visiting. "He responded to every beautiful vista, every paintable crag or tree. . . . His polite manner, his camaraderie and ready sense of humor won completely Mrs. Netherland. Every passing day proved the value of our friendship" (351).

But then, suddenly, Mrs. Netherland's demeanor changed. She would not tell Swan, when he questioned her, what was wrong, but said she had to send them on their way. "I knew really what it was and I was asking her to openly voice her reasons for such an ill-concealed change of heart" (352). Had she discovered that Fred was more than a secretary? Before the trip, she had arranged for a commission of a painted stage curtain for a theater in Paris, money Swan counted on to get them through the approaching winter. A few days after he and Fred returned to the city, he was informed by the theater that his services were no longer required.

September 1930 arrived. Helen, Paula, and Flora did not join him. Helen told Paul that she would try to live in New York again but would not take the girls out of school to live in France. Raising money to pay off bills and support himself and Fred in the cold months ahead was getting difficult. It was time to return to New York and his family. That "hospital for broken wings" always had its doors open: "Fred and I had been partners now nearly six months. His artistic efforts had made great strides, and I had produced several serious canvases during this stay. Finally, hoping against reason I wrote to Mrs. Netherland explaining the critical situation and asking for a loan—not a gift—so that Fred could go to New York also. At once a telegram from Switzerland arrived: 'Regret impossible.' She could have easily granted my urgent request, but now she saw where she could wound me most" (353).

Like many another artist, Swan had difficulty understanding why anyone would hesitate to help him. In the midst of this trouble, Alfred G. Pelikan, director of the Milwaukee Art Institute, visited the studio. He was known at the time for bringing the latest in painting and sculpture from Europe to the United States and for encouraging those artists to visit. Impressed by what he saw, he invited Swan to hold an exhibition in Milwaukee. It was the final push the artist needed. Swan sailed for the United States, while Fred, who was unable to get enough money together for a ticket to the States, returned home to London.[4]

New York, Winona, and Paris

What greeted Swan in New York was shocking.[5] Helen hadn't mentioned that she was now in a wheelchair. At fifty-five, she had become debilitated with arthritis. Swan was upset that she had given quite a bit of money to faith healers. He wanted her to get better medical care, but she refused. Like any caring husband, he didn't want her in pain (or spending money uselessly). And he felt guilty. "I'm not a dancer," she would always tell him. "I don't miss my legs as you would." But he thought it a cruel joke of fate that Helen's legs were rendered useless. Was it a message that he was being allowed a carefree life for which someone else would have to pay? (354–55).

Shortly after returning to the United States in 1930, and with Helen's blessing, Swan left for Milwaukee. The exhibition took place in November and resulted in additional commissions.[6] Then he spent a week in Winona, where he painted several portraits, including society personalities Mr. and Mrs. Charles Choate, Ms. Sarah Allen, Mrs. Theodore Vogel, and theater director J. P. Jones. A final count sent him back to New York and Helen with two thousand dollars, an impressive amount for an artist during a national economic depression (SB).

Helen always understood that her husband was not going to stay in New York. She knew about his "secretary," Fred, but no record exists of how she felt at this juncture. Swan simply told her that he was more artistically appreciated in Paris, and he wrote to Fred to meet him there. Helen asked him to stay through Christmas "for the two lovely cygnets," and he did. He sailed for France at the end of February. The *New York Times* announced his arrival on Sunday, 7 March 1931, with the headline, "Mauretania Lands Passengers from America for Paris: Paul Swan and Prince Murat Among Cunard Arrivals."

He and Fred were able to rent the same studio he had used in the mid-1920s, at 39 rue Delambre. In cleaning away the debris of a former tenant, they made an amazing discovery. Covered with some old sheets and much dust was Swan's own signed sculpture, *L'Opprimé*, which he had left behind in 1924. At the time he thought he would not be long away from Paris, but his plans changed with the death of his father and the tour to South America. After several years' absence, he simply forgot what he had done with the piece. Swan was a prolific artist, but it is strange that he would have been so nonchalant about a sculpture that had been shown at the Salon des Artistes Français in 1925. Now, in 1931, *L'Opprimé* would be re-patined (356). Later in the decade it would win a Salon medal.

Swan began holding Saturday receptions, and once more his atelier became a place for artists to congregate. Esoteric dancer Nadja often performed there. Another guest, Prince Chula Chakrabongse, the great-grandson of King Rama IV of Siam, attended a Saturday reception on a whim and, because he liked Swan's dancing, thereafter visited often. The race car enthusiast and the eccentric artist became good friends. Feeling that the prince "was very handsome in his Oriental way" (357), Swan painted and drew several portraits of him.[7]

Performances in Berlin in March 1931 were not as successful as Swan had hoped. Several publicity shots of him dancing on the steps of the Reichstag appeared in German papers. On opening night of the show there was much applause and several curtain calls, but Swan thought the audience too restrained. He was used to French adoration and didn't like "German indifference." People apparently thought they were going to see an acrobatic show. Swan correctly deduced that his *Study in Curved Lines* was too rhythmic and graceful, and "lacked point" in Berlin (359).

The trip and production had cost him several hundred dollars. Depressed by the situation, he decided it was once again time to return to his family. Within a few weeks, he bid Fred good-bye at the St. Lazare station. His faithful partner would return to London until Swan could raise enough money for Fred's transatlantic ticket.

New Art

Little Maiden and the Fairies (with Flora Swan as subject) and *Paula and the Bluebird* made Swan a popular children's portrait artist in the United States. The reproduction rights to *Little Maiden* were purchased by the City of New York, which had posters made for all the elementary schools in the district. In July 1930, *Paula and the Bluebird* appeared on the cover of *Literary Digest*.

One of Swan's most popular portraits of this period was *A Modern Madonna*, which had as subject his sister-in-law Olivia holding her little daughter, Cynthia. It was chosen for the cover of *Literary Digest* in January 1932. "The young mother sits in profile, head slightly bowed, arms clasped gently around her little girl, who is looking wide-eyed at the painter, perhaps ever-so-slightly frightened by the sitting. Even though the mother's eyes are closed, the emotion they suggest resonates" (*PFR* 339). The reviewer for *Literary Digest* explained why the painting merited the cover: "The technical treatment is forthright and simple, with a harkening back to the ideals of Ingres."

23. Paul Swan dancing in front of the Reichstag, Berlin, 1931.
Photograph courtesy of Dallas Swan Jr.

Literary 𝒯he Digest

Vol. 112, No. 1
Whole No. 2176

January 2, 1932

Price 10 Cents

"A MODERN MADONNA"—By Paul Swan

24. *A Modern Madonna*, Paul Swan's portrait of Olivia Buranelli Swan and Cynthia Swan, as it appeared on the cover of *The Literary Digest*, January 1930. Oil on canvas, 24 x 24 in. From the collection of Cynthia Swan Klemenger.

During Swan's less than idyllic summer at home in 1931, Helen wisely decided to visit an old friend for a few weeks. She packed up the girls—even a rather rebellious Paula, who didn't want to leave her boyfriend at the time—and headed for Auburn, New York. There, Allie Harding happily greeted them, and Swan was left alone in their apartment in Jackson Heights (DS 368).

Acting on a new idea for an artistic series, Swan turned to composers Wagner, Ravel, and Rachmaninoff and to Negro spirituals. He played records as loudly as neighbors would allow, feeling the notes flow through him as he tried to create "abstract translations of musical compositions in their original colors, for it seems futile to attempt description by words" (369). Two decades of aesthetic dancing and conversations with Rosenkrantz about the use of color had prepared him for this new direction. Additionally, religious influences (he never could escape Adah) and an attraction to southern themes resulted in a creative tension and vision that possessed him during the summer and fall of 1931:

> I feel that this new expression which has developed in me during these last few weeks is so entirely my own, and I am sure that the rhythm of the lines weaving in and out of the patterns is the direct result of dancing . . . [and] of visualizing flowering lines created in space.
>
> In the pictures which have used the human figure, there is a tendency to become more concrete, but even then the figures are merely stylized and symbolic—they are a sort of focusing ego to the subject matter under consideration. . . .
>
> I repeat, this expression is the culmination of every art effort I have made since the beginning, when as a little boy of five I scrawled upon my slate at school. Certainly this work has been a glorious escape from the conflicting forces which have tortured my life. (370)[8]

Primitive Melodies (figure C) is an example of Swan's work during those weeks: a stream of nude male and female African American images on a vibrant yellow-orange background. The only real abstractions in the piece are the designs on the left side of the canvas, also falling from the top to the bottom of the picture. Suggesting blood cells, they become more pronounced as the figures next to them become larger. While composing this painting, Swan was often visited by an old friend from New Orleans, Robert Emmet Kennedy. A collector of Negro spirituals, Kennedy would play and sing songs from his latest music book, *More Mellows*, while Swan painted (375).

In the midst of his creative burst, Swan wrote to Helen that he was unworthy of her and that he still could not believe she loved him. He might have been concerned that her old relationship with Allie Harding still played too significant a role in her life. He wanted reassurance at these times, and Helen, like a virtual Penelope, was quick to calm his insecurities. She replied from Auburn:

> Oh, do not think that your love is a negligible thing to me, or that I easily dispense with your so tender and earnest ministrations. You are very dear to me always, else I should not be hanging on. And I need your petting!!
>
> . . . And you were surprised at my loving you! Dear, dear! How many times have you had to have that fact drummed in? How can I persuade you if I have not yet?
>
> And I wish you could hear your Paula talk of you sometimes. I can't remember always, but she was saying the other day something about your repartee, and remarked, " . . . He has as brilliant a mind as anyone I have ever known." (371)

Could this have been Helen's attempt to help father and daughter grow closer? Nothing endeared someone to Swan more than a compliment. In any case, Helen was obviously answering his plea to be coddled, and she ended her missive with, "I'm glad you have told me your trouble: I'll know what to do from now on." No matter how one may judge the unusual nature of this marriage, it is clear that these extraordinary people shared a deep and genuine love for each other.

When Swan's family returned to Jackson Heights, his art changed again, from the experimental, suggestive symbolic work to large paintings that looked more like magazine illustrations. He did not abandon the former, but why he began to concentrate on more traditional work is not clear. Did the return of his family sap his creative juices? Did he find that story murals brought better money? During the depression, the federal government was encouraging this sort of work by artists in WPA programs, and Swan might have jumped on the bandwagon for the cash.[9]

Mrs. Cornelia Whiting of Connecticut, who saw his nine- by five-foot mural called *School Under the Arbor* (commissioned by the Jackson Heights Garden Country Day School and hung in its entrance hall), decided to become his patron. She sent him six hundred dollars, not for art but to help him with "daily supplies" (375). A similar mural titled *Come Unto Me* was commissioned by the Community Church in Jackson Heights.[10]

Fred Bates arrived in the States at the end of the summer, about the time the girls came back from Auburn. A joy that had been missing from Swan's life returned with Fred's "sunburned face, the sparkle in his eyes the sea had given him, and his wholesome grin" (376). Paul Swan was in love. Now he knew it for certain. The separation had only intensified his desire. The Jackson Heights residence suddenly became very crowded. Helen wisely suggested that her husband would have more room to work if he and Fred took a separate studio.

They moved into an apartment at Carnegie Hall and soon began to collect an array of friends. Ballet school founder Mikhail Fokine was often there, chatting over the state of American dance. Frank Bagot, a friend of Swan's from his Chicago tours, sang for the gatherings. Occasionally, Fred would pantomime through the performance, to the general amusement of all. *New York Herald Tribune* city editor Stanley Walker, fashion designer Martha Andrews, and Mexican singer Riña Reyes commissioned portraits by their new friend. Artist Emily Nichols Hatch, known primarily for her seascapes, painted a portrait of Swan in his *To Heroes Slain* costume in exchange for one he did of her in an evening gown (376–78). Swan effectively transformed his Carnegie Hall studio into his Paris atelier.

Fred charmed everyone. Always able to keep the two compartments of her husband's life separate, Helen became such good friends with Fred that whenever she needed to go anywhere in her wheelchair, she insisted that he take her. Swan was never allowed to push her chair when Fred was present; only Fred would do. The handsome young man was gregarious, good-humored, and got on famously even with the recalcitrant Paula (380). Although Swan was now approaching fifty and increasingly concerned about his physical appearance, he didn't seem to mind the attention his younger friend received. Uncharacteristically, there seemed to be no jealousy of Fred, except, perhaps, in the heart of little Flora, who wanted "Poppa" to herself.

A quick trip to Washington DC in March 1932 to paint Senator William E. Borah of Idaho gave Swan another handsome commission. The portrait is realistic, nearly photographic. Swan must have liked the senator, for he spent more time on the work than usual. Senator Borah was especially pleased and arranged to have a photograph of the portrait appear in a Sunday edition (3 April 1932) of the *Washington Star*.

By that spring, tensions began brewing at home. Swan wanted to assume the role of patriarch, but Paula, now eighteen years old and long used to his absence, was not amenable. She liked a boy her father did not, and even worse, she told him she detested the theater, which Swan thought was "incomprehensible." (Perhaps she knew how much it would irritate him.) She seemed embarrassed by her father's aesthetic compositions. She "scorned all dancing . . . and saw to it that she avoided a performance of mine where her contemporaries might have beheld it." It is not, of course, unusual for teenage children to be embarrassed by their parents, but Swan found it difficult to understand why Paula did not appreciate him. In fact, their rows were a frightening reminder of his conflicts with his mother. He usually backed down from the disputes, perhaps a little in awe of Paula's independence. She "possessed a supreme honesty and candor, and was busy searching for her own truth, and for her rightful domain" (363).

Flora was more pliant and graceful and became "Poppa's favorite." She enjoyed accompanying him to several dance recitals given by his friend Harold Kreutzberg.[11] She could also draw, "without models or patterns," and "seemed most promising to her eager father, who gazed ambitiously into the years to come" (364). This lovely brown-haired girl of fourteen also wrote poetry, perhaps as much to please her exotic parent as for love of verse. When Swan danced for a function sponsored by the American Woman's Association in February 1933, Flora joined him in one number (385). On 22 March she performed with him again in front of a larger audience at the National Arts Club. "We two were very near in understanding," Swan wrote at the time (364).[12]

Perhaps because of his daughter's hero worship, Swan's intensified stage fright made it almost impossible for him to perform on this second occasion with Flora. He had a "blinding, nervous headache" for two days prior to the event. He wrote afterward that "the will which had taken me often before by the back of the neck, rabbit-wise, and 'put me there,' prevailed this time also and as soon as I was really in costume and pushed into the arena, my headache left me" (386).

He was not so understanding when it came to Paula, who at nineteen decided to marry Charles Abbott on 27 March 1933. The ceremony was held at St. Marks Church in Jackson Heights on a cold, overcast day. A photograph of the event doesn't reveal much joy in the face of either father or daughter (SB). Within the year, Paula would be divorced. Swan never mentioned any of her five marriages in his memoir, letters, or interviews, preferring always to think of his daughters as little girls.

During the same month as the wedding, Swan received troubling news from friends in Paris. The magnificent German Reichstag, upon whose steps he had danced only two years earlier, had burned on 27 February. The Nazi leader, Adolf Hitler, was delighted at the destruction of the German parliament building, calling the blaze "a God-given signal."[13] The next day, he pressured President Von Hindenburg into granting him dictatorial powers. Hitler would no longer need the votes of the Reichstag deputies to deny citizens all civil rights, which he then did on 29 February. Even more ominous, Germany's first concentration camp, at Oranienburg, opened on 12 March. Swan only heard of vague "concerns." He worried, but like the rest of the world, he didn't know very much, and he had no idea of what was to come. For now, he was enjoying dancing with his lovely daughter.

"A parent is a sort of a filling, refueling, or rest station, at those interims between the child's real preoccupations and interests" (364), he wrote, and yet, how often did he call his wife and children *his* "hospital for broken wings," and then leave them again? As the years wore on it would be the fiercely independent and passionate Paula who would be closest to her good-bye-saying father. Flora's efforts to please him did not convince him to stay in America, and so she felt a deeper betrayal, first when Fred arrived and next when her father left once more for Paris.

After a dance program held at Emily Hatch's studio on the old

Gould estate in Tarrytown, New York, Swan began to pack his bags. He departed on 5 April 1933. Helen did not see him off at the docks. On shipboard, he wrote in his memoir that she told him she was "glad she would not have to see me suffer. Her personal loss of my 'doubtful' company was less than her satisfaction at my release." Swan's tone suggests that he sensed her anger, but he decided she acted this way "to keep from weeping, as the skies were with their tap-tapping on the blurred window pane" (387). Paula, her new husband, and Flora drove Swan and Fred to the ship. His daughters did not cry when he kissed them good-bye, and he was a little hurt: "I have always been the dispensable member of the Swan family." After living with them for so many months, he felt that he had lost "all the importance or originality that other people, in Paris for instance, granted me without question. I have protested this attitude often but the beloved family never seemed to hear me or realize the resentment in my words" (389). What he didn't see was the resentment in the eyes of children he kept leaving, and especially, on this occasion, a quiet anger in Flora, who had tried so much to please him. When she reached adulthood, she attended the Jung Institute in Zurich as part of her program to become a psychoanalyst. She told friends about all the hours of self-analysis she had to undergo. "I learned only one thing: I hated my father," she would say, half-joking.

Swan did not visit Nebraska or see his mother on either of his trips home in the early 1930s. On Christmas Day 1931, Adah had written to him from Crab Orchard:

My dear son Paul:
    I'm just writing a few lines to my wonderful son, Paul. I am feeling lonely this afternoon, as it seems I cannot get used to living alone. I live in the past like old ladies do.
    My home is very comfortable but it is too large. Do not forget me, Paul. I need your love and comforting.

Your Mother.

The writer didn't sound like the Adah of his youth, stern and righteous. But he was ill-equipped to help her, and he did not want to visit, knowing old conflicts would arise. [14]

Love is not blind, but all-seeing. His measure for me was the highest I aspired to. **Paul Swan,** concerning Fred Bates

9 Winds of War, 1933–1938

At Peace

By the time the two travelers saw the shores of France, other outrages had occurred in Germany. The Nazis had established a boycott of Jewish-owned shops and were burning books.

But when Paul Swan and Fred Bates reached Paris, they knew nothing of this, and both "felt at once the zest for life . . . of our lives" (DS 395). Away from his family and a more moralistic New York, Swan's love for Fred deepened: "I had now found perfect companionship; trust, faith, inspiration had come back to me, as spring comes over the black hills" (396). It seemed as if his stars were finally in the proper alignment. The manic behavior of his previous life abated, and a twenty-five- by fifty-foot cavernous room at a somewhat rundown 10 rue Campagne Première became the place where Swan felt more at home than anywhere else in his life, before or after. There he could sit by one large balcony window at the north end and observe the goings-on of fellow artists who lived across the twelve-foot-wide cobblestone passageway. A group of umbrageous old trees at both ends of the building made him feel as if he were spending summer in the country: "Many people stopped in passing on the street to rest their eyes at this sequestered *ruelle.* One journalist said that in the winter it was a splendid place for a murder" (402).

Inside, Swan decorated the enormous, cracking plaster walls with several mural hangings (oil on cloth) he had brought from home. One was called *Annunciation*, a symbolist painting of three figures on invisible crosses, placed diagonally on the cloth, left to right with each higher than the previous, and with arms outstretched, like wings, as if the images were already angels in the process of ascending. In the lower right, another figure watches. Swan's old teacher, Baron Rosenkrantz, would have noticed his influence here, having created his own version of *Annunciation* for a stained-glass window: "archangels with great sweeping wings, Mary in a field of lilies [watching their ascent]" (Fletcher n.p.).

The front of Swan's homemade stage was curtained by his painted tapestries, *Paola and Francesca* and *Medieval Group.* He devised a way to raise these with side pulleys and placed a rather elaborate homemade switchboard (for lights) in the wing on stage left, where an assistant could remain hidden. A violet carpet displayed stripes of red and burnt orange. The large side windows were blacked out, and there he traced the horizon of his Nebraska farm on the pane. This left only a high skylight, "the only source of subdued light, giving the whole place the effect of a fabulous temple of beauty" (403).

Furniture included pedestals for his sculptures, large coffers, benches, and tables all built by Fred, an able carpenter. They painted these black, with bright red tops, and with terra-cotta-colored Greek figures surrounding them, to suggest the designs on Grecian urns.

Fred rewired the lighting so that at night the studio, with lights placed to bounce off several silk hangings, gave visitors the sense of an Arabian palace: "The sheer triumph of taste and talent over limited means caused Fred and me to chortle a little at the lavish compliments our place elicited. Of course we did not tell these enchanted ones to look behind the scenes and behold the kitchen table which was in reality the cover to our bath tub" (404).

By 1 May 1933 the temple was ready; all he needed were clients to commission art and an audience to watch him dance. He would simply advertise, and they would come. Swan's old lover, Cabanel, was the first to walk through the door, but she did not enter "with diamond dust sparkling from her eyelashes and lips," as she had a decade earlier. She was no longer the sumptuous courtesan of Paris; her opium addiction made the ravages of time more damaging. Her lover, the banker, had found younger beauties on which to bestow his money. The sum she had given Swan for his debut at her Babylonian palace would now cover her expenses for a year (de Pougy 250).

More people attended the second week, and by the third Saturday there was busy activity at 10 rue Campagne Première from dawn to midnight. After a meager breakfast, Swan and Fred cleaned and arranged the place into a theater, moving chairs, benches, stools, and dozens of cushions. Curtain pulleys and lights were tested. Fred ran his errands to the local grocery for tea and butter, to the baker for whole-wheat bread, and to other merchants for candles (in case of electrical outages, which were not uncommon). Fred was in charge of cutting and buttering the sandwiches, while Swan assembled cups and saucers and lit the incense. He always lit one candle in the swinging oriental candelabra to give a faint glow when the studio lights were off during certain dance scenes. Fred would dress in conventional attire, while Swan did warmup exercises and donned his first costume. He never danced nude until late in the program.

Fred greeted guests, gently reminding them to pay, while Swan scrambled across the studio to disappear behind the front stage curtain until the first dance began. A guest book was passed, soon followed by the tray of tea and sandwiches. Then, darkness for a moment, stage lights up, and the accompanist would begin to play the old piano. Fred, who had by now positioned himself behind the curtains, yanked the ropes to reveal a black cyclorama, lighted in the mellowness of an orange glow from the oriental candelabra.

One dance quickly followed another. Usually, Swan led with *The Théâtre Chinois*, but the repertoire varied from week to week. He often included *The House that Jack Built* to the music of Percy Grainger's *Molly on the Shore*, and always performed his two most famous pieces, *The Sphinx* and *To Heroes Slain*. After a short break during which his audience could wander about and view the paintings, tapestries, and sculptures (and sometimes make purchases), the program would resume. Usually *Danse Orientale* would be the final number. Swan would then walk to center stage and recite a poem by Tristan Klingsor while Fred, who had donned a Persian costume, beat a drum. The audience got their money's worth, for a usual Saturday consisted of twenty-eight dances.

Although shy by nature, Fred was a natural comedian. As long as he had the security of a costume he didn't mind performing, and sometimes he entertained guests while Swan caught his breath between dances. In one routine, he would appear dressed as a clownish stage carpenter hanging panels. Trying to hammer something on the top of the panel, he would grab his pantaloons and try to lift his weight. His exaggerated and athletic acrobatics delighted everyone and earned him the nickname "Dan," after the famous Danlino of the London music halls.

More times than not, the two hosts would have an intimate dinner for several friends at the end of the Saturday, using the long benches as a table. Fred was always the cook. "Suppers were happy and reposeful moments. It was so as life should be" (472). After the dinner guests left, the kitchen table reverted to the bathtub, where Fred would help his friend wash off body paint and makeup. Tired but happy, Swan would climb the stairs to the loft that had been converted into their bedroom. Still a young man in need of excitement, Fred often left for an evening at the American Students and Artists Club, where he danced with the girls, or played pool with the boys. Like a mother waiting for her child to come home from a date, Swan never slept until his return: "I hear his key in the latch—a most musical sound—and the *Samedis Artistique* in the rue Campagne Première is over, that is, until the following week" (473).

During this epoch, not only did the fifty-year-old Swan surpass his previous popularity on the Paris dance stage, but his art was accepted yearly for exhibitions by the Société des Artistes Français and the Société Nationale des Beaux Arts. Some of his best work decorated the Grand Palais.[1] By the time World War II ended almost all had disappeared, some likely into Nazi hands. A few photographs remain at The Ringling Museum of Art.

Swan had acquired a new patron by now, a young woman from Massachusetts named Jennie Stevens. She had written to him of her admiration, and he graciously sent her a small painting as a gift. She was overwhelmed, she said, and sent him twenty-five dollars. Then she ordered a portrait of her deceased brother, which Swan created

25. Paul Swan (*right*) and two of his students in his studio at 10 rue Campagne Première, Paris, 1933. Photograph courtesy of Dallas Swan Jr.

from photographs and for which he was paid several hundred dollars. After that, she wrote often, always tucking in twenty dollars for "living expenses." He did not know until later that she was terminally ill and that he was fulfilling her romantic dreams, a safe but mysterious lover who was in good part a figment of her imagination. For three years the letters continued. The last contained a photograph of herself as a little girl, the only picture Swan ever saw of her. A second photograph showed a wall in her home where hung a number of his works. His letter of reply wasn't answered, so he wrote again. It was returned after many months, stamped "Deceased, return to sender."

But in 1933, blessed with patrons, consistent audiences, and clients, Swan was making easy money. He was engaged to dance at a number of venues, including La Potinière, where he had appeared a decade earlier. Fred was almost always by his side, which made the artist feel settled and familial. He would visit the United States occasionally to see his family, he decided, but from now on, Paris was home. Besides,

Helen and the girls had now moved permanently to California, and the added distance provided an excuse to visit less often. In Paris he could live with Fred, work on his art and dance, and be free. Almost.

One day they were visited by an official from the police department, who inquired about the nature of Swan's relationship with Fred and the objectives of the weekly receptions. It was a disturbing interview at first, but not unexpected. "I wish my other tenants were as earnest and acceptable," the inspector told them after a thorough examination of the studio. "Mr. Swan is the most proper man in the world, and Mr. Bates is his servant" (408).

It is sometimes difficult to remember that until recently being a homosexual was criminal in most countries, a fact Swan had to deal with for almost all of his life, and a factor in his peripatetic travels. Even in Paris, supposedly the capital of tolerance, certain factions were concerned with the relationship between Swan and his partner. Although it appears that the inspector was willing to be convinced that the association was that of artist and assistant, a satisfactory story had to be concocted, and Swan's considerable charm had to be exercised before the two men could live together without official interference. It seemed at first a minor annoyance, almost on a par with a zoning regulation, but remember that it was only a few years before Hitler's infamous pink triangles were the prelude for gays to be killed in the gas chambers.

The days of bliss continued, while the Nazis were opening another concentration camp in Dachau (June 1933); but with old friends and new devotees congregating around the temple at 10 rue Campagne Première, all was lovely in Paul Swan's isolated world. He was still a favorite of reporters. In times of slow news, they always found something interesting to say about his gatherings or exhibitions. Magazines like *Candide* and *Art et Pensée* acclaimed his work. Hélène de Colligne wrote in *Diapaison* that Swan was creating "extraordinary frescoes," "sculpture of a tumultuous harmony," and "very clever drawings of profound inspiration." "He dances nude, a Greek bas-relief animated by the immortal spirit. One would like to understand what is the chemistry which could create such perfection" (SB; DS 422).

All this praise in his sixth decade was intoxicating: he thought he could stave off the effects of age indefinitely. After a successful performance at La Potinière, he wrote in his memoir that he had "real inward satisfaction . . . in the definite proof that I had kept 'Old Father Time' completely at bay. . . . I could still express my art as fully by my sculptured body. . . . I could feel that my career was just now beginning. The interim of time was merely a bad dream." Remembering his patient wife back in the States, he added, "not always bad but still a dream" (437).

In fact, one reviewer of an exhibition held at the American Woman's Club in the rue Boissière exclaimed, "Mr. Swan's talent is so versatile and his medium of expression so novel that he has already at a youthful age received recognition all over the world" (SB; DS 434). This was a six-week-long two-man show with Walter Neville (noted for his watercolors of Venice). The *Chicago Tribune*'s B. J. Kospoth reported from Paris that "Paul Swan is one of America's foremost portraitists" who displays "virtuosity in capturing a vivid likeness of his sitters." Seymour de Ricci of the *New York Herald Tribune* wrote that Swan's work was "perfect."[2] Selections that both critics applauded were portraits of American singer Victor Prahl, Nazimova, and André de Fouquières (known as Paris's "arbiter of elegance") and a decorative wall hanging called *Romance*.

Swan's portrait business—oils, drawings, and sculptures—was brisk, and in 1934 the Société des Artistes Français accepted several pieces for its exhibition. His bust *Homage to Debussy* was admitted to the Société Nationale des Beaux Arts. One paper called him Paris's "magnificent sculptor."[3] His dancing was equally celebrated. *Comoedia* (10, 14, and 17 June 1934) reported that "le célèbre danseur Paul Swan" would perform at Gala Yves Renaud at Théâtre Albert-I. *The Temptation, The Legend of Narcissus, The Great God Ra*, and *Danse du Desert* (in which Fred and two dance students also appeared) made up the program. Afterward, Swan was greeted (and praised) by one of the guests, Madame Albert Lebrun, wife of the president of France.

Also at the gala was the acclaimed Italian actress Emma Grammatica, who was then appearing at the Théâtre Madelaine in Paris. Soon after meeting Swan, she commissioned him to do a portrait drawing. They spent an afternoon laughing, talking, dancing together, and working. As he did with most of his subjects, he asked Grammatica to move freely about the room while she chatted about her life; he never liked his subjects to be completely still. She was so pleased with the drawing that she arranged for a photograph of it to appear in *Nouvelle Italie* (SB; DS 426).

Nouvelle Italie had published articles about Swan before. In a previous issue (21 July 1934) a critic had not only praised Swan's bust of Prime Minister MacDonald but raved about one of Mussolini, for whom the artist (the newspaper wrote) had "grande ammirazione." In 1934, Swan, like so many others, did not understand how dangerous Mussolini was. The dictator had gotten the trains to run on time in Italy. What was bad about that?

The weeks and months of Swan's life had taken on an easy rhythm, but when the Nazis murdered Austrian chancellor Engelbert Dollfuss on 25 July, real news was hard to ignore. On 2 August, German president von Hindenburg died, and Hitler became chancellor. There were rumors about purges and mass murders in Germany, but Swan still could not believe such horrors.

Fred kept Swan focused on work, work, and more work, and protected him from the realities of the world outside of France as much as possible. Soon after the Gala Yves Renaud, in June 1934, Swan was invited by the Fédération des Artistes Français on boulevard Haussmann to show ten of his paintings (the musical experiments from the summer of 1931) in the fourth Salon des Peintres-Musiciens. He also provided entertainment at the opening with several dances.[4] He was busy dancing again in November at La Potinière.

In the spring of 1935 the Salon des Peintres-Musiciens accepted another sculpture, *The Serenity of Fred*. One day Swan disguised himself and visited the Grand Palais to observe reaction: "I noticed, standing as artists do at exhibitions, just a little apart, that the admiring spectators seemed to be waiting for the eyes [on the bust] to open. Art is so much more than a visible prototype of the sitter. The soul of the artist has mingled with the soul of the model, and when deep bond has united the two, only great production is the logical result" (427).

Although Swan was complimented in many reviews over the years for his rendition of fine hands and penetrating eyes, by the 1930s he wanted to create more of a sense of mystery in his subjects. Downcast, half-opened eyes became his trademark in paintings like *A Modern Madonna* and sculptures like *The Serenity of Fred*, *Fernande Cabanel*, and *Tête de*

Femme. Photographs that remain and several extant paintings suggest that Swan successfully captured that last moment before eyes open, when the window to the soul is still a mystery. Like Mona Lisa's smile, the eyes fascinate.

By the end of September 1935, Swan's own eyes began to open. He learned that German Jews had been stripped of their rights by the Nuremberg Race Laws. Rumor became truth.[5]

Le Célèbre Artiste

From 2–15 December 1935, Swan exhibited two sculptures and a painting in the American Artists Professional League, 261 boulevard Raspail.[6] By the following May, Paris papers were touting his dance performance at Lord Neville Lytton's grand ball at Le Gardénia, an event to celebrate the work of Thomas Gainsborough. *Comoedia* paid its usual tribute to Swan, as did the *New York Herald Tribune*'s (Paris edition) reviewer, René Richard, who wrote that Swan evoked the inspiration and spirit of Gainsborough in his art.[7] One need only look at Swan's 1927 mural of the Wielich family (figure A) to observe how much the works of Gainsborough influenced him.

Swan's artistic vision—in painting more than in dance—was sometimes shaped by the need to cater to the tastes of the patrons he might meet at a lord's grand ball, and he was not above creating art to order; it paid well. Sometimes called "the perfect painter," a master colorist and superb draftsman, Swan was Paris's twentieth-century version of Andrea del Sarto.[8] But he was never able to hang onto the vast sums that passed through his hands. It may be another example of his insecurity that he continually complained about the prices he got for his work and yet seemed to rid himself of his money as soon as he touched it. Maybe he felt that if he had too much money, he would become artistically lazy; but his need for constant infusions of cash may have in some instances weakened his art. It was always easy to get a commission for a portrait, and portraits were work he could do quickly and well.

By 1936 he was feeling the need to push himself in another direction, as he had when he created his musical paintings in the summer of 1931. He began to experiment with sculptural masks. *Douleur* had been a success in the 1920s, but he wanted to go further, concentrating—perhaps in part because of his friendship with Prince Chula of Siam—on the oriental face. Certainly the masks did not reflect the prince's good looks but were instead bizarre, if not grotesque. The results may have caused some of his supporters from the conservative Paris Salon to frown, but other critics who were waiting for Swan to break free of convention were pleased. *La Nouvelle Dépêche* called the masque series "extraordinaire," transcending everything that was traditional and expected.[9] The masques show definite influences from Chinese and Japanese theater, particularly the Noh, possibly because of Swan's growing interest in the Orient, which also manifested itself in his dance. He had once written that "the more advanced an artist's work becomes, the more stylized are his efforts. So in life, the more truth is perceived, the more all things become symbolic."[10]

The business of art was brisk, but Swan began to worry about the current political climate. Some of his associates were getting in trouble. Among them was artist/critic Georges Turpin, who was a friend of Jacques Faneuse (pen name for Marthe Bertin-Conrads), one of Swan's staunchest supporters. Turpin (as famous for his *lundis* [at-home Mondays] as Swan was for his *samedis artistique* [artistic Saturdays]) and Faneuse joined organizations Swan avoided, including the Comité de l'association de la presse artistiques and Comité de la sociéte des gens de lettres. Both were involved in the anti-parliamentarian demonstrations and riots in Paris in the mid-1930s.[11] Although Swan had been an agitator for women's rights in the second decade of the century, he felt now that "politics were for politicians, and private citizens did not discuss their issues, except to fill up a gap in lagging conversations." In Paris, "irony and playful aloofness had become the prevailing fashion" (DS 536). His friends' timing was inappropriate, he thought. By 1936, Germany's aggression concerned him more than problems with the French government. He tried his best to remain oblivious to the sounds of war, but as weeks and months passed it became impossible.

One day he was having tea with a woman at the Hôtel Grand in Versailles. A group of fighter planes flew overhead and his friend exclaimed, "I love seeing those birds in the sky!" He retorted, "I hate them!" "I never forgot that brief instant as the formation flew across the vista of the tall window, nor the hellish noise their motors made, drowning out the orchestra and the chatter of that artificial assembly"

(465). In the years that followed, the image would return to him again and again of that peaceful day broken by the noise of military aircraft.

The woman who invited him to tea that day was Madame Delabuse, whom Swan called "Tendresse." She was so named one day when "she laid her fat cheek upon [Swan's] shoulder, looked up with her small black eyes and murmured, 'I really need some tenderness' " (462). This amateur author self-published books of her poetry under the pen name Jacqueline de Rosemonte.

Swan's description of her is unkind: "round melon-like face with a receding chin" (462). He used a quote from Edith Wharton to elaborate: "Her figure looked like an even tussle between her cook and her corset-maker."[12] Swan had met Tendresse by accident one day in the foyer of the Hôtel de St. Ives in 1936. He noticed her rich furs and engaged her in conversation. After that meeting she attended every Saturday performance, paying more than the stipulated entrance fee. Soon she invited the artist to her home on boulevard Montparnasse.

Love letters began arriving at Swan's studio. Then, bouquets of flowers, food, and more invitations to the theater. He danced for her when she held her own "at homes" but charged a thousand francs, more than his usual fee. He learned quickly that if he began to talk of other women, of their generosity and devotion, of their youth and beauty, she would give more gifts.

Fred called him a gigolo. Swan knew his partner wasn't completely amused. He had given three gifts of art to Tendresse, he reminded Fred: two portrait drawings and a landscape called *The Song of the Sea*. "Those gifts are my real alibi, by which I keep my self-respect," he argued. In fact, he had sold her the art, but at a discounted price. As usual, Swan believed that he had parted with his work too cheaply. Any money she gave him simply made up for that transaction.

"Whatever self-respect means in Paris," Fred muttered (463).

The relationship continued, off and on, depending on Swan's cash flow, until he left Paris.

Jacques Faneuse was another matter entirely. The forty-seven-year-old spinster was a well-regarded art critic for several journals who championed the old Wilde-Pater aestheticism that had once excited Swan. "Life is greater than art," Swan decided, "but art is life's truest expression nevertheless" (450). He had never really committed to "art for art's sake." There were too many other considerations, including Swan's own sense of the beautiful, the supremacy of life over art, and the need to please a patron.

"Evasions," one of Faneuse's many articles on Swan, appeared in *L'Elan Universaliste*. In it she describes how natural it is for a painter and a sculptor to move from "picture" to dance. In the same way that the negative space in a simple sketch becomes the perfect line (because we complete it in our imaginations), dance becomes the perfection of the movement toward the abstract in painting and sculpture. There is no concrete line; the line keeps changing, and that is its perfection. It is never static; paradoxically, its very ephemeral nature ensures that it transcends the temporal: "Does not dance possess the power to reach the height and depths of humanity like the absolute of certain words which stretch into illusory bounds of the infinite abysses of consciousness" (SB).[13]

Swan embraced the ideas of Noh actor and playwright Motokiyo Zeami (1363–1443), who said that the actor intones his lines until they take over his body, and then they resolve into a wordless dance, because the movement transcends speech. Because an artifact is deliberately separated from reality (we are not deluded that a picture or a sculpture is other than a representation), it exists in its own universe. Dance, therefore, creates a space and time that is thus its own, responsible to no other laws than those it imposes on that time and space.

How well Swan and Faneuse were acquainted at the time she began to promote him and his particular vision of dance can only be speculated. She agreed to write the preface to his new book of poetry, *Ma Vie Intérieure*, in December 1936, but she remained an unobtrusive presence at his Saturday performances.[14] He saw her in the crowd at the seventh Exposition des beaux-arts et arts décoratifs in 1937, where he exhibited *L'Opprimé* along with one of his oriental masks, *Maquette pour Monument*, and his painting *Prince Japonais*. She never spoke to him, but her reviews were positive. Like other critics, she focused on *L'Opprimé*, and so did the judges, who presented the sculpture with an award. He was offered a generous price for it but refused, thinking that, draped with its large medal, *L'Opprimé* would be an advertisement for his work when people visited the studio.

It was a good idea. Many artists had "at homes," competing for business, and Swan was clever at self-marketing. Delphine Marti of *Les Études Poétiques* wrote on 10 January 1937 that Swan's studio still fascinated, still had an "atmosphere of mystery." He was "the great artist" of dance, painting, and sculpture who could capture tragic, Shakespearean-like emotions in his work. He was, in fact, an "*Incomparable virtuose*" (SB).

A month in London in 1937 gave him time to see old friends again and provided Fred with an opportunity to visit his mother. Swan painted a portrait of Mrs. Hylda Hunter (sister of Sir Eldon Gorst), whom he had first painted in 1910 in Egypt. She also hired him to paint a pale green and gold landscape around the entire hall of the dining room of her home. "Birch trees formed the vertical lines. . . . The water and skies were gold. Swans floated about repeating the light tones of the trees, weeping willow fronds gave the rhythm to the whole effect." At the end of the hallway he designed a Spanish mural featuring a señorita, "like my portrait of Raquel Meller, sitting on a balcony while a red boleroed toreador strummed his guitar" (480).[15] He earned additional money by restoring paintings owned by Miss Gorst, Hunter's sister. Kitty Gorst, Hunter's niece (who Swan had also painted in Egypt), commissioned a portrait of her son, Paul, with his pony, and another of his wolfhound. That last was titled *Bird's-eye View of a Sleeping Dog*, one of the few animal portraits Swan ever painted.

When he and Fred returned to Paris, Swan and Jacques Faneuse became better acquainted. In his portrait of her, she wears a soft felt hat with a feather in it and looks elfish and more youthful than her years.[16] She could easily be mistaken for a character in *A Midsummer Night's Dream*. But her slight size belied her power in journalistic circles. She could, if she so chose, make life difficult for an enemy.

Swan saw her in the audience when he performed between acts at a production of Euripides' *Electra* at Salle Pleyel (252 rue de Faubourg Saint-Honoré). The play starred a well-known actress from Greece named Angèle Cotsali, but Faneuse gave Swan the most space in her review.

He wouldn't have her support for much longer, though. She was ill, her fragility caused in part by an unspecified disease. When Swan found out, she was only a few months from death. Still, she summoned the strength to see him perform one more time in Le Gala Paul Swan at salle Marcelin-Berthelot in late April 1938. Underwritten by the ever loyal Cornelia Whiting and produced by impresario Alfred Lyon, the event attracted the interest of almost every paper in Paris.[17]

Swan arranged for several of his artist friends to perform: musicians played, poets and actors recited, and he danced. Even Fred was onstage, looking "superb as he sat by Miss Hansen [the accompanist], turning her pages." Of course, Swan had his obligatory case of nerves and "blinding headache" at the outset, "But when the faint murmur of the accumulating crowd grew from a little into a loud, happy, anticipating blur of voices," he calmed down and performed brilliantly, according to all reports (SB; DS 476). In fact, he defined stage fright as the instant when "my spirit is purified and winged . . . just before the curtain goes up on my first number. That lifting of the veil is so symbolic of the lifting of darkness and the dawning of freeing truth. . . . In those moments I reach out across the ocean to my family" (476).

"His harmonious body is ever enhanced by the art of his ideal attitudes. Always searching new rhythmic figures, poetic and original expressions, this astounding artist was warmly applauded," wrote a critic from *Le Matin*. Maurice J. Champel of *Paris-Soir* observed that Swan was "the very apotheosis of movement applied to an inner dream. The originality, the sincerity, the universality of Paul Swan has already filled a golden book of critiques. This recital only confirmed the merits of his great renown" (29 April).

Wanting to have one last chance to praise him, Faneuse published her last article in *La Politic Nouvelle* a few weeks later: "What is more satisfying for a great artist of the dance than to bring forth silent tears on the faces of his spectators by no other than the pathos his own face inspires and by the *rythme-évocateur* of his steps. It is thus that Paul Swan in his magnificent festival . . . knew how to move the public in executing *Before the Great Silence* to Chopin's Funeral March" (SB; DS 479).

When Swan called at Faneuse's home to thank her, he was greeted by her mother, who informed him that her daughter had died the day before.

26. Advertisement for Paul Swan's gala at Centre Marcelin-Berthelot, Paris, 1938. Photograph courtesy of the collection of The John and Mable Ringling Museum of Art, the State Art Museum of Florida.

Only he creates truly who rises above
sense perceptions . . . and who in his inner
life seeks the universal . . . seeing beyond.
Baron Arild Rosenkrantz

10 Farewells, 1938–1939

Crab Orchard

Swan's sculpture *Époque* and his memorial bust of Maurice Ravel were
celebrated at the Paris Salon that spring. One reviewer wrote that the
Ravel sculpture "elegantly evokes the tormented visage of [the musician's] last months" (April 1938, SB), another that it was "particularly
worthy of attention."[1]

But after Jacques Faneuse died, Swan became depressed and began
to worry about his loved ones in America. He hadn't seen his wife
and daughters for five years, and felt the "pull of family heartstrings"
(DS 486). There were hints from the stoic Helen about her pain from
debilitating arthritis. All her husband knew was that she was no longer
the young, energetic woman who had walked miles with him down
Adirondack mountain roads. She was now in her sixties, and she felt
eighty. Flora's letters had been formal in tone, and that worried him.
Paula, on the other hand, wrote long, graphic letters (perhaps hoping
for some reaction from her long-absent father) confessing indiscretions
with her new lover, trying to control her "white-flame-like emotions,
her completely artistic outlook" (486). He was curious about her conduct and wanted to see in person what his firstborn had become.

Swan also knew that his mother, Adah, could not live many more years, and (feeling guilty about avoiding her on several previous trips) he didn't want to miss seeing her at least one more time. When the Salon show was finished, he brought *Époque* and *Maurice Ravel* back to his studio, told Fred to pack a bag, and bought two tickets on the German Red Star Line from Antwerp. Swan knew the ship had been nationalized from the Bernstein Line, but he didn't consider then what that might mean. He only wanted to get to America.

Except for avoiding a woman they suspected might be a German spy, the two had an enjoyable trip across the Atlantic. An attractive young woman sailing with her mother set out to capture the young men aboard, and Swan enjoyed watching Fred fall under her spell. "Even I was susceptible," Swan confessed, and so drew a portrait of her to gain favor. "A young French count fell in love with her, and wanted to marry her then and there. Fred was her slave for ten days" (494).

Dallas and Olivia Swan opened their home to the wanderers, who stayed several days. The house in Garden City, New York, now contained two children. Cynthia, famous for her portrait with her mother on the cover of *Literary Digest* (*A Modern Madonna*), had been joined by a little brother, Dallas Jr. "These completed the ideal family," Swan wrote in his memoir: "I was sensitive to every aspect of their welcoming home. I was eager to notice all the attitudes, manners, niceties of their warm hospitality; their candor, openness, unrestrained self-revelation, their confidential, naïve relation to each other and to Fred and me. . . . The simplicity of everything was ideal" (495).

Swan always enjoyed spending time with his beautiful sister-in-law: "Her oval head, white skin and dark parted hair made her the ideal model for Italian madonnas. Her pure *other-world* eyes reflected her nature's intrinsic goodness." Even his brother Dallas, with whom he had "philosophical differences," seemed "strong" rather than "callous" on this occasion: "Dallas has had the same urge to accomplish that has always driven me on, although his direction has led him to the rigors of West Point, combined with the practical experience of psychology in salesmanship and business promotion." The family accepted Fred without question. Dallas was probably relieved to see his volatile brother

27. Undated photograph of Paul Swan, which he gave to Olivia and Dallas Swan Sr. Courtesy of Dallas Swan Jr.

under the gentle influence of someone who had a more practical view of life (494–95).

After the visit, Paul and Fred headed by train for Lincoln, Nebraska, and then Tecumseh. Swan recognized the red brick courthouse in the city where he had lived with the Appersons almost forty years earlier. But Anna had died a few years earlier, and this time it was Adah Swan who met them at the train station. With her was Swan's favorite sister, Harriet, whom he had once dressed in costume to perform in his corncrib theater. Adah, now seventy-six years old, was "clad in a beautiful blue frock" of her own making. Swan was struck by how wrinkled and withered she looked: "Poor lady! . . . Much change had come to her face since that day of my father's funeral in 1926, when she had looked so surprisingly youthful in spite of her grief and ordeal of the last weeks of his illness. She wore a sort of peering expression in her still blue-eyed-Corson-girl-eyes but when she saw me she wept a little through her happy smile and embraced and kissed her eldest baby boy" (499).

Adah immediately recognized the resemblance her son had to his younger friend. "Why, he is just like one of my own boys!" she exclaimed. She could not have imagined them as lovers. No doubt, the entire family was determined to acknowledge Fred publicly as the trusted secretary and adviser. Their private thoughts were their own.

There was a joyful reunion a few days later. Six of Adah's ten children, with their children, were there. It was a glorious but difficult time. Adah wandered from person to person, always afraid to miss a hug or a snippet of important talk, knowing that soon her family would separate again. "My mother craved for love she never got and never gave," Swan noted. "Only in respectful pretense was it given to spare her loneliness, of which all of us children were conscious. But the sad truth was she never gave unqualified, all-forgiving love to any one, though she did not know it." His opinion has been at least partially supported by several younger relatives who remember her as "a difficult woman." For some reason, it was easier for Adah to give her best version of love to her grandchildren. Even Swan observed this, but still he could not let go of the old resentment: "It was almost as if to say, 'See, these love me! These love their Grandmother!'" (499). Of course, Adah was not the first person to discover that dealing with grandchildren is much simpler than rearing one's own. When the feast was over, the grandchildren would go back to their parents, who would have to deal with the day-to-day quirks and rebellions of this latest generation.

The visit with Adah soon became an ordeal, as such times always were. Swan felt unloved. "She was thoroughly artistic in viewpoint," never "ordinary or common." There was "a sort of imperious quality which was completely unrealized." It might have done Swan some good to consider this observation more carefully, for he was also describing himself.

"I hate death! I hate death!" he said after visiting his father's gravesite. "Whoever say Death is only a slight transition is a liar! . . . My father is dead and now disintegrated. I shall never again see him as he was" (504). Swan, utterly depressed, placed a little bouquet of his mother's zinnias at his father's gravestone.

The final hours of the visit were the worst. It was a beautiful, sunny, late-August morning in Nebraska, one that reminded him of the day, a lifetime ago, when a boy ran away from home to high school in Tecumseh. On the way to the station, he and Fred decided to make a quick stop at Harriet's home to say good-bye. To prolong the time she had with her wandering son, Adah wanted to go with them. He told her that they were in a rush and would be calling on Harriet only for a minute. He confessed later that he didn't want his mother to eavesdrop on a conversation with his favorite sister:

Why didn't we grant her this last wish? Why couldn't we see this was the last time on earth I should ever look upon her face?

. . . My mother kissed me goodbye and held on to my hand, looking tenderly, resignedly, as the car jerked into action. She was almost thrown to the ground, but the car did not stop and we moved on faster and faster, farther and farther. We waved back to her. She waved in response to us, until her bright blue frock that she wore had faded out of sight. We had gone. (505)

It is a scene worthy of the cinema, with the mother forcibly thrown by the car jerking forward, then diminishing in the distance until only a blue speck dissolves in the rear-view mirror.

Adah Swan was stricken with apoplexy at her home in Crab Orchard on 3 February 1939, four months after her eldest son had returned to France. The "blue-eyed Corson girl" died six days later, on Thursday, the ninth of February, at 9:15 a.m. The *Tecumseh Chieftain* ran a long obituary the next day: "Good Woman Is Gone." Adah was, the paper explained, "an active and consecrated worker in His kingdom wherever she resided. She was a lover of truth and beauty, and possessed a fine and artistic nature."

California

Swan learned early in his career to lie about his daughters' ages. Some smart reporter might start doing the math and discover that he was probably not nineteen in 1918, or a "youngster" in 1935. Sometimes Swan himself seemed to forget the real truth. He certainly wasn't prepared to see two adult daughters greet him and Fred at the station in Los Angeles.

Paula, now twenty-four, immediately endeared herself to him. She espied a young man in the crowd and told her father, "He probably thinks you are my latest catch. He'd never guess you are my father!" She was all full of news about her latest love. "Is it the one you sent me a little photo of?" he asked. "Oh, no, not *that* one! This is a new one." Then she shocked him again. "I hope you will go up in my airplane with me. It's wonderful up over the clouds." He silently promised his nervous stomach, "Never!" (506).

When they finally arrived home in Van Nuys, Swan found his wife "plumpish, and much more gray, though her hair was still as luxuriant as ever. She was bent over by her malady, but her eyes still had that mellow sparkle and her smile was the same reassuring smile" (507). She usually took her meals alone, while listening to the radio program *Amos and Andy*, and Swan felt diminished: "I had become a stranger" (509). He didn't know how to help her and knew that if he did carve a useful niche for himself, he would soon be gone anyway. He had no control and so, like many loved ones who must adjust to a disabled person (and he would have more trouble than most), he got irritated: "Being an invalid, she was invested with all the trappings of tyranny which no one could take from her. She was 'down' physically but this gave her decisions 'the strength of ten.' Her gentle, passive, acquiescent mien, concealed a stubborn will which in spite of her inability to move freely about, made her always the center of her world" (510). And that meant that he was *not*.

He loved Helen deeply; and in a different way, of course, he loved Fred. After both were dead, it was Helen he would always speak of to friends, never Fred. But in 1938, Fred was much more his life partner than Helen ever would be again. Perhaps in later decades a deceased wife gave him an aura of heterosexual respectability; perhaps the thought of Fred was too painful to articulate.

A rift with the once adored Flora, now twenty-one, was apparent from the start of his visit. Paula had become an expert cook and helped keep the household running on track. Swan liked her more and more. To the dinner table were often invited several aviator friends, and Swan dubbed her "queen of the skies." But the dark-haired Flora who had danced with her father and written poetry for him was now out of favor. He wrote: "Intensity and contrasted apathy is characteristic of everything Flora undertakes. Zeal is followed by indifference. Her intelligence outruns her realizations and turns upon itself destructively. She has not the self-discipline or patience to wait the harvest of the seeds she sows. . . . She is complex, contradictory and inconsistent" (508). Flora had a lot of getting even to do, so when her father tried to pick up the relationship where he thought it had left off, she had her chance for revenge. He believed that she would want to avail herself of the opportunity to learn from him during his stay, for she continued to dabble in drawing and painting. She told him, "I don't want to lose my individuality by working with anyone." "I pleaded with her," Swan recalled. "I explained how, in Paris, an advanced pupil or two from the Beaux Arts Academy had so admired my bold and vigorous technique and . . . had asked to study painting with me. But finally, I gave up trying to persuade her. It was a summer wasted, as far as Flora's painting was concerned. . . . 'Serves him right' would echo down the valley where my family lived" (509).

October meant returning to Paris, and Swan was relieved when the day came to depart. He had come six thousand miles, he said, to " 'look again upon thy face,' but no one but Fred witnessed what the pilgrimage did to me" (512). Among all the tension, there "sat Helen

28. *Flora Swan* by Paul Swan, about 1938. Location and size not known. Photograph courtesy of Dallas Swan Jr.

on her throne [wheelchair] like the holy Lama of Shan-gri-La, while the vortex of family energies seethed about her" (511). It was, perhaps, the meanest criticism he ever uttered about his wife.

In addition to his family concerns, Swan was worried about what was happening in Europe. When he heard about the signing of the Munich Pact on 29 September 1938, he was overjoyed. Prime Minister Neville Chamberlain was his hero. "We all had so little grasp of the colossal problems involved," he later reflected. On 15 October, German troops moved into the Sudetenland. Swan wanted to be back at his studio. He was worried about years of artwork left behind, "trembling in Paris." He cried often, with little comfort offered from a wife who was dealing with her own pain. He thought he might have a breakdown but for the steady hand of Fred. He couldn't wait to get home once more to begin a new season of *samedis artistique*. He would concentrate on his work; somehow the rest of the world would rediscover its sanity.

To pay for their tickets, Swan sold a large mural of a mountain scene to Miss Belle Meller, who had bought some of his work the previous decade in Chicago. He also painted several other portrait commissions at a week's stopover in that city on the way to New York. Finally, with great relief, he and Fred boarded the ill-fated Holland American liner *Statendam*. Less than two years later, in August 1940, it would be lost at sea, a victim of a German torpedo. [2]

Paris was as beautiful as ever. Swan later told friends that he "lived in a fool's paradise." He wrote in his memoir, "Fred and I were in our own self-built world, where everything we touched or could see, had been placed just where we would have it" (516). Like most, these two didn't want to acknowledge political realities. Within a few years, life would be changed, utterly.

But on the day they returned to Paris in October 1938, all was joy at 10 rue Campagne Première.

"Things fall apart"

George La Rogov, tall and graceful, with golden hair, danced often now at Swan's studio. He became a popular entertainer, in part because of his intriguing self-made costumes. Swan, always concerned with the element of masculinity in dance, was bothered by the effeminate nature of La Rogov's performances, observing that his friend had a tendency toward the *précieuse*; but he admired his dedication and good spirit. One evening in late 1938 La Rogov gave a great dinner for some friends who were leaving Paris. Swan remembered that night clearly because several partaking in the festivities disappeared into concentration camps during the war. No one at the happy dinner understood that they were saying good-bye forever.

In February, Swan received news from Nebraska of his mother's death. Years of lost opportunities to forge a connection with her suddenly overwhelmed him, and he "broke down and wept aloud like a baby who awakes to find himself alone" (521). The death of parents is always traumatic, no matter what the relationship, and in the case of Adah and her son Paul, it was undeniably complex. Parents are our last barrier against death; when they are gone, we can begin to gauge our own dissolution. Adah was both his deterrent to a freer life and the genetic link to his talent. In her case, however, Swan believed that talent had been subsumed by an unrelenting religious absolutism. It is impossible to say how much her passing was a son's sorrow or the realization that the time remaining for himself and his art was now more precisely measured.

Life kept pulling him back; there was business at hand. On 2 March 1939, the second Gala Paul Swan was presented at the Salle Marcelin-Berthelot. "Another nerve-straining experience," he wrote to Helen, but also a "glorious experience" (521). The program was a repeat of the one he presented in 1938, with the same friends performing. Singer Ginette Guillamat and actor Jean Varillat joined him, as did accompanist Evelyn Hansen. In the final number, Swan danced to "Asia," a poem by Tristan Klingsor, recited by Varillat. Fred (whose stage name was Fred Eric) played the tambourine. Many curtain calls followed, with flowers tossed onto the stage, and several ardent ladies from the audience rushed up to kiss Swan (papers did not mention kisses for others in the show). Maurice J. Champel of *Paris-Soir* was only one of many who sang praises: "une exceptionnelle démonstration d'art" (SB).

Two weeks later, on 15 and 16 March, the Nazis took control of Czechoslovakia. Still, the art world remained staunch. On 5 May, B. J. Kospoth of the *Herald Tribune*'s Paris edition ("Art Immune to War 'Jitters,' Paris Salon Exhibition Reveals") wrote that important shows would continue "despite politically critical times": "The Paris Salon, uniting in the vast halls of the Grand Palais the combined art exhibits of the Société des Artistes Français and the Société Nationale des Beaux Arts, was inaugurated by President Albert Lebrun yesterday." Several American artists had work accepted that was considered "excellent and interesting," and in particular, "a touching plaster bust called *Petit Soldat Inconnu* by Paul Swan."

"The beautiful, the ugly, the sacred and profane" shifted into "strange kaleidoscopic patterns," wrote Swan in June (527). He was "saddened beyond the scope of words." Now his own world began to disintegrate. His landlady informed them that he and Fred would have to move. Reasons are unclear. She explained that the building (built as a tapestry-dyeing atelier in 1883) must be handed over to the owner of the ground underneath it. In reality, she—or the owner—no longer wanted to house tenants at risk. They knew that if the Germans arrived it would be dangerous to be connected to homosexuals in any way. Rumors of Nazi atrocities against gays had by now been documented.

In Germany, the Law for the Protection of German Blood and German Honor was passed in 1935, and paragraph 175a of the Reich Penal Code, which gave police the power to imprison males who committed "an unnatural sex act" and to take away their civil rights, had been amended. The unnatural acts included not only sex but also kissing, embracing, and having homosexual fantasies (how this last was to be determined was not made clear). As the Nazis later began sending suspected German gays to concentrations camps, those prisoners wore pink triangles to identify them. As the war progressed, Nazi viciousness extended to the countries they occupied.

Paris was still safe in June 1939, but landowners were beginning to prepare for the worst. Paul Swan and Fred Bates were told that they had one week to leave their home of six years. Undoing, unnailing, unpinning, pulling down was every day's exercise. Rugs were rolled up; dishes were packed. Paintings that once hung from floor to ceiling were now stacked in piles around the sides of the room, reduced to heavy baggage that must be moved. Busts were the hardest to pack, and Fred's carpentry skills came in handy as boxes were quickly constructed.

Even Fred's habitual good nature was tested at this juncture. Swan was gloomy and moody, and his hardworking, quiet partner was some-

29. *Petit Soldat Inconnu* by Paul Swan, about 1917. Plaster and bronze versions. Locations and sizes not known. Photograph from authors' collection.

times the target of his frustration. One can only imagine incessant directions, like "Be careful with that sculpture" or "Don't scratch that painting." Blowups were not infrequent, but their duration was short:

> [Fred] would fly into a violent rage, saying "then do the job yourself. I'm fed up. I'm going out!" He would seize his bérét and reach the door, turn the handle, but already the sudden storm was over! He would linger a moment in silence and then giving me a sly look with a twinkle of a smile in his eyes he'd say: "Nev' mind, perhaps you were right, Maître." He knew that his use of Maître teased me a little as so many Parisian women had used this salutation in addressing me. . . .
>
> I still wonder how anyone who knew every hidden nook and corner of my life and character as Fred does could unwaveringly respect and honor me, for through moments of strength and moments of weakness he remained with me and for me without admonition or censure. He believed in my soul's integrity. This must have been why he forgave and forgot without question. His own soul is so honest he saw mine as it is. (531)

They were fortunate to find a place to live. The address was 15 rue Simon Déreure, on Montmartre, the heights of Paris, not far from the Cathedral of Sacré Coeur, and owned by an Italian insurance company. They were glad to have a large apartment. Seeing his companion's dejection, Fred immediately pulled the stepladder out of the pile of belongings stacked in the dusty room and located Swan's painted tapestry *Yesterday, Today, and Tomorrow* rolled up in one of the rugs. "Where shall we hang this," he asked, getting to business at hand, as always. There was a lot of work to do. "You are my balance wheel," Swan told him (534). Within two weeks they hosted a housewarming, followed by a short dance performance. As August arrived, life did not seem quite so hopeless. In fact, *Maurice Ravel* and an oil, *Portrait of J. M. le R.*, were shown at the salon of the Société des Pientres-Musiciens in June and July (SB).

But history was set on its inexorable course. By late August they heard that some civilians were being evacuated from London, and they didn't know what that meant. Swan was concerned. If he had to return to the United States, would Fred be able to go with him? Nothing was clear. He painted a new portrait of his partner, "to imprison his image, which I feared even then would sooner or later be taken from my sight. This experience was somewhat like that of the great Renaissance artist who painted his dead son before he was put into his tomb" (539). He worked frantically, as if sheer production would keep war away. From photographs he made a bust of Paula. He never had a chance to cast it; it was the last work he did in the studio.

With only a few days left in August, they became concerned about some commercial photographers who had moved into several rooms in their building. Although the newcomers said they were French, Swan was quite sure they were not. There were mysterious arrivals and exits, and the photographic equipment was never unpacked. He suspected it was all there to camouflage less innocent purposes. When he heard a very German-looking youth sing "La Marseillaise," there was no doubt: "French people never sing *La Marseillaise* casually; only on proper occasions" (541). One day the Paris police arrived unexpectedly and arrested the entire group. Swan knew they would be caught eventually, as "these Germans possessed no dramatic talent, or feeling for their assumed roles" (542).

On 1 September, news came of the invasion of Poland. On the afternoon of 3 September, an actor-friend, Alexandre Ryonel, arrived at the apartment, breathless and crying. War had been declared. Fred was out at a club. Swan was worried about him and had to wait several hours more until his return. When he did, he had already heard the news. He spent the remainder of that day calming both Swan and Ryonel, who was worried about a younger brother "called to the colors."

That evening Swan, Ryonel, and Fred said good-bye to Ryonel's "petit soldat." The sight they observed at the Madelaine station was disheartening:

The [station] was crowded with stoical, silent soldiers and their families. There was no shouting, no bragging, and [no] zest for what faced them. They were obliged to go whether they believed or not, and hardly anyone did believe. They loved their *patrie*, but all was somehow too unreal and too *fantastique*. So, stoically, like all good Frenchmen, they thus said *au revoir* to all the joy of living, and most of them who have not since been killed, have not yet returned to their loved ones they left behind that night.

From the Madelaine, the Grand Boulevard was transformed by darkness, the crowds moved to and fro, mostly in uniforms. These seemed like the phantoms in "In Flanders field the poppies blow." All war is a kind of dream, from which each person expects to be suddenly awakened. (544)

At four o'clock the next morning, Swan and Fred jumped from their beds at the sound of air-raid sirens and antiaircraft guns. Thinking that Paris was under attack, they hastily dressed and sat together by the light of a little candle, not knowing what else to do. They heard dogs barking and the meowing of a bewildered cat.

Nighttime air-raid sirens continued for several days. One morning, while Swan was standing in line for a visa (something he now needed to stay in Paris), it all began again. Hundreds of people started running; he ran for his studio, some distance away, but it was a false alarm. The best he and Fred could do was stay in their steel-girded building as much as possible: "We had taken the precaution to tape up the cracks of the window and door of the bathroom for a 'safety place' in case of a gas attack, and had always by our bedsides improvised gas masks which Fred had made. We had failed to get regulation ones, as hundreds of others had done, and it was against police orders for one to go into the street without a mask strapped over the shoulder" (548–49).

Another concern arose. Not knowing whom they might meet in the street, and knowing that being an artist offered no special protection from political madness, they began to fear arrest. Fred did all the necessary errands, and Swan felt a surge of relief each time he returned safely.

They tried to determine how they could both get to the United States, but Fred knew that was highly unlikely, because he was not a citizen. He would soon have to make plans to return to England. For the moment he began, quietly, to pack his companion's art once more in protective boxes. It was the beginning of a heartbreak from which Swan would never fully recover.

They saw each other for the last time on 12 September 1939. Fred encouraged his partner not to delay another day; he must get a ship to the States, and the number of people trying to leave was growing. Soon it might be more difficult. On 3 September, U-boat no. 30 sank the steamship *Athenia*, a liner carrying 1,100 passengers, 300 of whom were Americans trying to get safely home. Fortunately, other ships in the area came to its rescue, but 112 people died. Swan mentioned the *Athenia* in his memoir, but his fears were more for Fred's safety. After purchasing his ticket, and carrying as much art as he could, he boarded the train that would take him to Bordeaux.

"When the moment actually arrives and one is in an outgoing train and the other is waving 'farewell' from a platform, we have no philosophy to meet this pain in our breasts," wrote Swan about his last glimpse of Fred (550). Normally the ride to Bordeaux took five hours, but at that time it took all night and most of the next day. The train often stopped on sidings to allow flatcars full of cannons and soldiers to pass by. Finally at his destination, tired and despondent, Swan took a room at the Gasgoine Hotel. He would have to stay there for three days, until he could secure passage on a ship whose name he never remembered.

A letter from Fred arrived on the fifteenth, dated the thirteenth:

Dear Paul:

You are gone and I can't bring myself to realize it. What we are to each other is too real and sincere "au fond" to ever find an end in this life.

Parting is hard but few can feel as I do now. If I hadn't come back to the studio where you are still on every inch of wall-space and in the very atmosphere and silence of the room, I could have stayed the profound emotion that has taken everything from me, leaving me completely weak in mind and body.

M. Bernard, the concièrge and his wife, insisted that I eat with them and their eulogy of you was almost more than I could stand without breaking into tears again.

I took all the sculpture off the stands, just "in case." The head of me and the other busts I put in the closet and padded all around them with blankets. I hope it was unnecessary.

If I ever lost sight of what you truly are, I see clearly now. Forgive me for my shortcomings and know I am your true friend, and when we take up where we left off, I will promise to try and be worthy of what you have done for me, in spite of me. I'll write again soon.

Fred

They were never able to take up where they left off. Hitler had other plans.

Rare bird, I saw you leap . . . Into a lake of air.
Hyacinthe Hill, "On Having Seen Paul Swan Dance"

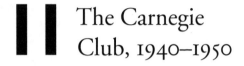

The Carnegie Club, 1940–1950

"Rendezvous for the Famous"

On 20 October 1940, *PM Weekly* ran a feature story on Carnegie Hall as the new concert season opened.[1] The New York Philharmonic scheduled recitals by Marian Anderson, Fritz Kreisler, and Sergei Rachmaninoff. But the article also told the story of another Carnegie Hall, a "city in which 653 men and women eat, sleep, work and make love." It included small photos of the philharmonic and the hall's director, Robert E. Simon Jr. A larger picture showed Carnegie's famous new resident, Paul Swan. Still in excellent physical condition (but obviously no longer in his twenties), Swan chose to pose in a brief Grecian garb, complete with headband and cape. He is greeting someone at his studio door. Behind him, walls are decorated with his art. The caption explains that he is a dancer, painter, and sculptor who "spends 80 per cent of his life within the confines of Carnegie City. Ads that once appeared on Parisian billboards now decorate one side of his studio. There he sleeps, works, entertains, and has his breakfast brought in." Another description provides additional details: "The high ceiling and the huge dimensions of [Swan's] studio afforded it an air of solemnity. The floor was covered with numerous Oriental rugs. Beautiful rugs of dark colors and drapes of red framed the scene. The gravity of the place where I found myself reminded me that da Vinci preferred his studio to have dark walls and preferred to paint on cloudy days as he felt that was the perfect lighting" (Cluzel 42).

But when Swan settled into Charles Dana Gibson's old Studio 90 and 91 at Carnegie Hall, his primary concern was not art. Fred Bates was working at a munitions factory in London; other friends were in concentration camps or at the front lines. The war was everywhere, and he was determined to do whatever he could to aid those who were suffering. For several years he gave performances at his studio every Thursday and donated all the proceeds to relief organizations. A year after his return to the United States, he danced at the Guild Theater in New York (17 November 1940) for the Queen Wilhelmina Fund, raising money for Belgian refugees. He performed benefits for wounded soldiers and orphaned children.[2] Swan had always campaigned for causes in which he believed, including suffrage, education, and war relief. In addition, his art reflected his concern, memorializing the plight of soldiers in sculptures such as *Petit Soldat Inconnu* and *Lest We Forget*, in paintings such as *Refugees*, and in dances such as *To Heroes Slain*. His charitable activities sometimes caused a shortfall of working capital, which he expected to be remedied by infusions of cash from his younger brother Dallas.

A month after his performance for the Queen Wilhelmina Fund, Swan was heard on air, at radio station WEVD, speaking for fifteen minutes on "If Artists Ruled the World" (18 December). No transcript remains, but Swan often suggested a social structure in which the artists and poets who so concerned Plato would assume leadership over the philosopher-kings. The artist, because of his search for beauty, was the true philosopher. Above all, there would be no war. The military man would be stripped of his toys and retrained in music, dance, and drawing. Men and women would be equal in every aspect of life.

Swan dreamed of re-creating his old Adirondack society in Stony Creek at Skiwaukee, which was still owned by Helen. Hoping that Fred would be able to join him after the war, he decided that together they would establish the Swan Theater there, "wherein impoverished artists may exhibit their works."[3] Even though he never had the financial means to execute such plans, Swan always did what he could with what he had (or with what he could borrow) to help other artists. Sometimes he was simply, incomprehensibly, extravagant. Once, when he received a large commission, he rented the ballroom at the Waldorf Astoria and threw a grand party for his friends, leaving himself more in debt in its aftermath.[4] Brother Dallas, of course, was not informed of the occasion.

Swan's first exhibition after his return to the States was at the Montross Gallery at 785 Fifth Avenue.[5] The director signed him to a contract as soon as he heard Swan was back in New York, and the Macbeth Gallery, where Swan had exhibited on several occasions in past decades, was not far behind.

The Montross exhibition, which ran from 3 to 22 June 1940, received generally good reviews, but the art world had changed a great deal since Swan had made his first big sale to *Putnam's Magazine* in 1908. Critics began to discover more sentimentality in his work, but most were still drawn to the poetic impulses he captured in his sculpture. "Much of the work is efficient technically but in its imaginative aspects much overdone on the sentimental side," wrote a reviewer from the *New York Times.* "It is Mr. Swan's evident conviction that there is a haunting mystery in the eyes of people which calls for a far-away expression that is anything but prepossessing. But when he avoids this psychological mannerism, as in his 'Prosper Burranelli,' and his handsome Holbeinesque 'Mrs. D.D.S.' [Mrs. Dallas Dewitt Swan, RMA], Swan's portraits are more persuasively characterized."[6]

Not seeming to mind these reservations, Swan carefully pasted the review in his scrapbook. Business was good, and he felt secure. He was of course more pleased by comments from people like Angelo di Benedetto, who wrote that Swan's portraits combined "the sense of harmonious design and pattern of the astute craftsman . . . with the imprint of the penetrating psychologist" (SB). *Art News* called him "versatile . . . and particularly aware of movement in the forms of nature. His portraits are self-confident."[7] When Michael Engel, director of exhibits for M. Grumbacher, visited Swan's studio, he offered similar praise. These were the judgments Swan remembered: "Your . . . sculptures are worthy of the highest approbation of the critic, art lover, and museum director alike."[8]

In November, Swan returned in triumph once again to his home state of Nebraska, where the Joslyn Memorial Art Museum in Omaha held a one-man show in his honor.[9] Although family members were proud of his success, most didn't understand how renowned he really was. Even if they had known, they probably still would have been embarrassed to introduce him to their friends. For conservative midwesterners, Swan—with his facial makeup, long fingernails, and eccentric style of dress—was a genuine oddity. He was perceptive enough to know how they felt and sensitive enough to be hurt by it. From the day that a neighboring farmer had asked Randolph "What's wrong with your oldest boy?" until the end of Swan's life, he never felt at ease in Nebraska.

The following January, the *Orlando Star* noted a private exhibition of Swan's work in that city, produced by New Yorker Ernest Briggs. Two months later, the *West Palm Beach Post* reported that three of Swan's landscapes and two portraits were the latest additions to the exhibition of contemporary artists at the Biltmore Hotel Art Gallery.[10] These exhibitions attest to Swan's continued popularity as an artist, even after a decade away from the United States.

But Swan still felt out of place in his own country. His journey through the 1940s is marked by a search for inner peace and the solace of a special companion, and as much as he mused about enjoying "aloneness," he wanted people around him, and he wanted them to like him. He always seemed to gather an interesting coterie, and this period of his life proved no different.[11] One of many was Clare Booth Luce, whose portrait Swan painted. She lived in a neighboring studio and was for a time a frequent visitor to Swan's.[12] On several occasions, writer William S. Burroughs and his friend David Kammerer stopped in.[13] Whether they admired Swan, or whether he was an interesting eccentric, or both, is not recorded. Swan disapproved even of caffeine and would not have approved of the drug culture that Burroughs described later in *Naked Lunch*.

Agnes DeMille, who lived nearby in Studio 61, was another associate, though not as close to Swan as other dancers-in-residence. In the early 1940s DeMille was busily refining the choreography for *Away We Go*. Swan would have liked a role, and thought he could improve the dances, so their friendship may have been strained when nothing ensued. In any case, when *Away We Go* opened on 31 March 1943 with its revised title, *Oklahoma*, new stars were born as a younger generation of performers took the stage. Although Swan was certain that *Oklahoma* needed his magic touch, it's difficult to imagine how his classical Greek interpretation could have fit DeMille's rambunctious choreography.

Christine Fokine of the Fokine School of Ballet was much closer to him. Glad to list the school among its occupants, Carnegie Hall's administrators placed Swan's oil portrait of Fokine in its entranceway: "Almost all my friends have called," she wrote to him in her thank-you. "What a wonderful painting it is to have attracted the attention of a large part of the dance world. . . . I always thought of posing as a task, but after sitting for you and having those enjoyable and inspiring talks I will never think so again." [14]

At this time a long and mutually fulfilling relationship with Australian-born British composer Percy Grainger began. He had been struck by the beauty of Swan's portraits at an exhibition in Omaha years earlier and hoped to meet the artist. Grainger didn't know that Swan had created a dance based on the musician's arrangement for *Molly on the Shore*. Living in White Plains, New York, Grainger wanted a portrait painted of his wife, and on 15 December 1940 he wrote to Swan:

> When I saw your marvelously beautiful and lifelike portraits in Omaha I was greatly touched and impressed by them, and the wish came to me to have you paint a portrait of my wife for my music museum in Melbourne . . . if I could afford it.
> . . . In the domain of art there must also be a high place for portraiture such as yours, in which the meticulous detail of a Bach and the sweet skill of a Scarlatti unite to make a portrait art that is wholly lifelike and faithful. I admired your work boundlessly. [15]

Swan painted portraits of both Grainger and his wife, Emma, and drew a separate pencil sketch of Grainger. A photo of the Grainger sketch is at The Ringling Museum, but no images of the oils and none of the originals have been located. The portraits never made it to Melbourne, and the Percy Grainger Society continues to be on the lookout for them. Although Swan said that he corresponded with

PAUL SWAN

30. *Percy Grainger* by Paul Swan, about 1942. Graphite on paper. Location and size not known. Photograph courtesy of the collection of The John and Mable Ringling Museum of Art, the State Art Museum of Florida.

Grainger until the composer's death in 1961, only three letters from 1940 and 1941 remain.

Tragic news from England arrived late in the summer of 1941. Fred's mother wrote to say that her son was dead. He had been killed by a German bomb while working at his assigned defense factory in London on 11 May, the seventy-ninth anniversary of Adah Swan's birth. No other loss, not even the death of his parents, affected Swan as much. Brokenhearted, he paid one last tribute to Fred in his autobiography. Then he put down his pen and left "The Distorted Shadow" forever unfinished. His life now would be "forlorn waiting outside a locked door" (DS 565).

Swan started a memorial portrait, but he was unable or unwilling to complete it until November 1943.[16] Never again would he allow himself the kind of intimacy he shared with Fred; he could not risk the pain. A later companion, Forrest Frazier, would be treated more like a servant than a partner.

In surviving papers there are no letters from Fred Bates, though Swan mentions that many were written in those last years (563).[17] Except for the portrait he finally completed, and one more in 1944, he excised Fred from his life. He may have destroyed letters that were too upsetting to reread. He never mentioned Fred in correspondence after 1945, and friends who knew him during his last two decades do not recall hearing Fred's name.

In September 1941, Swan visited New Orleans for the first time since 1929. He needed a change; he needed to move, as if the train ride from city to city was his best defense against grief. Newspapers welcomed him: "Byronic," they said, "despite the years. . . . He seems to have taken up life again with zest, exhibited paintings and sculpture last season . . . in New York City, appeared at the Guild Theater," and was preparing for an exhibition in Los Angeles a few months later.[18] While in New Orleans he painted several portraits, including one of Mrs. J. Oscar Nixon, the founder of the New Orleans Little Theater.

Clearly, Swan was trying to reinvigorate his career, and he wisely refused to own his bisexuality publicly, always concerned about U.S. laws. As he had often done in interviews throughout the years, he emphasized his marital status and his masculinity: "I'm just a normal man. I have two daughters. I'm in good physical condition, and I like

31. *L'envoi, The Memorial Portrait of Fred* (also known as *Destiny*) by Paul Swan, 1943. Oil on canvas, 32 x 40 in. Private collection, Florida.

people. I even think I'm robust. Now, why do people think a male dancer is a sissy?"[19]

During the summer of 1943, Swan was with his family in California. He told *Dance Magazine* that he had an "apprehension" that they were in trouble. "When he called them, the cook had just left, Paula was ill, and they all needed him. He, therefore, hurried to Los Angeles to spend the summer."[20] That they would call on him in such difficulty is questionable. When had he ever "hurried" to them in their time of need? More likely he would only have been in the way. But Swan was adept at putting his own spin on the situation.

In fact, he was looking forward to meeting his first grandchild, Paula's son, Lance Morris, born a year earlier in Glendale, California. Swan didn't want to mention in print that he was a grandfather, and his references to Paula made her sound as if she were still a young girl. Even though he rarely saw Lance or his only other grandchild, Gregory

Morris (born in 1945), he felt a masculine pride that more than his art would continue after he was gone.[21]

A newspaper clipping in Swan's scrapbook that noted "Handsomest Man Arrives from East" mentions that Swan expected to "engage in motion picture work." If he tried, nothing happened. His greatest enjoyment centered instead around his friendship with another artist, Bennett Bradbury. They worked together, painting landscapes and talking art. There was probably an affair. Bradbury's friends remember him talking about a man with whom he had a passionate but short liaison at this time, and Swan is the most likely candidate. Recently, one of Bradbury's seascapes was located in a box of Swan's belongings.[22]

Perhaps because of his association with Bradbury, Swan's work focused primarily on landscapes during his California visit. Family life tired him, though, and he longed to return to New York. Helen was nearly seventy and seemed very old, and being around her only reminded him of his own age. There were moments of great affection between them; they had been friends for most of their lives and had fulfilled in one another a need that no one else ever met. But Swan didn't like seeing his wife so infirm. When he left in August he tried to keep dark thoughts at bay, but the image of his last visit with his mother no doubt preyed upon his thoughts.

Art as a Way of Life

In spite of Swan's personal pain—or perhaps because of it—the 1940s became one of his most successful decades. His art encouraged him to prevail, in spite of the destruction surrounding him. The impression one gets of his work from this decade is eclectic, for his attempts ranged from the abstract to the photographic. Central to all of it was Swan's sense of the virtuoso artist who first perfected technique before he moved to experiment. What connected Swan's work in the 1940s was his belief that artistic *method* should be the central concern of all artists. Only through understanding form and color can the artist create an accurate record of his emotions, and therefore of truth. When Swan took the time to follow this premise, he produced his best work. Portraits from the mid-1940s illustrate this point, particularly *Lisan Kaye as Empress Theodora* and several of actress Nance O'Neil.

The beautiful Lisan Kaye, the dancer who had teamed with Yeichi

Paul Swan, qui est peintre aussi bien que danseur et sculpteur, fait ici le portrait de la danseuse Lisan Kay en Impératrice de Byzance, Théodora, dans son studio de New-York.

32. Actress Lisan Kaye sitting for her portrait. *Lisan Kaye as Empress Theodora*, oil on canvas, 29½ x 25 in. Courtesy of the Carnegie Hall Archives.

Nimura of Ballet Arts to captivate so many audiences in New York, commissioned the portrait in 1944. A story about Swan in *La Presse* (Montreal, 24 June 1944) includes a photograph of him painting Kaye, who sits on her throne, her right hand in mid-air, as if granting boons to her subjects. In 1990 Kaye donated the painting to Carnegie Hall, where it hangs today.[23]

Nance O'Neil, a major stage star who played Lady Macbeth, Hedda Gabler, and Camille, knew Swan by 1943. A striking, tall woman, she, like Swan, was always in financial trouble, from the time of her first big screen role in Tolstoy's 1915 *The Kreutzer Sonata* until her death in 1965. Swan understood her sense of artistic entitlement better than many of her friends, and they remained close.[24]

33. *Nance O'Neil* by Paul Swan, 1944. Oil on canvas, 16 x 20 in. Private collection, Florida.

In the mid-1940s, Swan executed one drawing and three oils of O'Neil. The drawing is a profile. O'Neil is leaning forward slightly, in a graceful pose, as if listening intently to someone nearby. The considerable presence she had onstage is captured by Swan's expert line. The work was a study for one of the oils, one of Swan's best portraits of the decade.

The life-size *Nance O'Neil as Lady Macbeth*, now hanging at The Players on Grammercy Park in New York City, is stunning.[25] In this study Swan uses his flat illustration technique, as he did in the Kaye portrait. Especially appropriate for theatrical poses, the style suggests Japanese wood-block prints, especially those of Toshusai Sharaku, who painted many actors of late-eighteenth-century Japan. John Singer Sargent's influence is also apparent. From the early days in Swan's career, when he copied and "improved" Sargent's work that he had seen at the Tate Gallery, Swan used the same kind of deft, fluid technique in many of his portraits. The bright colors and decorative qualities he learned from studying paintings like *Fanny Watts, Carmela Bertagna,* or even the theatrical *Javanese Girl at Her Toilette* are all visible in *Nance O'Neil as Lady Macbeth*. A second version of this painting, almost an exact copy, is owned by Swan's niece Eldonna Swan Critchfield and is every bit as magnificent.

Success now seemed to present itself in each facet of Swan's life. On 1 February 1944 the *New York World-Telegram*'s Irving Johnson admired Swan in his article "Greek Gods Cast Spell over Dancer's Career." In November, *Dance Magazine* ran a three-page story on him called "The Dance as a Way of Life" and remarked on his portraits: "More beautiful than you ever could hope to be, but with such a truthful likeness that even your worst enemies wouldn't dare make comment" (9). This statement encapsulates Swan's unique skill in portraiture. For though he often "improved" his subjects, the results were striking, as if he had penetrated and portrayed a dimension hitherto unseen.

The *Dance Magazine* article called Swan a true artist who had "the heart of a child and an infallible feeling for fantasy" (25). This manifested itself in his dance; of all the arts, "he believes the dance to be the greatest" (9). While the interview was taking place, Nance O'Neil arrived for a visit: "He has recently done a lovely portrait of her as Lady Macbeth. Miss O'Neil's beautiful voice and exquisite diction still delight the ear. Her sweet, modest personality contrasts charmingly with her fabulous career. But both she and Paul Swan continue their reign as artistic personalities and remain true to their classic ideal at a time in the world's history when we need desperately to think of art as a way of life" (25).

One of O'Neil's friends, Joseph Cameron Cross, wrote to Swan on 25 March 1944, after *Nance O'Neil as Lady Macbeth* had been unveiled: "You have brought out very subtly the commanding histrionic art, the classical beauty, and the poetic quality of Nance O'Neil, whose voice David Belasco so often compared to a mighty organ! Your latest portrait is a thing of beauty" (SB).

Swan's scrapbook contains a number of similar fan letters from the 1940s, from people who visited him and were charmed by his person, his dance, or his artwork. He also saved several letters from an admirer he had not yet met. On 2 December 1945, Forrest Frazier, a young art critic from Huntsville, Missouri, wrote about a portrait Swan had drawn of Frazier's friend Arthur Corey.[26] "One of the finest figure studies I have ever seen," he explained, and apologized for his ignorance of Swan's work:

> I would particularly like to locate some detailed biographical material with photographic illustrations of yourself. . . . I would not trouble you for this information if I were not motivated by the deepest interest in you and your work. I cannot understand how I could possibly have remained ignorant so long of the work of so great an artist. The figure study of Arthur Corey is worthy to rank with the best drawings of the artists of the Italian Renaissance. Indeed, it shows the same appreciation of the poetic beauty of the human figure that was so evident in the work of Raphael, da Vinci, and Angelo.

Now, this was a man who knew art. Swan responded immediately, sending Frazier photographs of himself and his artwork. Frazier answered on 9 December: "I wonder if you will ever know what joy I felt when I opened the packet containing the material you sent—to have the very breath of Hellas here in central Missouri, it is an experience I never hoped to have. You have opened to me an entirely new vista of beauty—a conception of art that I never dreamed was being done in this country today."

Frazier's long letter is replete with worshipful praise. "These are the most exquisite drawings that I have ever seen." "No one can create such poetic nudes." "I have so much to thank you for that I hardly know where to begin." It didn't take him long to find his way to New York City. Perhaps he was there in time to see Swan work as dance director for Jules Denes's play *Eternal Cage*, opening at the Barbizon-Plaza Theatre on Fifty-eighth Street in Manhattan on 21 March 1945.[27] Within the year they were living together, and Forrest became the subject of a new series of paintings and drawings, as Fred Bates had been more than fifteen years earlier. Two of Swan's better portraits of his new friend (1948) show Forrest dressed in a monk's cowl. Swan had a particular talent for painting draped clothing, something he had learned under the tutelage of Lorado Taft in Chicago. The portraits

34. *Forrest Frazier as St. Jerome* by Paul Swan, 1948. Oil on canvas, 20 x 18 in. Private collection, New York. A different version (1948), with Frazier facing the opposite direction, is owned by The John and Mable Ringling Museum of Art, the State Art Museum of Florida.

show Forrest from two different angles. A caption could have read, "If you don't like it this way, I'm clever enough to do it that way."

Also like Fred, Forrest soon took his place at the door of the studio at Carnegie Hall on performance nights, greeting entrants to this latest "temple." An excerpt from an article in Newark's *Sunday Star-Ledger* allows readers today to reconstruct the experience:

A tall, slim, somber man, Forrest Frazier, Swan's secretary, opens the door to the studio a little before 8:30. A small group of disciples, who have been waiting patiently outside the door, file softly into the room, dropping their admission fees discreetly in a card-board box at the entrance to the room. They seat themselves on folding chairs. More are hoary-headed. Two little bent men wear white Van Dykes. They murmur softly among themselves, sometimes in French.

The air of the studio is heavy with incense. The stage is curtained in black. The floor is carpeted. The walls of three sides of the room are completely covered by Swan's paintings. His sculptures are scattered on antique tables at two sides of the room. There is a bust . . . of Senator [Robert A.] Taft. Many of the paintings are naturalistic and lifelike portraits. The others are religious and mystic in feeling. They bear such titles as "Cosmic Symphony," "Unborn Worlds," "Centers of Being."

The pianist [Evelyn Hansen], from behind a screen, plays a Chopin prelude. The audience applauds softly at the end. Frazier stands in the center of the stage and announces that Swan will dance one of his dances that was a great favorite "in happier days."

Swan, no longer the youth of Athens, but still intense and an arresting figure in a Florentine costume, enacts a pantomime-dance, the role of a man who lives, is deceived, fights a duel. All ends in tragedy.

Just before intermission Frazier comes forward and announces that he will display in a corner of the room some of Mr. Swan's watercolors, which may be bought at "a fraction of their actual value."

The watercolors are delicate things, finely executed, softly tinted.

More dancing. Swan interprets moods to the music of Debussy. . . . Then there is a curtain speech. . . .

The evening is over. The members of the audience come forward to shake Swan's hand and tell him which numbers they liked best. He greets each cordially and with great charm. The strand of gold beads of his Babylonian costume has broken and he offers the beads as souvenirs. An elderly woman stoops and scoops a few into her hand.

He chats lengthily with the last remaining couple. They would like an autographed picture. Next week he will have one ready, Swan promises. They leave happy and Frazier closes the door softly behind them.[28]

One who had been privy to Swan's Paris atelier might suggest that the only thing missing in New York was young Fred's clownish acts at intermission.

A photograph of Swan in a dramatic dance pose, with sculpture and tapestries behind him, appeared in *Collier's* on 1 June 1946. Stanley Frank, a staff writer from the magazine, had noticed Swan's work at the Grand Central Art Galleries exhibition in early 1946, became curious, and attended one of Swan's performances (SB).[29] "A profile that looks like a series of steps" is how Frank described the dancer's handsome face. Muscularity and elegance camouflaged the years.

Another article that focused on Swan's presence at Carnegie Hall appeared in the 6 July 1947 issue of *PM Weekly*. Written by Frances Herridge, the report suggests Swan's continuing popularity with audiences: "Most fabulous of the artists who inhabit the vast upper floors of Carnegie Hall is Paul Swan." But after praising his "vigorous personality," Herridge qualifies her remarks: ("His beauty like his dance is dated") and calls his performance (which she says she admires) "a museum piece." No doubt upset by the article, Swan enlisted Forrest to respond in a letter to the editor:

She dismisses his programme as a museum piece, but it is no more so than all great art which is preserved through the years as our cultural heritage. By the same analysis, da Vinci or Michael Angelo are museum pieces, but—in comparison—some of our modern artists are as dead as the dodo. . . .

Also, Miss Herridge stresses the age of Mr. Swan. It is true that he was dancing in the teens and twenties . . . [but] the recent photograph you published is adequate proof that he is not "dated" in any way, but transcends time. (SB)

Swan wrote his own letter to the editor, which prompted a pointed response from Herridge: "Your note to Mr. Lewis has been passed

35. Paul Swan in his Carnegie Hall studio, working on his bust of James V. Forrestal, 1949. Photograph courtesy of Dallas Swan Jr.

along to me. My use of the word 'museum piece' was not meant to be disparaging, but purely descriptive. It did not refer to you but to your program. And my dictionary defines 'museum piece' as a piece of art of a special value which makes it suitable for preserving."[30]

The article brought more curiosity seekers to Swan's studio. He became a popular lecturer. Topics included "Michaelangelo, from an Artist's Standpoint," "The Divine Sarah Bernhardt," "The Immortal Emerson," "Empress Elizabeth of Austria," and "Whistler, the Artist."[31] On 14 November 1947, for example, he spoke on "The Philosophy of Life from the Artist's Standpoint" at the Adelphi Academy, the first coeducational school in Brooklyn. Established in 1863 as a special cause of Henry Ward Beecher and Horace Greeley, the academy promoted scholarship, character, and—Swan's favorites—inquisitiveness and equality.[32]

Life continued without incident until the spring of 1948. A photograph of Swan sculpting while wearing Grecian garb appeared in the *New York Sunday News* ("Temple of the Muses," 8 February), the caption explaining that "Artist Paul Swan frequently paints or sculpts in his dancer's robes. Says it makes for greater freedom" (SB).

Swan, however, was apparently still not free from financial problems. Two months later he asked his brother Reuben for several hundred dollars for an "immediate and serious operation." Whether Reuben remitted the cash, or whether Swan even needed the surgery, is not clear. No mention of medical treatment is made again in any extant letters. There appears to be no obvious break in Swan's performance schedule.

In August 1949, Swan visited Broken Bow, Nebraska, at the invitation of his brother Karl. Relatives and their friends wanted portraits. Swan executed five pencil and eight oil commissions in five days, no doubt feeling somewhat abused and underpaid, but still grateful for the cash. He hurried back to the comfort of his studio in New York, where he completed his bust of former secretary of defense James V. Forrestal in October.[33]

By the turn of the new decade, Swan began to withdraw more and more into his studio at Carnegie Hall, no longer dashing about the country to perform. He was comfortable in this insular world, and enough people found their way to Studio 90 to keep his need for audience satisfied. Every week the pattern of Swan's life quietly repeated itself, as Forrest opened the studio door on Sunday evenings and invited people to enter the temple. People who knew Swan then said he could still leap and bound, wield his sword in *To Heroes Slain*, and charm audiences with his talks about art. In many ways, he seemed to "transcend time" exactly as Forrest had suggested to Frances Herridge.

What more tragic than to behold an old Narcissus still fondly gazing into his reflection pool, seeing no change. **Paul Swan**, *Philosophical Musings* (1939)

12 Holding On, 1951–1960

Death and Resurrection

On 14 June 1951, Swan and his assistant were preparing for the usual weekly performance at Carnegie Hall. The place had been cleaned, tea sandwiches had been prepared, and paintings-in-progress had been moved safely aside. As Forrest was arranging chairs and Swan was donning his costume, a telegram arrived from Van Nuys, California. Helen was dead.[1]

It should not have been unexpected, but death always is, especially for someone who feared it as much as Paul Swan. By the time she was seventy-six, Helen, immobile and miserable for nearly twenty years, had suffered too much pain. Her husband preferred not to think of her in such distress, wanting instead to remember the energetic woman who supported him at every turn. Perhaps that is why he hadn't visited her for some time. He didn't want to see an old lady. From afar, they wrote as if they were both still young. Whenever he unveiled a new painting, Helen was the first to wire him about its exceptional beauty and importance to the art world. "Deeply moved by your marvelous mural," one telegram in 1947 read. "A great work of art. Hope it will receive great acclaim. I have to tell you at once how wonderful it is."[2]

Swan wrote to her about all she meant to him. It remained an unusual but enduring love.

Now faced with the horrible news of her death, he didn't know what to do. People were going to begin arriving in a matter of minutes. Forrest could offer little advice in such a situation. He only watched his partner pace back and forth onstage and then disappear into the wings.

Some time later, Swan reappeared, in costume, ready to greet his guests. Years later he told a friend that he had pleaded for a sign from his wife about what to do. Then he heard her voice, "Paul, my dear, you know that the show must go on."[3] Whether or not there was such a spectral communication, it was exactly what the faithful Helen would have said.

And so it was a special performance, one of his best in years. When he looked out into the crowd that night, there in the front row sat the apparition of his beloved wife, smiling as she had decades before, giving him the strength to continue and the knowledge that she would always be with him.

But Helen's death did curtail future performances. On 24 June, *New York Times* dance critic John Martin (who owned several paintings and drawings by Swan) published a photograph of Swan and announced that the dancer would give a final program before closing his studio to guests until the fall. In the future, Swan would often call on his wife's philosophy to strike home a point: "As Mrs. Swan always said . . . ," he would begin. She was still very much a part of his life.[4]

There was never anything ordinary about Paul Swan. But his status as husband and father, so patiently maintained and supported by his wife, seemed to be his one great hold on a publicly acceptable life. When Helen died in 1951, Swan began, perhaps unaware, to change his image and move closer to the bizarre. He was nearing seventy, and like Gustave von Aschenbach of Thomas Mann's *Death in Venice*, he began to apply more and more makeup with an increasingly unsteady and desperate hand. Like Narcissus, he wanted the reflection staring back at him to be a beautiful youth. He had always gathered around him those who would reinforce his ideas and his image of himself. As he grew older that group dwindled in size, but as long as there was one person living who would believe as he believed, Swan would prevail.

One might argue that an artist needs a measure of delusion, of belief that he or she is the one whose view of truth and beauty will move the world. But an artist also requires some gauge of reality for progression and development in his art. Swan became stuck, living in a time warp, unable to accept the direction of contemporary art. In fact, according to him, the new art, including the art of dance, was ugly, destructive, silly. He never tried to understand Agnes B. DeMille's aesthetic in the 1940s, for example. He might have applauded the athleticism of movement, but he would have thought her dancers looked more like clowns and acrobats. Finally, he believed there was only corruption of form.

Swan had one characteristic of the tragic hero, a hubris that did not allow him to see his flaw, the "unswerving dedication to his increasingly anachronistic art form" that Callie Angell mentions in her essay on Warhol's *Paul Swan* ("Paul Swan" 23). And in fact, it is this inflexibility that later appealed to Warhol. There is an element in Swan's performance, as Warhol has preserved it, of a catastrophe in slow motion. We are both repelled and fascinated. We see the extraordinary delusion of the dancer while at the same time, like archaeologists digging up a fossil, we unearth the structure of past glory.

Unlike dance, which dies with its performance, extant paintings survive from each decade of Swan's sixty-year professional life, and there remain images and descriptions of others that were lost. Only one extant movie, *Diana the Huntress* (1916), shows Swan dancing in his prime. By the time Helen died, he must have been afraid that a proper record of his work might never be made. But in 1952, French art critic Magdeleine Cluzel's *Présences* appeared. This collection of essays about various artists includes sections on Paul Valéry, Paul Verlaine, Jean-Paul Sartre, and Louis Jouvet. But what made the book so special to Swan was that his portrait of Cluzel appeared as the frontispiece, the work was dedicated to him, and it discusses both his dance and his art. After Helen's death, the publication of *Présences* resurrected Swan's zest for art and life.

In her "Letter to Paul Swan," which introduces the book, Cluzel addresses him as "dear Master" and explains, "I want to reiterate to you my gratitude, and my expression of profound admiration." The first chapter, "Paul Swan: American Artist, Painter, Sculptor, Dancer, and

Poet," examines Swan's "inflexible will and attachment toward his art in all its manifestations." Chapter 14, "The Enchanted Circle: Paul Swan–Léonard de Vinci," calls Swan "a Master of color," "a mad man . . . served by an excellent technique": "Sometimes he would throw his head back, in a manner which is familiar to him, his chin out—and since I was admiring again his profile, I regretted not being a painter myself to immortalize his face, in that attitude, in front of his easel."[5]

An important contribution Cluzel makes to the story of Swan's life is her report of some of his dances. In "Paul Swan and His Dance Recitals" (chapter 2), she describes someone more attractive than the man Warhol would film fifteen years later:

> When he performs *Romance* (music by Jean Sibelius) Paul Swan is . . . asleep, lying on the ground [as] the music wakens him, and he goes looking for his ideal. He calls out for love, but none replies. Disillusionment, despair overtake him and he returns to his sleep, leaving us with an enchanting image.
>
> When he presents *Oriental Nostalgia,* the contours of his body clad only with jewels, precious stones—moving slowly, languorously to melancholy music—one is immediately transported to the past at the court of a Prince in a tale of the Thousand and One Nights. (10)

Cluzel includes full-page reproductions of six works: paintings *Mouvement de la Dance, Symbols des Credos,* and *Les Trois Parques*; and sculptures *James V. Forrestal, Maurice Ravel,* and *Icare.* In her critique of the first three, she argues for the symbolist nature of Swan's paintings. Executed in 1951, *Les Trois Parques* (The Three Fates) recapitulates his earlier style from the 1930s:

> *Les Trois Parques* shows us the skyscrapers of a large city abandoned as after some cataclysm. On the right, the inhabitants are frantic, desperate to run away. On the left a group of men, bronze statues, seem to want to resist the harshness of fate. But in the center of the painting the three fates, Clotho, Lachésis, and Atropos, as diaphanous as an apparition, continue to spin, to divide, to cut any way they wish the thread of human life, insensible to the

events that surround them. This painting puts us face to face with the tragedies of destiny, the impossibility to escape them no matter how we try. We are defenseless. (14)

Few artists have enjoyed such unqualified admiration as Cluzel's for Swan, and if modern critics challenge such absolute praise, they at least cannot question its sincerity.

Also in 1952, the popular WEVD New York radio program *Big Joe* boosted Swan's spirit when guest Kenneth Magruder talked about "the standards with which our nation grew great." One must dare to be a "creative self," Magruder explained. "Last Sunday, I witnessed the pantomimic dances of the world-famous Paul Swan. . . . He described beauty of face, not as a mask, but as symmetry through which the soul shines.[6] . . . Paul Swan is himself . . . and is determined to remain so. Why not encourage among mature Americans such constructive self-reliance as his?"[7] It's not clear whether Swan appreciated being lumped with "mature Americans," but he always loved a good review.

New enthusiasm was born from such publicity. In May he took his fame and his message to Auburn, New York. The city was giving a testimonial dinner for one of its most famous residents, landscape artist Frank A. Barney. Swan had painted Barney's portrait in 1920—Barney's favorite of himself—and Barney had especially requested Swan's presence.[8] In November he danced and recited poetry at the Goldwater Memorial Hospital in New York City, entertaining paraplegics unable to attend regular cultural events around the city.

Work continued on newer portraits, and there was little visible deterioration in this part of Swan's art. One example is his 23 April 1953 portrait, *Forrest Frazier in Raincoat*. Although the background of sepia tones is fitting, it lacks the meticulous detail of some of Swan's best work. But the half-body-length portrait is boldly painted, and close enough to life-size that one might feel compelled to extend a hand in greeting to this aristocratic-looking man with the aquiline nose.

It was not a memorial portrait, but it was the last one Swan painted of his friend. As quickly as Forrest arrived in his life, he disappeared from it. One story has him returning home to Huntsville to take employment at the nursing home to help defray costs for his mother, who was a patient. Another suggests that he simply returned home after his relationship with Swan ended. A nephew of Forrest's remembers his father telling him that he had to send bus fare, as Forrest was destitute and jobless. Forrest moved to Excelsior Spring, Missouri, around 1956 but returned to Huntsville in 1966. He died in 1970 and is buried in the City Cemetery in Huntsville in an unmarked grave.

Gifts of art that Swan gave Forrest during their association included at least several of his own drawings and paintings and a sketch by Swan's old associate John Butler Yeats. After Forrest died, his room in the family home was padlocked. His brother did not accept Forrest's gay lifestyle and finally hauled most of the room's contents to the dump, where they were promptly set on fire.[9] Little is left from the life of a man who was by all accounts a talented writer and a generous human being. Fortunately, the 1953 portrait survives and is part of the Swan collection at The Ringling Museum of Art.

Swan wasn't alone for long in his studio. He wanted immediate companionship. He needed someone younger to look at and to look after him; at this point it didn't much matter who it was. The fates intervened when a young, dark-haired Swedish man by the name of Sigvard Fors contacted him on 13 March 1953, only months before Forrest's departure. "It was a great experience to make your acquaintance," Sigvard wrote. "It is very unusual to meet someone who masters so many arts, including the art of speaking" (SB). It was a brief letter but enough for Swan to issue a personal invitation for Sigvard to visit again, and often. For two years, Sigvard assumed the role Forrest had held, and Fred before him. Several portraits of Sigvard were composed, and evening performances, with this new greeter stationed at the door, continued without interruption. The exchange had been made almost imperceptibly.

An exhibition in Havana, Cuba, now seemed like a good idea. Friends there had been after Swan for some time to reclaim the glory he had enjoyed in southern climes. *Bohemia*, a Havana magazine (27 June 1954), and *Diario de Cuba* (1 July 1954) both praised his work, mentioning how his "perfección fisica" had been hailed in Greece, and praising "la maravillosa cualidad de su arte." The trip was arranged around his summer studio break. On 4 July the *New York Herald Tribune* noted that "due to popular demand, Paul Swan will continue his weekly Sunday dance recitals throughout the summer." He was still

36. Sigvard Fors and Paul Swan at Studio 90, Carnegie Hall, 1956. Note the portrait of Nance O'Neil as Lady Macbeth behind Swan. Photograph from the collection of The John and Mable Ringling Museum of Art, the State Art Museum of Florida.

dancing in New York on 25 July, but then he closed his studio until September, in search of Caribbean dollars.

The journey was exhausting. Whether Sigvard accompanied him as an assistant is not known, but even so, Swan was a seventy-one-year-old man traveling by the cheapest fare he could find, hauling portfolios of artwork during the hottest time of the year. How much money he made remains a mystery, but one can only admire his tenacity in performing seven dances and lecturing on "Creators or Imitators" when he resumed his Carnegie recitals on 12 September.

In 1957 Swan exhibited *Portrait of Sigvard* at the Grand National

American Artists Professional League exhibition (31 March–14 April) held at the National Arts Club Building at 15 Grammercy Park, where sixty-three artists participated. At a thousand dollars, Swan's portrait carried the second-highest price in the show.[10] His brother Dallas, who never received credit for his years of support, eventually acquired it for an undisclosed sum. No doubt Swan thought that his brother was getting yet another painting at too low a price.

In a decision that foreshadows his Warhol performances, Swan agreed to be the featured dancer at Theater Macabre, Actors Playhouse, 100 Seventh Avenue South. The "offbeat venture," as the *New York Herald Tribune* called the theater, ran play productions like *Dr. Jekyll and Mr. Hyde* and *L'Affair de Mort* at midnight. Beginning on 27 July 1957 and running at least through 21 August, Swan presented several of his dances as well, including *Legend of Narcissus* and *Marche Funebre*. Playbills listing him as the star of the show suggest that he satisfied the audience's need for "Horror at Midnight in the grand Guignol manner" (SB). The situation was perfect for him; in this venue he would be applauded for his strangeness. It seems that either he did not recognize that his dance had changed in public opinion from beautiful to bizarre or, if he did, he decided that the exposure was worth it.

The first telegram to arrive on the day before "opening midnight" was from his old friend Nance O'Neil: "I wish you a great success tonight, with best greeting" (SB). Swan's mid-1940 portraits of O'Neil were still well known in New York. In 1959 he would draw her one last time. It is not his usual good work. The sketch was obviously hurried and looks unfinished, characteristic of drawings Swan didn't really want to do. Did O'Neil's physical decline trouble him?

Sigvard was probably still around when Swan made news at Theater Macabre in 1957, but by 1958 he had disappeared. He may have gone back to Sweden; he may have moved on to new friends closer to his age. No one who knew Swan then knows what became of this last companion. Without the surviving portraits and a few photographs of him with Swan in Studio 90, Sigvard might not have been even a footnote in Swan's life.

On 16 August 1958, the same month in which a full-page photograph of him dancing appeared in *Esquire*, Swan was a guest on the popular radio show *Long John's*, whose panel was known for its ruthlessness to

37. *Sigvard* by Paul Swan, 1958. Oil on canvas, 24 x 30 in. Private collection, New York.

guests. Letters from friends suggest that the panel tried unsuccessfully to bait him. Kenneth Magruder, who had praised Swan's work in 1952 on another radio program, wrote Swan a letter after hearing him: "It was quite a triumph for you to hold their high respect to the very end. . . . You kept on a high plane most admirably" (SB).

Balinese dancers Antonio Blanco and Ni Rondji (Blanco's wife) also responded:

> You did marvelously! Your well-modulated voice came on beautifully, as well as your rich thoughts. . . . [We] know that . . . the panel tries to arouse some form of controversy to keep up the interest during the long interview . . . but must they ask such silly questions of a man of your integrity about blemishes and moles on the skin! Good Lord! That in itself is indicative of how America skims the surface of life.

However, [we] did like their attitude towards you, almost verging on reverence and respect for your artistry. . . . It is we poor minority that must man the firing line. (SB)[11]

The attention didn't end there. A telegram from pediatrician Dr. Virginia Lent informed Swan that "Everything you stated re art is great" and asked, "would you do a portrait of a golden retriever?" Although Swan had painted a dog's portrait only once before, long ago in England, the fee convinced him. His portrait of "Sir John Copper," for which he received $350, delighted Lent and was the star attraction at the Country Art Gallery's "Dogs in Art" exhibition in January 1959 (Sky Island Club, Roosevelt Field).[12]

In the midst of this resurgence in the business of art and life, Swan heard unsettling rumors. Surely they were only that. Who could imagine the great Carnegie Hall being razed? On 18 February 1954 a Carnegie events program ran a column by Swan about the importance of tradition: "When one considers the fine things that Carnegie Hall represents both in the auditorium and in the surrounding studios, one realizes what an important word 'tradition' is. . . . All one has to do is say: 'Home, James, to Carnegie Hall,' to a taxi-chauffeur, and no matter how little he may know of the arts, he knows where 'home' is!" Eight months later, on 24 October, the *New York Sunday News* published a feature on the "Biggest Beehive of the Arts," hailing "a staggering parade of talent" who lived at Carnegie, including (with photos) the Fokine Ballet School, musician Emilia del Terzo, violin maker Luthier Rosenthal, and the man once billed as "the most beautiful man in the world."

Hoping to dispel disastrous thoughts, Swan exhibited *Sigvard* (a different portrait from the similarly named one in the 1957 Grand National exhibition) and *Dorcas Palmer*, two oils priced at a thousand dollars each, in the May 1959 Thirty-first Annual Exhibition of the Hudson Valley Art Association at the Exhibition Hall (Westchester County Center), White Plains, New York. By this time he had begun to wage his own campaign to save Carnegie Hall, writing letters to board members, testifying to the historical value of the little city where art lived. On 18 October 1959 the *New York Times* ran a large photo of him and sympathetically explained that he would be opening his farewell season that night.[13] The *New York Herald Tribune* ran a similar story about him, regretting the hall's impending demolition (11 October). In the November–December issue of *Music Journal*, Swan's friend Robert Cumming quoted him in "Carnegie Hall's Deadline": "I won't leave until the bricks begin to fall! I think it is sacrilegious to tear down such a shrine to beauty and art. . . . The marvelous acoustics alone are worth preserving! And where will the pigeon tenants go? They are surely the most cultured and privileged of all!" Some of Swan's neighbors at the time included actor José Ferrer, playwright Paddy Chayefsky, and musicians Gerry Mulligan, Don Shirley, and Thomas Sherman.

During this troubled time, Swan finally met his youngest grandson, Gregory Morris, who in 1959 flew from California to meet his mother's sister. After a vacation with Flora at Skiwaukee in the Adirondacks, Woody (as Gregory was nicknamed) accompanied his aunt to Carnegie Hall to meet a rather extraordinary-looking grandfather: "He was bigger than life, and for a thirteen-year-old was not exactly what one expected. The studio was huge and he had many paintings scattered about in various stages of completion: statues, theatrical sets, and the very strong smell of oil paints. We spent the afternoon together and he did a pencil sketch of me which I still have. I always thought of my grandfather as an incredibly talented artist in everything he tried. He was certainly unforgettable."[14]

Barnes, Duchamp, Matta, and Calder

As the 1950s drew to a close, Swan gathered a new group of artists around him. When Marcel Duchamp, Roberto Matta, Robert Barnes, and Alexander Calder called upon him, it was because he was both a curiosity and a talent.[15] Barnes explains: "The interest that Marcel, Matta, myself, and Alex Calder had in Paul Swan was not so much aesthetic but in the capacity of collecting interesting and oddly representative characters . . . in this case vanity. Marcel and Matta were always generous and appreciative . . . and were also admirers in an oblique way. They did much the same for people like Arthur Craven [Oscar Wilde's nephew] and the ubiquitous musician Moon Dog."[16] According to Barnes, the four made an excellent audience: "Marcel—all of us—enjoyed entering into weird situations with unusual people without being judgmental. Swan was a benevolent egomaniac."[17]

The term *egomaniac* is useful in understanding Swan's appeal as an artist and a person. Those who remember him describe the sweetness of his nature yoked to an unwavering conviction of his magnificence. The passage of time did little to alter this conviction, for Swan still thought of himself as the beautiful artist he had once been. Perhaps because of this innate sense of superiority, he was able to be generous with the lesser mortals he befriended. As long as you paid proper deference, Swan would do anything for you.

Matta had met Swan first, possibly when the former was a fifteen-year-old boy in his native Santiago, Chile. Swan was on tour there that year (1926), eliciting raves wherever he danced or exhibited his artwork. Now, in 1958, he was in his late seventies and could not disguise the effects of gravity, no matter how hard he tried. And try he did. In an interview with Thomas Girst in the Duchamp journal *Tout-Fait*, Barnes said Swan revealed that "the reason why his body was in such great condition and why his skin was so perfect was that he bathed daily in a vat of olive oil and that everyone should do that if they wanted to stay as young as he is. And he was one of the first health food addicts. . . . The trouble is, only Paul Swan thought that he still had smooth skin that looked really young. He was really a wreck" (Girst 6).

No matter how old Swan was, or how vain, these new friends "liked the way Swan liked himself. There was never any doubt about how he felt." [18] Barnes recalled that they admired his nerve and determination to hold on to his art form:

God, if there was a Duchampian theater, it was Paul Swan. I did paintings with Paul Swan [as subject] . . . when Carnegie Hall was great and real before it was fixed and made up for the deluxe world. . . .

Paul would have his soirees. . . . If you timed it right, you would get in on Paul's bacchanal. And Marcel introduced me. Matta found Paul Swan, made Marcel go, and then he became a fan. And the best thing that he did was the Bacchanal of the Sahara Desert in which he danced naked, virtually; he had veils, very gay. All by himself, he would do the bacchanal . . . losing his veils and ending up totally naked. . . . And of course everyone would throw money into the box afterwards because it was such a marvelous event. (Girst 5–6)

Barnes's Swan pastels are inspired by the Bacchanal dance, in which Swan appeared garbed in the veils Barnes mentions.[19] Two of the pastels in Barnes's sequence, *Bacchanal of the Sahara Desert* and *Swan Song* (1958), are an unique homage to Swan's lifelong dedication to dance. The reference to Bacchus emphasizes the resolutely pagan temper of the piece, and Barnes's work echoes lavishly illustrated medieval altarpieces. For an illiterate churchgoer of that time, these depictions of biblical stories served as a text to supplement the Mass and a focus for the piety of the faithful. Barnes's pictures serve the same function for a modern audience, for in spite of the fact that Swan was once lionized and celebrated internationally, we now need an exegesis in order to interpret Barnes's work. These pastels stand by themselves as art without the necessity of a conceptual reference, but our understanding of his subject intensifies our perception of his vision.

Swan continued his dance performances long after his reign as "the most beautiful man in the world" had ended, and in his works Barnes captured the tension between what was and what remained when the artist saw the dancer perform in the late 1950s. In a way, the pastels are like frames in a movie, suggestive of Warhol's filming of Swan during the latter's decline in 1965. In *Swan Song*, the clothed Swan is at center stage. All lines of force are directed at him, but he seems less a dancer than a pedestrian. Nevertheless, the audience is tilted toward him like acolytes, adoring and expectant, while amorphous ghostly forms, perhaps indicative of bygone fans, swarm toward the stage.

In *Bacchanal of the Sahara Desert* (figure D), the naked Swan is displayed more like an erect cadaver than a god of dance, while members of the audience move toward him with cloths, either to cover his nudity or to sheathe the sacred being before his next revelation. Although Swan almost always danced alone, there are two other figures in this work, like afterimages on one's retina. One is to Swan's left, his nudity apparent but obscured in shadow. Above Swan, however, there is a dark figure with arm raised in a more conventional dance pose, conceivably emblematic of the earlier dancer who thrilled thousands with his art. As the cloths are drawn toward Swan, they uncover more ghostly shapes, less distinct than in *Swan Song*, while anthropomorphic stick figures outlined on a theatrical backdrop imply another kind of dance.

Again, as in the previous painting, all the lines of force direct viewers to Swan, and the energy created by these lines suggests the reverberation of the dance still resonating in the collective mind of the audience. The bold use of color and the relentless sweep of line demand that attention be paid to both Swan—who will never willingly abandon his dance regardless of his ability to execute—and Barnes, the artist who recognizes and celebrates that commitment without constraint.

Shadows

Robert Barnes doesn't recall meeting the mysterious figure who lived at Studio 90 and occasionally appeared at performances during the late 1950s. Helping Swan defray costs, she created a little room for herself behind one of Swan's hand-painted curtains. How he first met actress-writer Anita Loos, famous for her 1926 novel, *Gentlemen Prefer Blondes*, is unclear. Perhaps he painted her portrait and got to know her during sittings. Whatever her reasons for sharing Swan's space (one would think she had enough money from movie royalties to do as she wished), they seemed to get along. With Sigvard's departure, Swan appreciated the companionship. Loos was ten years younger than he, and they never shared a romantic relationship. His last real sexual affair with a woman had probably been with the infamous Cabanel in the 1920s.

Most who attended Swan's Sunday recitals didn't even know about his famous roommate. Nephew Dallas Jr., who had by now returned from duty in Korea, knew that Anita enjoyed bringing younger lovers back to the studio to enjoy private trysts away from the public eye. She was polite and unobtrusive, more like an obscure painting hidden in a corner. When others were not around, she and her roommate no doubt enjoyed trading stories, for which both were acclaimed. "Show business is the best possible therapy for remorse" was a Loos principle both lived by. One pictures the two of them sharing a meal in the studio, discussing philosophy and art. In such private moments of companionship, Loos's oft-quoted "Pleasure that isn't paid for is as insipid as everything else that's free" might have been countered by Swan's own "Ecstasies are always so expensive to pay for, and the Piper adds whimsical sums each time the bill is presented."[20]

While Loos was living with Swan, she worked on her memoir and various screenplays, but other than her 1951 dramatization of Colette's *Gigi* (before she moved in with Swan) her work was not finding the same audience it had in the 1920s.[21] In 1966, however, she published *A Girl Like I*, and in 1972 she collaborated with Helen Hayes on *Twice Over Lightly: New York Then and Now*. Friends who knew Swan when he lived at the Van Dyke Studios during the final decade of his life knew little about his relationship with Loos and don't recall seeing her there during his performances. Their association probably ended when he left Carnegie Hall.

As his departure from Carnegie Hall began to appear imminent, everyone who knew Swan gathered forces. Dallas Jr. wrote to the board of directors, hinting at legal action if his uncle and others were forcibly removed. Longtime friends and even more recent admirers made sure Swan had enough money for his rent, not wanting to give Carnegie an excuse for eviction. Duchamp, Barnes, and Matta all helped. Barnes explains:

> In Carnegie Hall there were apartments and they were slowly getting rid of people . . . because they wanted them back either for space or for rich people. But Paul Swan held on. . . .
>
> The thing is, he must have made a fortune [from donations] because no one wanted Paul to get kicked out of Carnegie Hall. I don't know what happened. I went to Europe after that. . . . Oh, those performances were so superb. It made the happenings seem mundane. You know, they think they started that stuff down at Judson Church. No! Swan's soirees were a million times more exciting. . . . I know Matta always loved to go there and a whole group would go up there. (Girst 5, 6)

But calamity was inevitable. The eviction notice arrived on 23 February 1960: "To . . . all persons occupying said premises: You are hereby notified that the Landlord elects to terminate your tenancy . . . and that unless you remove from the said premises on the 31st day of March

38. Paul Swan at seventy-five, dancing at Studio 90, Carnegie Hall, 1958. Photograph courtesy of Dallas Swan Jr.

39. *EP* (Ezra Pound) by Paul Swan, ca. 1958. Oil on canvas panel, 20 x 16 in. Collection of the authors.

1960 . . . the Landlord will commence summary proceedings under the Statute to remove you from said premises."[22]

"I need every encomium and praise possible to keep me from suicide," Swan wrote to Jeanne Robert Foster (*DY*169). The former Gibson Girl and poet, who had listed among her friends W. B. Yeats, Ezra Pound, Pablo Picasso, and Constantin Brancusi, was now in her eighties, living quietly and frugally in Schenectady. Most of her wealthy and influential associates were dead. Like Swan, her day in the sun was past, and there was little she could do to help her desperate friend.

The age demanded an image
Of its accelerated grimace,

. . . .

Not, at any rate, an Attic grace.

Ezra Pound, "E.P. Ode pour
L'election de Son Sepulchre"

13 Diminuendo, 1961–1972

An Old God's Attendants

On March 12, 1963, the Metropolitan Opera House was filled to over-
flowing for Frederick Ashton's ballet *Marguerite and Armand*. One
sensed more anticipation than usual in the hum of the crowd. The
twentieth century's foremost dancer was about to make his entrance
in one of the last performances before the great old building was torn
down.

The lights dimmed; the crowd hushed. An old man wearing a thread-
bare suit that looked like it had been taken off the wardrobe rack of
one of William Powell's *Thin Man* movies reached over and grabbed
the hand of his young friend. "This is it," he whispered. "This is the
most exalting part, these moments before the curtain rises."[1]

The friend smiled, a little sadly. Once, another audience waited for
this dancer to make his leap onto the stage. Once, it was Paul Swan
who had been behind the curtain, feeling the fear and excitement that
always drove his performances. People watching him gasped; some
fainted. In Paris a headline had read, simply, "*Une Révélation*: Paul
Swan"; in Chicago, "He Heralds Spring," with a large photograph

of him leaping through the air; in South America, he was praised as "Nijinsky's Successor."

Now almost eighty years old, Swan heard the audience gasp for Rudolf Nureyev, who had begun his great leap in the wings so that the first view of him was mid-air. Gravity had not just been overcome; it had been annihilated. Tears of joy, of admiration, of longing welled up in the old man's eyes. Nureyev was perfection. At the end, Swan stood with his friend and applauded during twenty-one curtain calls, honoring Nureyev and his partner, Margot Fonteyn.

Determined to hang on to his art as long as he could, and almost certainly longer than he should have, Swan still collected a group of loyal followers. He had given his last performance at Studio 90, Carnegie Hall, on Sunday, 28 August 1960.[2] No longer able to afford the rent Carnegie demanded, he thought about returning to Paris but could not manage it financially. Now he danced at Studio 508, his new home at the Van Dyke. The place left something to be desired, but it was affordable, and Swan usually had incense burning to cover up a permanent musty odor. There he would be able to commiserate with other well-known but impoverished artists, like Charles Avery Aiken, who was given an honorary dinner in the mid-1960s by the mayor of New York City, John Lindsay. Swan attended the grand affair, but afterward both artists had to return to their shabby digs.[3]

The spectators who drifted into Swan's new studio were an interesting, obsessive lot—for the most part older women who had been regulars at Carnegie Hall. Seeming to regard Swan and his performances as a link to their own youth, they were willing to overlook his arthritic jetés. Although he sometimes offered withering comments about his "claques" (Swan's term) to Richard Nealy, his accompanist, their presence was a tonic to Swan. He could make those around him feel as if they were the most important people in the world. He looked directly into their eyes and listened intently. In return for such consideration, many of the eyes that looked back at him still saw images of the most beautiful man in the world, and he was grateful for that. But when they left, he unleashed his frustration. They were not like the young beauties who had fainted when he appeared at Hammerstein's Victoria Theater in 1914. They were wizened old hags.

With his movie-star good looks, Richard Nealy, on the other hand, represented youth and vigor, and Swan was fond of him. "He was like a grandfather to me," Nealy explained, "a loving and supportive mentor, a friend, someone who would stand behind me no matter what difficulties I might be facing. He seemed wise, and always generous in his praise of whatever I did." Young people were Swan's center, for these were the beings who existed in his imagined Greek community. In fact, he spent many hours cutting out pictures of beautiful people from magazines, as if by collecting their photographs he made them part of his world. He loved the lovely, and feared his age. Once when Nealy was visiting, he observed Swan standing in front of a full-length mirror, dressed in a brief Grecian garb. "Look at this," the dancer moaned as he grabbed his thigh. He shook his head and turned to see another angle, but it was no better. "This is terrible."[4]

Raymond Duncan, Isadora's brother, often visited Swan's soirees during the early 1960s. He brought with him an odd assembly of followers. Even on the coldest winter night, they would arrive dressed in something akin to Greek togas, white shifts made of material they had woven themselves, their sandals still showing traces of the snow they had just walked through. They admired Swan's homemade costumes, including jewelry made from old sardine tins.

Isadora's brother had known Swan for decades, and each appreciated the other's unswerving commitment to life and art. Duncan had once established his own nation in Albania, and later he became a fashion guru in Paris, Nice, and New York. "A vegetarian in a toga, without socks, pure San Francisco moxie," his biographer, Adela Roatcap, explained.[5] In the last years of their lives, both Swan's and Duncan's ideas and lifestyles became increasingly eccentric. They, however, still thought of themselves as uncorrupted searchers after truth.

Occasionally, Swan's Sunday evenings were sparsely attended. One night only four guests arrived, though there were chairs arranged for thirty. He still gave the best show he could. At its conclusion he addressed the audience "with great good humor," Nealy said: "Thank *both* of you for coming." They laughed and relaxed, spending a little extra time enjoying the artwork. "He was always able to turn the miserable into the good, and never seemed phased by poor attendance."[6] Now he danced for himself. In his heart, there was always a packed house.

The grace and elegance noticed by Swan's aging audience was not completely illusory in the early years of his residence at the Van Dyke. "When we would go shopping, he would be the old man, shuffling along, stopping to rest and look in a window of a store, and then shuffling on again," Nealy said. "But when I began playing the music for a performance, it was as if his love of dance gave him new energy. It could be magical; it was certainly impressive." When the music ended and guests were gone—when Cinderella's coach turned back to a pumpkin—Swan again became "the old wreck" that artist Robert Barnes remembered from his visits to Studio 90 in the late 1950s.

In public, Swan could be as peculiar as he was charming. Sometimes he would exasperate Nealy by suddenly asking passersby, "Do you know who I am?" They usually didn't, and so he would summon the powers of his rich, theatrical voice and declare, "I am Paul Swan." He expected to be acknowledged, yet at the same time he feared he would not be. When he was not, his feelings were hurt.

His daughter Flora, who lived in New York City at the time, told friends of her embarrassment when she saw her father in public. For at least a decade, he had been stuffing his pants with a sock to make himself look more endowed. His heavy makeup (applied with a shaky hand), the long fingernails, strange dress, and hair darkened by shoe polish or eyebrow pencil—it all mortified her. Flora had overcome most of her old anger toward her good-bye-saying father, but there was still little contact between them.

Everyone who knew her said she was a charming, sensitive, and intelligent woman. She was a Jungian psychologist with a thriving practice, but nothing in her training enabled her to bond with her father the way she had those few months in 1932, when they danced together in a performance at the National Arts Club.[7] The stable, professional child was now continually vexed by the bohemian, outlandishly garbed parent.

Flora's husband, Walter ("Arnie") Arnold—who, like Swan, had been a model when he was younger—was closer to his father-in-law. He often stopped at the Van Dyke to see if Swan needed food or clothing. No one saw a refrigerator in the place, and everyone was concerned about storage. On one occasion, Swan was fixing lunch for a young friend, Alberto Jaccoma. Alberto was as nervous as everyone else about eating the food, but he didn't want to hurt Swan's feelings and so swallowed, saying a prayer as a charm against botulism. Arnie dropped by unexpectedly. "Oh, sorry. Excuse me. I'll come back later. I didn't mean to disturb you," he apologized, and quickly closed the studio door. Alberto smiled. He knew Arnie mistakenly thought he was interrupting a private moment between Swan and a boyfriend.

Alberto first met Swan when the younger man was a clarinet student—barely eighteen—in the early 1960s and looking for interesting cultural experiences in New York City. He saw SWAN in a bold-type newspaper advertisement one day and decided to attend an evening show.[8] He was fascinated. He agreed with Nealy and others: "Paul looked ridiculous most of the time, but when he moved, he floated across a room. This old man, then almost eighty—he had a way of moving that was unforgettable. With subtle gestures of his hands, he expressed a powerful emotion and energy. You could see the past shimmering through."[9] Swan knew that Jaccoma and Nealy were not interested in a sexual relationship with him and never expressed anything to them other than grandfatherly friendliness.

During this period (1961–65), Swan developed an odd relationship with a nearly deaf eleven-year-old boy from the Albany area. The boy's grandmother brought him to see Swan once, and after the performance Swan spent extra time with him, gesturing, making clucking noises, and pointing out items around the studio. The boy responded. Several other visits were arranged, and by the time the boy returned home they were able to communicate. Somehow Swan had figured out certain sounds—tapping and clucking, mostly—that the boy could understand. They made up their own code and were able to "speak" on the phone. Swan was sympathetic because of his own, age-related hearing loss. He acted stone deaf at times and often snapped, "What? What?" Even so, he never missed a compliment about himself, as if he had a special sonar for those glorious words.[10]

Friends and family worried about Swan's relationship with the young boy. Richard Nealy, Alberto Jaccoma, nephew Dallas Jr.—all watched as Swan became more and more obsessed. The boy was to Swan what Tadzio had been to Mann's Gustav von Aschenbach in *Death in Venice*, "the physical embodiment of the ideal of pure beauty which he had been striving to achieve in his work."[11] The child's hearing disability only made him more attractive, as if he had been marked by the gods. Nealy remembers long phone calls of clicking and clucking, and he sometimes wondered if there was really anyone on the other end. Perhaps Swan felt more needed than he had in a long time. Whatever the motivation, the old Adonis and the young boy spent hours communicating. What finally happened to the boy is not known. Perhaps his mother decided a break was appropriate; perhaps Swan, as he drifted into senility, simply edged away from the relationship.

Swan's determination to continue to dance and paint was his greatest buffer against senescence; it had always been the way he confronted pain and dealt with the death of those he loved. In 1962 he was saddened to learn that his favorite little sister, Harriet Swan Spence, had died at the age of seventy-five.[12] She had been his first artistic compatriot. When she was an adult, she wrote music and poetry and was known throughout the state of Nebraska for her dramatic readings, while serving as the Poet Laureate of the Midwest Federation of Chaparral Poets. But she chose primarily to be a wife and mother, helping her husband, a farmer who also served two terms in the Nebraska State Legislature.[13]

Now Harriet was gone. Swan dreaded these telegrams of death, and he quickly got involved in new projects, trying to forget. Fred, Helen, Harriet—they were all people he loved, and they had all left him. His sister Belle had died in 1946, and brothers Rollin (1949) and Karl (1953) were also deceased. A year after the news about Harriet, another telegram came. Eldon, the youngest Swan (b. 1904), was dead. There was no other way to survive the pain but to dance and paint.

A few months after Harriet's death, Swan received a two-thousand-dollar grant from the Nebraska Hall of Fame Commission to create a bronze bust of Willa Cather. The bust was placed in the capitol building in Lincoln, where it remains today. A 26 November 1962 article in the *Lincoln State Journal* announced the award, quoting Swan: "This opportunity is an incentive to call on the gods of Greece to lend me the skill to do my very best for posterity." Swan's plaster version is owned by the University of Virginia at Charlottesville and is on display in the library.

In late 1963, after John F. Kennedy was assassinated, Swan studied dozens of pictures and set to work on a bust of the president. It be-

40. *Willa Cather* by Paul Swan, 1963. Bronze, 25 x 10½ x 11 in. In the collection of the state of Nebraska. Photograph courtesy of John and Helen Swan. A second version of the bust is owned by the University of Virginia, Charlotte.

came noticed by a New York press searching for memorial images. Swan's rendition captured the youth and vitality of the slain leader. Photographs appeared in all the papers, including *Forward*, a Hebrew-language journal, which published an article that detailed plans for JFK's memorial library and Swan's donation of the sculpture.[14]

The Cather and Kennedy sculptures showed no indications of a deteriorating artistic talent. Whether he was studying photographs for a future piece or looking directly at his subject, Swan was still meticulously observant. He watched even the casual visitor. "He looked with an artist's eye. You could see him measure you—the way he turned his head to look at you. He was painting a portrait in his mind."[15] On occasion, though, Swan's extraordinary talent allowed him to be careless. He claimed at times that he could paint a portrait in an hour. He could; but when he did, the work often showed it, and there are several paintings, especially from the last years, that seem hurried. To be fair, these are mostly gleaned from his studio after his death, and we can't be sure that they are finished versions.

When he embraced an idea, however, as in *Ophelia* (1911, figure 9), *Jeanne d'Arc* (1922, figure B), or *Nance O'Neil* (1944, figure 33), he made exceptional art.[16] For those mortals who struggle with color and proportion, it is difficult to understand the ease with which Swan could conquer such elements and penetrate to the essence of his subject. *Ophelia*, for example, owes a great deal to the Pre-Raphaelite movement, but, while referencing that period, Swan is able to place his own stamp upon it, showing the girl at the height of her beauty and innocence. There is in her eyes, however, a tinge of sadness that foretells how soon that beauty will be obliterated.

Jeanne d'Arc, which may be Swan's most successful work, combines Christian iconography with a semi-mythological figure. Again the subject is a beautiful young girl just before her immolation, ironically by the church she loves. Swan, perhaps remembering his own early problems with Methodism, is commenting on the capacity of religion to destroy those who take it most seriously. In the background are the soldiers who revere her, but soon they will be the agents of her death. Her arms are crossed in imitation of Christ's sacrifice and in submission to God's will, which she interprets as the rescue of France. As in

Ophelia, Swan shows us the moment of greatest beauty, the moment before the realization that this world will not tolerate perfection.

Nance O'Neil, a work of his later years, presents a different view. Swan is older now (sixty-one) and has experienced what happens when the beautiful youth is not fortunate enough to die at the height of glory. O'Neil has also survived from ingenue to character actor, and experience is reflected in every line of her face. She seems not to be looking forward, but her head is tilted as if in reflection. The portrait is heavily painted, and instead of the near-transparent tinges of youthful beauty in the earlier works we see how the many colors of age and experience leave their marks. Swan recognized in himself the inevitable diminuendo, but we have no record of a self-portrait as real or as intense as this one of his friend. It may be that O'Neil's portrait is a projection of Swan's own physical decline. It seems highly unlikely that he could see himself that clearly; or if he could, he was unwilling to capture his decline in paint.

Swan's efforts often produced excellent results in the mid-1960s. A portrait of Pope Paul VI was one such example. People who visited Swan's studio at the time still remember the stunning painting. A representative of the Vatican suggests that because the portrait was the pope's private property, he may have sold it to raise money for charitable concerns. Its location today is not known. Portraits of author Malachy McCourt and of the children of Nelson Rockefeller were also admired by those who saw them before they left Swan's studio with their owners.

But Swan no longer worked on the sort of art he had been praised for in the 1940s. The artist who had been "particularly aware of movement in the forms of nature" (*Art News*, 8 June 1940) and recognized as a "symbolic" painter (*Art Digest*, June 1940) now embraced an increasingly conservative idiom.

Swan was still sought after for exhibitions, but travel was more difficult. At the request of his niece Eleanor Anderson (sister Belle's daughter), he made a trip to Lincoln in August 1964 to paint portraits of herself, her husband, and several of her friends. Among those who sat for him on this occasion was the governor of Nebraska, Frank B. Morrison.[17] Swan brought a few other works with him, and the Andersons held a large reception so that their friends could enjoy a viewing. Although Swan's artistic talents were appreciated, his physical

41. *Nihon-jin* (Japanese Man) by Paul Swan. Oil on canvas, not dated. Location and size not known. Photograph courtesy of the collection of The John and Mable Ringling Museum of Art, the State Art Museum of Florida.

appearance was a problem. One of his grand-nieces was surprised when she saw him because all she had heard was that he had been the most beautiful man in the world:

> I was stunned to find an eighty-year-old gentleman who was rather disheveled and who smelled. He refused to wear a hearing aid, so we had to shout everything we said. I noticed he had a pronounced bald spot that was rather unusual looking. Mother explained to me that he was living as if he were still the most beautiful man in the world and the strange looking bald spot was actually paint that he used to cover it. My mother bought him clothes, fed him, arranged for many portraits, and understood the importance of his work.[18]

On the evening of a reception to exhibit the new portraits, the car sent to fetch him arrived so late that the party was over by the time he arrived. He suspected that he had been left out of the festivities on purpose.

The new portraits stayed in Nebraska, and the Johnson County Historical Society held a one-man show at the Tecumseh Library in October 1964. Swan was safely far away in New York by then, so there was no need for subterfuge on this occasion, if indeed there ever had been any.

The Death of Adonis

On 7 February 1965, as preparations for the filming of Warhol's *Paul Swan* were under way, Nance O'Neil died. It shouldn't have been a surprise, but each loss now eroded Swan's stamina. He often railed at death, as if the cursing would keep him safe (*DY* 169). On the day of O'Neil's funeral, Swan's niece Helen (Mrs. John Swan) was in New York for a nursing convention and visited him at the Van Dyke. He asked if he could share her taxi so that he could get to the service. While she waited, he dressed in the corner of his studio, behind a long black curtain which separated that area of the rest of the room. When he emerged, he was wearing wrinkled old black trousers and a jacket—hand-me-downs, he told her, from his brother Dallas. He found a black eyebrow pencil in a drawer and colored the bald spots on his head. He patted white powder on his face in a futile attempt to hide wrinkles. Then they were ready to depart. "Not knowing the full story of their gifts, I was angry that his brothers would not provide decent clothing for him," Helen recalled. "At the same time, I was embarrassed to get in a cab with him. I had never seen anyone who dressed and looked like that."[19]

Those who watch Warhol's Paul Swan movies today know what Helen meant, though, of course, Swan purposely designed his "look" for those productions. According to Richard Nealy, Swan "always crafted the style and color of his costumes meticulously, to create the illusion of the real thing, and the costumes were very specific to his vision of the message and the beauty he wanted to convey. When I consider the film, I'm impressed even more, now, with his ability and determination, in the face of the adversity of age, to continue to move, to remember the words, to keep the details of the extreme stylization alive, to summon the energy, and to still have the absolute sincerity of the characters he portrays. Despite his age and experience, I can still see the beauty, innocence, wry humor, and compassion in his eyes during the close-ups."[20]

In the year following the making of *Paul Swan*, it was time for Swan to attend another funeral. His brother Dallas died on 30 March 1966. Arguments between the two brothers had never abated. "I think I'll take that painting back. You didn't pay enough." "You can't have it back. I bought it. You'd have enough money if you would stick to the painting and give up that damn dancing. And get your hair cut, while you're at it." Their irritation with each other was exacerbated by the fact that Dallas was Paul's greatest and most reliable source of income, although Paul thought that Dallas never gave him his due, financially or artistically.

Swan's monetary situation changed immediately with the death of his brother. How would he live? He was too old to raise the kind of money he spent. He wrote to his niece Helen, still angry at Dallas: "I was at Dallas' funeral and my emotions were so mixed it is still hard to get the impression out of my consciousness. The funeral was a great success. This is the only word which seems to apply! However, when I go, which does not seem in the offing yet, I'll leave many things that were not bought somewhere. He seemed to imagine he could take them with him. Alas!!! I was met at the station in his $6000 Cadillac which he bought while I didn't have enough to eat!" It is a minor but revelatory note on the relation between Paul Swan and his family. He never ceased to believe that his better-off siblings should support him.

That same year, Flora was diagnosed with lung cancer. A few months later, Paula discovered she had breast cancer and underwent a mastectomy in June 1967. Flora wrote to her about her own treatment and how much better she could breathe after having fluid drained from her lungs. Their shared pain brought them together after years of estrangement.[21] Although neither daughter burdened her father with the details of their illnesses, he must have been heartsick for them. How does a parent—especially one like Paul Swan, who was a champion of physical fitness and long life—deal with such grim prognoses for his children?

Then, on 20 May 1968, his lovely "Modern Madonna," his sister-in-law Olivia Swan, was accidentally killed by her sister while crossing in front of the car to get in on the passenger's side. Her sister's foot slipped off the brake as she leaned over to unlock the door. When she realized the car was rolling, she quickly put her foot down on what she thought was the brake, but it was the accelerator. Swan's favorite model, the woman he loved most in the world next to his own Helen, was gone.

Although Swan had always exhibited a degree of paranoia, now the onslaught of bad news and his advancing dementia combined to erode his grasp of reality. He began to make up fantastic stories. He told Dallas Jr. that the emperor of Japan had called to ask him to dance in Tokyo. Then, supposedly, the director of the Folies Bergère contacted him, offering a huge sum of money for performances in Paris. Swan refused this, he said, because the man also insisted that Swan perform risqué acts with him onstage. It was a sad time in the life of the great Adonis. In March 1970, word came that his sister Julia had died. In September another telegram arrived. His brother Jesse was dead. Now only Paul and Reuben were left of the ten children. Several days later, Swan heard that ninety-one-year-old poet Jeanne Robert Foster had died in Schenectady. She was his last tie to the idyllic days.

He didn't dance anymore. He simply couldn't. He tried to paint and draw, and some of the work was still excellent, but those pieces

42. *Olivia Buranelli Swan* by Paul Swan, 1942. Oil on canvas, 26½ x 36½ in. From the collection of Dallas Swan Jr. and Margaret Swan.

were few. Two that show the old genius are a drawing and an oil of photographer Vince Grimaldi.[22] As time went on and his hand became unsteady, Swan gave up oils and drew only sketches. The pencil was easier to hold than the brush. What he valued himself—"the flame of his achievement that burned in him"—was all that was left.[23] He fought against the tide of life that would eventually overwhelm him, and he did not go gently. As each talent eroded, he grasped more firmly that which remained. This is his best lesson; it is what can be admired about his life: the unswerving dedication that attracted Andy Warhol to him. Now he could only retreat deeper into the part of his mind that allowed him to embrace a distant past.

Friends still visited, but he wasn't easy to deal with. Warhol had fallen away after he had gotten what he wanted, but Gerard Malanga continued to be his friend for several years. He genuinely liked Swan and thought his performance in *Camp* had been brilliant. Warhol had treated Swan rudely ("laughing and giggling," and "not even an invitation to lunch"), and Malanga wanted to do what he could to let the artist know how much he was admired. [24]

Grimaldi became a part-time caretaker, as so many of Swan's friends were then, making sure trash was emptied, checking to see that there was enough food, opening the mail to make sure bills were paid. He began to take photos of Swan at Studio 508, knowing the old man couldn't stay there much longer. They record the weary face of an artist whose life had burned across eight decades. [25] One of these shows Swan, ancient but watchful, standing in front of a nude he had painted three decades earlier. [26] Grimaldi's photographic portrait serves as antithesis to Rosenkrantz's 1912 portrait of the youthful Adonis: it is the final instance of Paul Swan not just making, but becoming, art.

In the fall of 1971, as it became apparent that Swan could no longer care for himself, his daughters moved him to a nursing home in Bedford Hills, New York. Paula visited for a few weeks and sat with him day after day, almost hoping he would die before she had to return to California so that he would not be alone at the end. Finally, she had to leave. She loved her father deeply, and it was difficult to go when she was certain she would never see him again. She later told her daughter-in-law that one of the reasons she had such difficulty finding happiness in her own life was because she never found a man who adored her as much as he did. [27] Both of Swan's children had been starved for his love; each reacted in her own way.

The most beautiful man in the world died on 3 February 1972, no longer beautiful and no longer famous. A memorial service was held two days later, on a blustery New York winter day, at the Little Church Around the Corner, where Paul Swan and Helen Gavit had been married in 1911. The service was attended by a small group of devotees—a few of Swan's loyal audience and close friends, including accompanist Richard Nealy, son-in-law Arnie Arnold, and daughter Flora. Dallas Swan Jr. had moved to Virginia by then and couldn't make the trip. Flora sent him the text of the service, knowing how much Olivia's son had cared for his uncle, even in the midst of long-standing tensions between Paul and his brother. Paula was in California; it was too long a trip.

Arnie and Flora chose Thomas Carlyle's words to begin the service: "There is no life of a man, faithfully recorded, but is a heroic poem of

43. Paul Swan photographed at his Van Dyke apartment in 1970 by Vince Grimaldi. Courtesy of Vince Grimaldi.

its sort, rhymed or unrhymed."[28] The minister continued: "What may be said of a man whose boy feet knew the black furrows of the cornfield and the lonely sweep of the Mid-western plains? . . . who ultimately found his idea in perfection while expressing his awareness of 'truth in beauty' in dancing on the steps of the Parthenon in Greece? Surely the ancient Muses looked in favor on the reverent youth." But when youth ends, so too does the Muses' favor. Swan lasted longer than most of his contemporary performers, but finally he was only an old man who bathed, vainly, in olive oil.

Return to Crab Orchard

Flora could not have known at the time of these eulogies for her father that she would be dead within a year; however, she was in so much physical pain by February 1972 that, after Swan's memorial service, she removed herself from other details involving his affairs.[29] The studio had long been closed, the remaining artwork sent to its appropriate owners. Some had disappeared. Perhaps a few friends removed mementos after Swan had been placed in the nursing home.[30] Sixty-six paintings and drawings that were discovered under floorboards in New Jersey in 2002 might have been taken during this juncture. There was too much art to keep track of, and the Swan clan had gone on with the business of living their own lives. Dallas Jr. hung many of his father's purchases in his home on the shore of the Chesapeake Bay. Others were put in storage, some for thirty years before they were cleaned and restored and hung again in places of honor. Several of these became part of the collection at The Ringling Museum of Art.

Flora was grateful when Reuben, the only surviving sibling, offered to take his brother's ashes to Nebraska if she would mail them to Reuben's home in Missouri. Now eighty-one, he found the drive to Johnson County difficult, but he mustered his strength and made the journey. On 16 March 1972 the *Tecumseh Chieftain* printed a small article about Swan's death, announcing that he had been cremated and would be buried in the family plot in the Crab Orchard Cemetery on Saturday, 18 March, at 2:30.

On that chilly, early spring day, when the ground was just soft enough for local farmers to start plowing their fields, Reuben dressed warmly against the biting Nebraska wind. He would be glad to be done with the ordeal. The cemetery was located in a rural setting of hilly grasslands and trees, a meandering creek nearby. A few nieces and nephews joined him, and he was happy they were there. When he knelt to read the simple pink granite tombstones of his parents—only their names and dates given—he wondered what they might think about this insignificant service for their famous, firstborn son.

Reuben dug out a small portion of grass and dirt between the graves of Adah and Randolph, removed a small coffee can he had been carrying in his overcoat, and buried it in the hole. Carefully, he replaced the grass divot, tapping it down it with his hand. Willard, his sister Harriet's son, directed the brief service. Then the gathering bid adieu and walked back to their cars. Reuben wasn't sure how his oldest brother would feel about being buried in Crab Orchard, between the parents who had been the cause of so much angst. No, Paul would probably rather be in Paris somewhere, with a great headstone that read, "Paul

Swan: Dancer, Artist, Philosopher, The Most Beautiful Man in the World."

In 1981 the Swan clan held a reunion in Tecumseh, a gathering of nieces and nephews and cousins and grandchildren, most of whom knew little about their famous relative. Flora was dead, and no one could reach Paula or her two sons, but other, more distant kin seemed eager to hear about Paul Swan. Dallas Swan Jr. took up a collection for a headstone. It wouldn't be grand, but at least Paul Swan's name would be visible in the family plot. Today a small bronze headstone marks the approximate spot where Reuben buried the ashes, rescuing the gravesite from complete anonymity.

Few visitors to the Crab Orchard Cemetery know that the man who was once dubbed "America's Leonardo" is buried there. If they happen by after the winter snows have melted and warmer breezes turn the grass a deep, rich green, they may not even then notice the little marker tucked in between the gravestones of John Harper Randolph Swan and Adah Sutton Corson Swan. Next to them rest other Swans, including Reuben and his wife, Rose. Bushes of pink peonies bloom every spring, and meadowlarks are in constant voice.

It is not Athens, or Paris, or London, but at last it is home for Paul Swan.

Notes

1. Andy Warhol and the Rebirth of Paul Swan

1. Swan to Foster, quoted in *DY* 170–71, from letters in the New York Public Library, Foster-Murphy Collection.

2. For articles on Carnegie Hall's near demise and interviews with Swan see "Must Carnegie Hall Go?" (*Cue* 13 Feb. 1960) and "A Hopeful Reprise for Historic Hall" (*Life* 25 Apr. 1960).

3. From a copy of Swan's unpublished autobiography, "The Distorted Shadow" [hereafter DS], 246, and scrapbooks, located at The John and Mable Ringling Museum of Art [hereafter RMA]. Swan often cut off the names of newspapers and dates from articles before pasting them in his scrapbooks. Any information not otherwise noted in this biography is taken from articles and letters in Swan's scrapbooks [hereafter SB] at RMA.

4. Swan lived only occasionally in Paris before 1930, for a couple of years (and sometimes for only several months) at a time, between 1911 and 1929. His main studio was in New York City.

5. Quoted from Hammerstein's Victoria Theater poster, SB.

6. Gerard Malanga, e-mail to the Janis Londraville, 23 Aug. 2003. Malanga starred in several Warhol films, including *Couch*, *Apple*, *Kiss*, and *Camp*.

7. Official dates for *The Illiac Passion* are 1964–67.

8. "Gregory Markopoulos Biography," 20 Mar. 2005 <http://people.wcsu.edu/mccarneyh/fva/M/Markopoulos_bio.html>.

9. "Warhol's life's work was haunted by death in its many forms: death by celebrity, by accident, by greed, by boredom" (Blake 222). Some of Warhol's earlier work was inspired by a *New York Daily News* announcement, "129 die in jet." "That's what started me on the death series," Warhol said, "the Car Crashes, the Disasters, the Electric Chairs." The plane crash worried him. He often recalled the day it had happened, 4 June 1962, because six years later, on the same date, the headline in the *Daily News* read "Artist Shot" after Valerie Solanas nearly killed him with her gun (Warhol and Hackett 17).

10. Warhol qtd. in Blake 222.

11. See Sontag 285.

12. Anderson asserts that the actors "are inadequate but in their inadequacy lies their humanity; their performances are more moving than the super-real, carefully edited pastiches of personality we usually see on the movie screen" (58).

13. Swan was only an extra in *Ben Hur*, as were two other budding actors, Clark Gable and Myrna Loy. Swan's age (forty in 1923) and his desire to live primarily in Paris prevented further Hollywood success.

14. Callie Angell, e-mail to Janis Londraville, 18 Sept. 2003. Between 1970 and 1994, *Paul Swan* and *Camp* were not seen at all. By the time the Museum of Modern Art restored *Paul Swan* in 1994 and *Camp* in 1995, "the most beautiful man in the world" had almost faded into oblivion.

15. Compare to James Joyce's distinction between kinetic and static art in *A Portrait of the Artist as a Young Man.*

16. Francis X. Bushman, silent screen matinee idol (1883–1966). He may have met Swan when he played the role of Messala in *Ben Hur*. Gail Ambrose, phone interview with Janis Londraville, 24 Sept. 2003; Dallas Swan Jr., interview with the authors, Onancock, Virginia, 10 June 2000.

17. Vince Grimaldi, phone interview with Janis Londraville, 23 Oct. 2003. Grimaldi's work hangs in the Museum of Modern Art, the Metropolitan Museum of Art, the Guggenheim Museum in New York City, and the Tate Gallery in London.

18. Letter dated 8 Oct. 1965, Vatican accession number N. 54975 (SB).

19. Malachy McCourt's portrait was stolen from his New York City bar years ago, although a photograph remains (McCourt to Janis Londraville, e-mail,

7 Apr. 2004). The Rockefeller children were very young when Swan painted them (ca. 1968). Mark was born in 1964 and Nelson Jr. in 1967.

20. The letter is not dated but is a response to one that Jeanne Foster wrote to Swan in December 1960. Qtd. in *PFR* 343.

21. Julie Lesser, granddaughter of Dallas Swan Sr., remembers Swan's visits to her grandfather's house: "Uncle Paul was a frightening man to a small child. I know he told stories to me and my sisters, but I don't remember what he said. From what he looked like in the 1960s it's very hard to believe that he was ever known as a beautiful man" (Lesser to Janis Londraville, e-mail, 25 Nov. 2003).

22. Dallas Swan Jr., interview with the authors, 10 June 2000, and *DY* 343. Swan's portrait of his brother is in the collection of Dallas Swan Jr. and Margaret Swan.

23. Another visitor to the Van Dyke, Alberto Jaccoma, also observed Swan's frequent assistance to Aiken (Jaccoma to Janis Londraville, e-mail, 5 Dec. 2003).

24. Dallas Swan Jr., interview with the authors, 10 June 2000. Two oil portraits of Aiken (1872–1965) by Swan survive. Owned by RMA (gifts of Dallas and Margaret Swan, and John and Helen Swan), they are dated 1962 and 1965 and are the only known portraits of a man who was once the director of the Allied Artists of America. Aiken's papers are at the Smithsonian Archives of American Art. He was noted for mural work, watercolors, and portraits.

25. John Swan is the son of Paul Swan's brother Reuben. See chapters 2 and 13. The story of "Lunch with Uncle Paul" is adapted from Helen Swan's diary entry "Helen's visit to Paul Swan in February 1965," collection of John and Helen Swan.

26. Swan was bisexual during the first half of his life, becoming strictly homosexual from about 1930. He always considered his wife, whom he married in 1911, one of his best friends.

27. *Portrait of John Anderson*, collection of the authors. Swan attributes the quote from Henry Dobson (imitated from Theophile Gautier) to Goethe. The quote usually reads "Enduring stays to us," not "with us."

2. Cold Comfort Farm, 1880–1897

1. Swan tells the story of his parents' first meeting in *DS* 10–14.

2. Swan's sister Harriet, his closest ally in the family, became an avid geneal-

ogy student and later in life belonged to Daughters of the American Revolution (Swan line) and Daughters of Founders and Patriots (Corson line).

3. Death dates are as follows: Jesse (Sept. 1970, California), Harriet (June 1962, Nebraska), Julia (Mar. 1970, Nebraska), Belle (June 1946, Nebraska), Karl (May 1953, Nebraska), Rollin (July 1949, Montana), Reuben (Dec. 1977, Missouri), Dallas (Mar. 1966, New York), Eldon (Oct. 1963, Nebraska)

4. A newspaper photograph of Swan as "A Modern Leonardo" is reproduced on the cover of *Wild Swan of the Adirondacks*, exhibition brochure (Roland Gibson Gallery, State University of New York at Potsdam, 2001).

5. Postcard from Paul Swan to Dallas Swan Sr. (collection of Dallas Swan Jr. and Margaret Swan).

6. One of Swan's earliest carvings still exists — the profile of a young girl cut into a wooden beam in the old barn on the homestead in Crab Orchard.

7. See *DY* 168–71 and *PFR* 331–47.

3. Mentors and Lovers, 1897–1906

1. Jeanne Robert Foster, interview with Richard Londraville, Schenectady NY, 10 Aug. 1968.

2. A popular American stage actor in the late nineteenth century, Haworth was known particularly for his Shakespearean roles. See Stang, *Famous Actors*.

3. Swan's assistance to artist Charles Avery Aiken (chap. 1) is one example of his generosity. See chapter 13 for the story of the young mute boy.

4. John H. Vanderpoel (1857–1911) wrote *The Human Figure* (1908). Lorado Taft (1860–1936) is known for his "monumental, heroic sculptures, including a statue of the prominent native American Black Hawk, which was fifty feet in height and placed on a promontory overlooking the Rock River near Oregon, Illinois" (<http://128.174.36.155/projects/Taft/taftbio.htm> (acc. 22 Feb. 2004).

5. See chapter 9 for details about Swan's medal award from the Paris Salon.

6. Ulrichs (1825–95) borrowed the term *Uranian* from Plato's *Symposium*, in which Pausanias postulates two gods of love, the Uranian (Heavenly) Eros, who governs principled male love, and the Pandernian (Vulgar) Eros, who governs heterosexual relations. According to Ulrichs, who published several pamphlets supporting decriminalization of homosexuality, a Uranian "resulted when an accident in the differentiation of the fetus associated a preference for male partners . . . with a male body, or vice versa" (Greenberg 408). He thus

determined that Uranians developed "congenitally" rather than "hereditarily." Swan would certainly have been familiar with Ulrichs's work.

7. See chapter 5 and DS 222 for the story of Swan's reunion with Weaver.

4. Apprentice to Adonis, 1906–1911

1. Swan told people he met at this time that he was seventeen, and this is repeated in his *New York Times* obituary (5 Feb. 1972), but he was actually twenty-three.

2. There are few extant examples of Swan's murals, but SB contains a number of photographs.

3. In *Surpassing the Love of Men*, Lillian Faderman provides an example of a Boston marriage: women who "are generally financially independent of men, either through inheritance or because of career. They were usually feminists, New Women, often pioneers in a profession. They were also very involved in culture and in social betterment, and these female values, which they shared with each other, formed a strong basis for their life together" (190). See also Londraville, *On Poetry* 27.

4. Swan never mentioned the *Peter Pan* failure to his Nebraska family. In a postcard to his brother Dallas, he wrote how well he was doing at the time in his new studio, that art was everything to him, and that he hoped Dallas would enjoy some paints Swan had sent as a gift (collection of Dallas Swan Jr. and Margaret Swan).

5. Alla Nazimova (1879–1945), born in Yalta and named Adelaide Leventon, later changed her name to reflect her Russian heritage. Brandon Tynan (1875–1967) was an actor, writer, and director.

6. In DS Swan mistakenly says the play he saw in Albany was Ibsen's *A Doll's House*.

7. For example, in *Decay of Lying*, Wilde's Vivian explains: "As long as a thing is useful or necessary to us, or affects us in any way, either for pain or for pleasure, or appeals strongly to our sympathies, or is a vital part of the environment in which we live, it is outside the proper sphere of art. To art's subject-matter we should be more or less indifferent . . . in fact, Life is Art's best, Art's only pupil" (qtd. in Wilde, "The Decay of Lying" 41, 48).

8. Alberto Jaccoma to Janis Londraville, e-mail, 22 Dec. 2003. Jaccoma and Swan were friends during the 1960s.

9. As decades progressed, Swan took off more years so that he could be admired as the beau ideal, youthful Hermes returned. He began blacking out

age references in news articles he saved, and when he was nearly forty he told interviewers that he was twenty-six or (in several instances) twenty-two. Art encyclopedias today give his birth date as either 1899 or 1884, but rarely correctly at 1883.

10. Sadly, Nazimova never appeared at the Thirty-ninth Street Theatre again. On 15 September 1910 she starred in Arthur Schnitzler's *The Fairy Tale* in Chicago, which closed after only two weeks. Shubert sent her and Tynan on an Ibsen tour to the South and Midwest, which also failed. In May 1911, while Swan was in Europe, Shubert announced that Nazimova would no longer have a New York theater named after her (Lambert 152). What happened to the Swan portraits is not known.

11. Stories date from late 1910 and early 1911. Most clippings are pasted in Swan's scrapbooks, often with the date removed. Some of these and others are also noted in his memoir.

12. In 1916, when one of Swan's works appeared on the cover of *New York World*, a reporter for that journal repeated the Byron comparison: "Few visitors to Greece have been received with more acclaim unless it be Lord Byron" (SB).

13. A photograph of this portrait is reproduced in a Greek newspaper dated 1911 (SB).

14. Jeanne Robert Foster, interview with Richard Londraville, 10 Aug. 1968.

5. "America's Premier Dancer," 1911–1921

1. Swan left Greece on 27 Mar. 1911.

2. Albergo Fisher's Park was in Via Sallustiana in Rome, near the Palazzo della Regina Margherita, where the queen of Italy lived from 1901 to 1926 and which is today the U.S. embassy in Italy.

3. Salone Margherita (named to honor Queen Margherita di Savoia) is located at Via Due Macelli 75, Rome. It opened in 1898 as one of the first *Café chantants* in Italy. In 1908 it was restructured and used as a theater until the 1930s, when it was closed. Reopened in 1972, it is today being used once again as a theater and is protected by the Italian National Trust. Swan's Italian adventures are in DS 183–85.

4. See *Painting the Invisible*, a film by Bente Arendrup about Rosenkrantz's life and work (Charioteer, Christiansholms Parkvej 4, DK 2930, Klampenborg, Denmark). See also <www.arildrosenkrantz.dk>.

5. The story of Swan's first Salon appearance is reported in the *Omaha World Herald*, 13 Apr. 1926.

6. Rosenkrantz's *Portrait of a Young Boy* is in the collection of Bente Rosenkrantz Arendrup. The location of Swan's *Portrait of a Greek Poet* is not known, but a photograph appears in a July 1911 article ("Lionized Abroad") in the *Albany (NY) Argus* (SB).

7. Anthroposophy focuses "on the process of learning, the awakening encounter in collaborative work, and the healing made possible through the arts, rather than the acquisition of information alone" (18 Mar. 2004 <http://www.centerforanthroposophy.org/home.htm>).

8. Bente Rosenkrantz Arendrup to Janis Londraville, e-mail, 1 Mar. 2004.

9. Swan mistakenly indicates the year as 1912 in his memoir. Newspapers reporting the event are dated 1911, and this fits with his return from England, also documented in newspapers.

10. The painting's location is unknown, but Swan pasted one of the covers from the railroad's brochure in his scrapbook. See also DS 196.

11. Quoted from Hammerstein's Victoria Theatre poster advertising Swan's appearance, 1914 (SB).

12. The journal, called *A diary of a weary way across the Sea, 16 December to 24, New York to Glasgow, as a token of affection to someone he loves*, is in the collection of Dallas Swan Jr. and Margaret Swan. RMA owns a copy.

13. Swan had left London by the time *The Gate of Life* opened on 23 July at the Savoy Theater.

14. On the *Baltic*, Swan garnered more funds by drawing a number of portraits, including those of publisher Mitchell Kennerley's two sons, Morley and Michael, and Kennerley's mother, Mrs. Morely Cleveland.

15. The painting is pictured in an issue of *Southern Woman's Magazine* (SB, date trimmed).

16. Joseph Pulitzer had purchased the *New York World* in 1883. His son, Joseph Pulitzer II, took it over when his father died in 1911. In 1930 the publication was sold to Scripps-Howard and combined with the *Evening Telegram* to be the *New York World-Telegram*. It was the most important voice in the United States for Swan's work.

17. In "Egyptian Fete a Fine Spectacle" (5 Feb. 1914), the *New York Times* mentions that "Ruth St. Denis was the girl dancer and Iolaus [Swan] the boy dancer" (SB).

18. Romer, noted for her role in *Kismet* (1911), was starring in Louis N. Parker's *Joseph and His Brethren* (Century Theater, opening 11 Jan. 1913) at the same time she and Swan were performing.

19. Patterson is best known for her play *Love's Lightning*.

20. See Laura Sherry Dexter's correspondence with Stevens, Houghton Library, Harvard University (Series: MS.Am 1333.2: Correspondence with Bancel La Farge).

21. Swan wrote: "Why, at such a cost of nervous anguish do I put myself in such jeopardy? Then, no sooner is the dance over and I am relaxed and in my quiet room, then I at once plan to make the same venture over again" (DS 234).

22. Kelly won the O'Henry Award twice for her short stories. Her best-known novels are *Toya the Unlike* (1913) and *Sea Change* (1930).

23. Sergey Diaghilev (1872–1929) was a Russian ballet producer and choreographer.

24. The article is in SB, but part of the date is trimmed.

25. The second sculpture that Swan brought back from Paris was *The Serenity of Fred*. Its location today is unknown. See chapter 9.

26. The lines are from John McCrae's poem "In Flanders Fields."

27. "Shh! There's a Mystery Man in Greek Suffrage Play" (article in SB).

28. The date is trimmed off the *New York Times* article, but the *Brooklyn Eagle* is dated 3 January 1917 (SB).

29. Swan seemed everywhere at once in the second decade of the century. Selected engagements or articles not mentioned elsewhere are listed below. Swan almost always painted or drew commissioned portraits in cities where he danced.

1915

11 April	*New York World* publishes "Lament of the Most Beautiful Man in the World," with photos.
19 April	The Society for the American Renaissance. Dances by Swan, followed by an address by Dr. Horatio Dresser of Harvard.
June	*Southern Woman's Magazine* publishes Swan's article "Metropolitan Glimpses," on artist Alice Morhan Wright. One of Swan's Nazimova portraits is reproduced, as well as two by Morhan.

October	*Southern Woman's Magazine* publishes Swan's article "Wartime London as an Artist Sees It," with photos of his artwork.
November	Swan dances at Theatre Vendrome in Nashville and then in New Orleans (sponsored by Louis Grunewald), where he paints portraits.

1916

February	*Southern Woman's Magazine* publishes Elise Ward Morris's article "Paul Swan: The Most Beautiful Man in the Entire World."
8 February	Savannah Theatre, Georgia.
14–15 February	Columbia Theater, South Carolina. Swan lectures and exhibits art at the University of South Carolina; he executes a drawing of the president of the university.
21 March	Exhibition (New York): The Friends of Young Artists, Former Blakeslee Galleries. Swan exhibits *Blue Dance* and *Study* and performs a series of dances.
April	Exhibition: National Academy of Design. *Portrait Group*, painted in Stony Creek NY.
May	*Theatre Magazine* publishes photograph of one of Swan's Nazimova portraits.

Spring and early summer performances at various venues:

> Commodore Arthur Curtis James estate, Newport RI.
> The Blue Garden fete.
> Arthur M. Scribner Estate, Mount Kisco NY.
> Pitney Estate, East Orange NY.
> Frank Vanderlip Estate, Scarborough NY.
> New York University, Hall of Fame.

1917

10 May	Hotel Biltmore for National School Children's Gardens League Benefit. New York City.
21 May	*New York Herald*. Swan's portrait of Robert Treat appears in print. He dances at the Robert Treat Hotel.
24 May	Sylvan Theater. Washington DC.

July	*Theatre Magazine* publishes article about Swan's performances and artwork.

1918

13 January	*Boston Sunday Post* publishes photograph of Swan with his two daughters.
12 May	Performance at Orpheum Theater, as reported in the *Lincoln (NE) Sunday Star*.
19 May	"From Crop to Acropolis," article about Swan, published in the *Lincoln (NE) State Journal*.
Summer	The Rosemary Pageant at Huntington, Long Island; Red Cross benefit. Repeated at the Metropolitan Opera House. Swan was the principal dancer.

1919

11 April	Selwyn Theater performance reviewed in the *Globe and Commercial Advertiser* and the *Evening Mail*: "One of the most extraordinary interpretive classic dancers."
May	*Theatre Magazine* promotes Swan's upcoming appearances with the Post Film Company.
25 May	*New York Herald* publishes article about Swan and his dance that includes a photograph of his portrait of John Barrymore.
June	Dances at Alhambra Theater and Wisconsin Players Club in Milwaukee. Swan appears with several of his students, including Angna Enters.
	Dance performance in Omaha reviewed in the *Omaha Sunday Bee*.
8 June	"The Handsomest Man Draws His Ideal Girl," article on Swan published in the *New York Sunday Sentinel*.
13 June	*Milwaukee Evening Sentinel* reports "Highest Success Scored by Swan at Pabst Theatre." Similar articles appear in the *Milwaukee Journal* and the *Wisconsin News*: "A gentleman of grace and beauty. . . . To inner fire revealed in motion . . . Mr. Swan may grow. At present he seems to dance objectively . . . as one concerned chiefly with the limning of his pictures."

| July | Dance performance at the Atlantic Auditorium, Atlanta, Georgia. Dances in other venues in several southern states. An Atlantic paper reports ("Coming Attractions," 4 July): "The press and public in all the larger cities of the south have been loud in their praise of Swan . . . America's leading exponent of classic dancing." Swan returns to Stony Creek for the summer. |

6. All the World's a Stage, 1921–1925

1. A photograph of Swan's portrait of Russel is in SB. Desti was Mary Dempsey, later Mme Vely Bey. See Kurth.

2. Swan's story of his time with Duncan appears in DS 259–63.

3. In DS, Swan mentions the letter from Helen. The poems were the trilogy he wrote for the subject of his secret seven-year affair (chap. 5): "July 24th, '18," "Parting," and "Distance."

4. Le Pré-Catelan opened in 1870 and is at 27 avenue des Palmiers, Cannes.

5. *Death*, collection of the authors.

6. Swan discusses his association with Biegas in DS 263–66.

7. *Fête Romantique*, collection of John and Helen Swan.

8. Ghika's *My Blue Notebooks* (226) was published under her courtesan name, Liane de Pougy. She and Cabanel were close friends.

9. The only other women he confessed to bedding prior to his affair with Cabanel were several in Athens in 1911 (chap. 4), not a pleasant memory for him. Swan discusses his association with Cabanel in DS 267–72.

10. *World Traveler*, April 1922 (SB).

11. See also André de Fouquières's 1 March 1922 article on Swan in *Spur*, "At the Close of the Winter in Paris" (22), and *Le Figaro*, "Figaro-Théâtre: Courrier des Théâtres," 10 and 28 February, for reviews of Swan's first performances at La Potinière.

12. The article from the *Pittsburgh Dispatch* is in SB.

13. *Shadowland* 7.1 (1922): 22–23, 70.

14. *Laguna Life* photographs included Swan's *Portrait of T.M.* (15 Dec. 1922); Swan himself sitting on a rock, posed as Endymion (29 Dec.); examples of his poetry (19 Jan. 1923); his sculpture *Lest We Forget* (26 Jan.); his own article about Egyptian art, "Unconsidered Trifles" (2 Feb.); and more photos on 6 July. A self-portrait drawing based on Swan's *Endymion* pose (also sometimes called *Narcissus* in newspapers) is owned by RMA, gift of John and Helen Swan.

15. The self-portrait of Swan at the piano is owned by Dallas Swan Jr. and Margaret Swan.

16. In Europe, Western interest in orientalism dates to the eighteenth century and is noticeable in many nineteenth-century paintings. See Said, *Orientalism*.

17. Swan was still receiving good press in America. The *Boston Post*, for instance, published an article about him on 25 October 1924, with a photograph of him in his Paris studio, working on his bust of Raquel Meller. The *New York Times* followed suit a day later, running the same photograph.

18. Although not often listed as such, *Ben Hur* was directed by a quadrumvirate: Cohn, Fred Niblo, Charles Brabin, and Rex Ingram.

19. Swan's scrapbook contains photographs of the mural, which he named *Yesterday, Today and Tomorrow*. The critic's description reminds us of the mural Swan painted in Vermont while visiting George L. Turner.

20. Cabell's (1857–1926) *Jurgen* (1919) deals with the mythical and erotic medieval world of protagonist Poictesme. Pennell (1879–1958) was an American illustrator.

21. Shown at the Architectural League were the murals *My Yesterday*; *Yesterday, Today and Tomorrow*; *Youth Confronted by the Creeds*; and the sculpture *Homage to Debussy*. The painting *Mystic Portrait* came from the National Academy of Design show. The sculptures from the National Sculptors Society were *Douleur* and *Lest We Forget*. Although the location of these works is not known today, photographs are in SB. See also *Jackson Heights News*, n.d., p. 8, SB.

22. The 7 February 1926 *New York World* article was titled "Paul Swan Frankly Deplores His Classical Dancer Reputation as a Drawback to His Serious Artistic Work in Painting and Sculpture."

7. Death and the Celebrity, 1926–1929

1. Randolph Swan's words are quoted in DS 304 and in other written notes made by family members (n.d., collection of the authors).

2. "Exhibition of Original Portraits in Oil and Pencil by Paul Swan, October 1st to October 14th, 1929," Macbeth Gallery brochure, collection of the authors. The drawing of Randolph Swan is owned by RMA, gift of John and Helen Swan.

3. In "Nature," Emerson wrote: "Thus is Art a nature passed through the

alembic of man. Thus in art does Nature work through the will of a man filled with the beauty of her first works" (494).

4. "Chas. R." to Dallas Swan Sr., 5 May 1931. The letter also mentions Helen Gavit Swan's inheritance: "It is nice that Paul and his wife are heirs to such a nice big legacy, and isn't it a wonderful thing that it is fixed so that they just get an income and cannot waste and fool away the principal, for they would surely do it, the kind of a business manager Paul has always been." Collection of Dallas Swan Jr. and Margaret Swan.

5. Curtis Farrar to Janis Londraville, e-mail, 22 and 30 Oct. 2003; Dallas Swan Jr., phone interview with Janis Londraville, 23 Oct. 2003. In 1925, 1928, and 1929, Buranelli published best-selling cryptogram and crossword puzzle books with Margaret Petherbridge (who married John Chipman Farrar on 28 May 1926). A few years later, Buranelli became Lowell Thomas's ghostwriter. Thomas and Swan shared a correspondence for a number of years, and Thomas also attended Swan's performances at Carnegie Hall. Correspondence from Thomas is included in SB.

6. Laura Buranelli Huff, phone interview with the authors, 2 Dec. 2003.

7. "Paul Swan, Artist and Sculptor, at Edgewater Gulf," newspaper clipping, SB.

8. Bennett was the father of actresses Constance and Joan Bennett and grandfather of talk show host Morton Downey Jr. He divorced his previous wife, actress Adrienne Morrison (mother of his daughters), in 1925.

9. *Jeanne d'Arc* also appeared in exhibitions in Buenos Aires and in Santiago, Chile, in 1928 and in a Macbeth Gallery exhibition in New York in 1929. It is now in a private collection in Italy. In 1926, Paul Swan's studio was at 139 West Fifty-sixth Street.

10. In *Analysis of Beauty* (1753), Hogarth writes, "may we not also imagine it probable, that the symbol in the triangular glass, might be similar to the line Michael Angelo [*sic*] recommended; especially, if it can be proved, that the triangular form of the glass, and the serpentine line itself, are the two most expressive figures that can be thought of to signify not only beauty and grace, but the whole *order of form*" (xvii). *Writings on Art, a Virtual Library* (<www.bbk.ac.uk/hafvm/hogarth/contents.html>).

11. Thomas Gainsborough, British painter (1727–88). *Robert Andrews and His Wife Frances* is at the National Gallery, London. *Thomas Gainsborough with His Wife and Elder Daughter, Mary* is owned by the Marquis of Cholmondeley, Houghton UK.

12. Interview with James Kieley (Galerie Rochambeau, <http://www.galerie rochambeau.com>), who provided an analysis of *The Three Graces*, 25 November 2003. *The Three Graces*, collection of James Kieley.

13. Several articles about the Duncan memorial service are preserved in Swan's scrapbooks.

14. Michaux was a physician who directed Virginia's World War I Medical Advisory Board. Other portraits Swan executed in Richmond and Charlottesville in 1927 included those of Morgan Reynolds, William Clegg Monroe, and W. B. Shockley.

15. Some of the pieces Swan exhibited were *Head of Paula*, *Portrait of Paula Swan*, *Portrait of Oliver Dixon*, *Homage to Debussy*, and *Mystic Presences*.

16. Among the subjects Swan painted or drew in South America in 1928 were Enrique and Carlo Almeyra and Mrs. Orme Wilson, in Argentina, and Richard Crighton and Ms. Crighton, in Chile. A photograph of Swan's portrait of Señora Quintana is in SB.

17. See also Martín and Fèvre. Although the location of the Martin portrait is not known today, a photograph of it appeared in *Aurea: Revista Mensual de Todas Las Artes*, which is preserved in SB. The same article contains a photograph of Swan with his bust of aviator Charles Lindbergh. Swan presented Lindbergh with the sculpture a few years later at a ceremony in Paris.

18. Many articles about the South American trip that are in SB have the date of publication trimmed. Articles contain photographs of Swan and his work. Some dated articles (all 1928) include *La Prensa* (2 June), *La Nación* (21 June, 12 and 14 Aug.), *Buenos Aires Herald* (1 July, 20 July), *El Diario Illustrado* (16 and 21 Aug.), *Boletín Consular* (Aug., vol. 3, no. 42), *El Mercurio* (18 Aug.).

19. Pauline Palmer (Mrs. Potter Palmer) paid Swan $150 for the drawing (SB). Before her death in 1918, Mrs. Honoré Palmer had helped to make Florida's central west coast a southern hub for art and culture, purchasing large sections of Sarasota County. Around 1911, she welcomed two of her friends, circus baron John Ringling and his wife, Mable, to the Sarasota area. No one then could have foreseen that a century later The Ringling Museum of Art would house the largest publicly owned Paul Swan collection in America.

20. Ochsner is best remembered for contributing the words to Paul Ambrose's song "The Nights O' Spring" (ca. 1900). No copy of Swan's play has been located.

21. Subjects for portraits in the exhibition included Mrs. Leeds Mitchell, Miss Bertha Palmer, Mrs. Stuyvesant Peabody, Prof. S. Chylinski of the Univer-

sity of Chicago, and Mrs. Herbert Steger. Swan's *Portrait of O.D.* was pictured in a Chicago newspaper, courtesy of M. Knoedler Galleries.

22. The location of *Paula and the Blue Bird* is not known.

23. The *Post* article appeared on 1 October 1929. The *London Times* is quoted in the Macbeth Gallery brochure, 1929 (collection of the authors). Among the paintings Swan exhibited were *Paula Swan, Mother and Child, My Children, Raquel Meller, Mme. Cabanel, Louis eleventh, Mr. Wu, Miss Van Arsdale, Nelson Bennet, Electra Doren—Memorial Portrait,* and *Jeanne D'Arc.* Drawings included *Butler Mandeville, Bertha Potter Palmer, Miss Lamson, Mr. Frederick Norcross, Mr. Pabst, Pavlowa, Violet Hemming,* and *Mr. J. R. Randolph.*

24. An undated article of the same period about his one-man show at the Milwaukee State Teacher's College explains that Swan has given up dancing, except in private life (sb).

8. Ateliers, 1930–1933

1. Harvey (1887–1954) was the director of the Old Vic theater in the early 1920s.

2. The Climas portrait was sold by Phillips art auction house in 1998; it is listed in its 1 June 1998 catalog as lot 559.

3. Although newspaper reports of the time verify this information, as does Swan's memoir (ds 340; sb), the Royal Academy today has no record of Swan's bust of MacDonald, and its location is not known.

4. Among the shipboard portraits he executed on the 1930 trip to the United States was a drawing of the Christian pacifist Muriel Lester. The drawing later appeared in several papers in the United States (sb). A photograph of the drawing is in the collection of the authors.

5. The Swans resided at The Chateau in Jackson Heights. Between 1930 and 1933, Helen made her last attempt to live in New York.

6. *Bulletin of the Milwaukee Art Institute* 4.3 (1930); see also "Noted Artist Exhibits Here," *Milwaukee Journal* 6 Nov. 1930.

7. Swan's portrait of Prince Chula (1908–63), oil on canvas, and a composite board containing two head studies of the prince are in a private collection in Italy.

8. Swan went on to say, "The color represents the emotional quality, or mood, and the prismatic effects and combinations of harmonies or dissonance portray the same effects, translated, that the combinations of sounds produce to our minds" (ds 370).

9. "Artists [for the WPA program] were selected on the basis of their sketches [and] were compensated for finished art works." See <http://lsb.syr.edu/proj ects/wpafolder/AboutWPA.html> (acc. 25 Mar. 2004).

10. Both murals have disappeared, but a primitive-looking mosaic of *Garden Country Day School* still hangs at the school. This may have been a school project Swan designed for the children so that they could paste small tiles on the piece to create their own artwork. Swan often encouraged children to participate in art projects.

11. Kreutzberg was Germany's leading expressionist dancer.

12. Swan was interviewed on several radio talk shows in late 1932, lectured on "The Artist in a Democracy" at The Morons' Discussion Club on 13 February (Old London Restaurant, 130 West 42nd St.), and danced at the Pleiades Club, Hotel Brevoort, on 19 February. See SB for news articles, and also *Jackson Heights News* (2 Dec. 1932).

13. See <http://www.idid.essortment.com/nazireichstag_rghx.htm>. Historians speculate that Hitler himself was behind the plot to burn the building. Nazis blamed a Dutch Communist named Marinus van der Lubbe, who, they said, was trying to destabilize the nation.

14. Swan copied his mother's letter into DS 369. Flora's story about her experiences at the Jung Institute are taken from interviews by Janis Londraville with Richard Nealy (3 Feb. 2004) and Dallas Swan Jr. (10 June 2000).

9. Winds of War, 1933–1938

1. Two of the works on display were *Prince Japonais* (oil on canvas) and the *Maurice Ravel* (sculpture).

2. Both articles are dated 3 October 1933 (SB).

3. Letters of acceptance from the jurors of the societies and articles praising Swan's works are in SB.

4. Swan also exhibited in the fifth Salon des Peintres-Musiciens.

5. Swan exhibited in the November–December 1935 Le Rève et l'Image exhibition on Champs-Élysées.

6. The sculptures were not identified by name. The painting was *Prince Japonais.*

7. Richard's article ("Lord Neville Lytton au Bal Gainsborough") is pasted in Swan's scrapbook, without a date. The *Comoedia* article is titled "Quand les toiles de Gainsborough s'animent sous l'oeil de Bacchus" (When the canvases of Gainsborough come to life under the eye of Bacchus) (SB).

8. Andrea Del Sarto (1486–1530), Italian painter. See also Robert Brownings's poem "Andrea Del Sarto." Articles in SB refer to Swan as the perfect painter.

9. The article in SB is titled "Masques d'Extrême-Orient" (21 Nov. 1936).

10. Paul Swan, *Philosophical Musings* (privately printed, n.d.). Swan said he wrote this booklet in the early 1930s. Some extant copies are dated 1939 (SB).

11. See Faneuse's article on Swan in *La Nouvelle Dépêche*, 21 Nov. 1936 (SB). See <www.Getty.edu/research/conducting research/finding aids/turpin m6.html> (acc. 15 Jan. 1904).

12. Wharton's story "The Hermit and the Wild Woman" appeared in *Scribner's Magazine* Feb. 1906: 145–55.

13. Faneuse reiterated these ideas in "Artistes du Temps Présent: Paul Swan," *Restauration* 10 Oct. 1936.

14. Swan's poetry is conventional at best, and Faneuse was generous to call it "enriching," "possessing a universal harmony" (SB).

15. See the cover of the January 1930 issue of *New York World*.

16. A photograph of this portrait is in the collection of the authors, but the portrait's location is not known.

17. Among them were the *New York Herald Tribune* (Paris edition, 17, 24, and 30 Apr. 1938, by Edmund J. Pendleton), *Le Figaro* (25 Apr.), *La Semaine à Paris* (23 Apr.), *La Fédération de la Seine* (23 Apr. and 7 May, by Paul Douet), *Le Matin* (16, 23 Apr.), *Excelsior* (17, 27 Apr.), *Le Temps* (28 Apr.), *Le Ménestrel* (6 May, by Claude Altomont), *L'Art Musical* (n.d., by Esther van Loo).

10. Farewells, 1938–1939

1. Another sculpture that received attention in a Salon exhibition for which we have no exact date was Swan's *Georges Achille Lemoine*. Well into his eighties at the time of the bust's creation, Lemoine had been an archaeologist in Egypt. Some of the jewelry Swan wore in *The Enigma* and *The Great God Ra* after 1935 was a gift from Lemoine.

2. A new *Statendam* was built in the 1950s and still sees service as a cruise ship today.

11. The Carnegie Club, 1940–1950

1. "Rendezvous for the Famous" is quoted from a description of Swan's studio at Carnegie Hall. See *Fashion Digest* 9 (1953–54): 44.

2. A letter of 5 January 1943 to Swan from Mrs. Julius Ochs Adler (Chairperson of the New York City Defense Recreation Committee) reads, "The

men of the Armed Forces will never forget your hospitality and generosity"
(SB).

3. "Studio Notes," *The Musician* Dec. 1941. The article also mentions that Swan's art work was "featured in the Montross and Carnegie Hall art galleries."

4. Richard Nealy, phone interview with Janis Londraville, 14 Feb. 2004.

5. Some of the works shown at the Montross were *Elegy*, *The Masses against the Individual*, *Garden of Narcissus*, *Apres*, *Return of Pegasus*, *Lost Horizon*, and *Afternoon of a Faun*. He also exhibited *Homage to Debussy*, but this may have been a copy of the one shown earlier at the Paris Salon.

6. The review was cut from the *New York Times* (n.d.) and pasted in Swan's scrapbook.

7. *The Art News* June 1941: 3.

8. Engel to Swan, 5 Feb. 1941 (SB).

9. One of Swan's self-portrait oils appears in the Sunday *Omaha World Herald* (17 Nov. 1940), in conjunction with the Joslyn Memorial Art Museum exhibition.

10. Briggs resided primarily in New York City. See *Orlando Star* (15 Jan. 1941) and *West Palm Beach Post* (7 Mar. 1941).

11. Those who visited and/or corresponded with Swan regularly included his old friend Ethel Traphagen, Kitty Cheatham (singer and music anthologist), Harry Green (actor who starred with Fanny Brice and Charlie Chaplin), Edith Ellis (playwright and director), and artists Chester Snowdon and Dorothy Furniss. Letters are in SB.

12. Swan mentions Luce's portrait and her friendship with him in "About the Hall," *Carnegie Hall* 18 Feb. 1954 (SB).

13. Burroughs and Kammerer were in their early thirties when they visited the sixty-one-year-old Swan.

14. The location of the Fokine painting is not known.

15. Collection of the authors.

16. *L'envoi* (also called *Destiny: Memorial Portrait of Fred*), collection of the authors.

17. The only letter from Bates is the one Swan typed into DS. See chapter 10.

18. There is no further documentation in Swan's scrapbook or letters about the Los Angeles exhibition; however, he did exhibit in California on several occasions during the early 1940s.

19. *New Orleans Item* 15 Sept. 1941.

20. *Dance Magazine* Nov. 1944: 8.

21. Paula Swan married Elliot Merle Morris, her second husband, in 1941, after they had known each other only a few weeks. She married five times.

22. Collection of the authors. Bradbury told the story of his affair "with a gorgeous lover" to his friend Marshia Brown. Brown to Janis Londraville, e-mail, 12 Nov. 2003.

23. Kaye and Nimura, her husband, lived in Carnegie Hall at Studio 60–61 until 1975. Nimura died in 1979 at age eighty-two. At the time of this writing, Kaye is still living but suffers from Alzheimer's and no longer recognizes anyone.

24. O'Neil was rumored to have had an affair with accused (and acquitted) murderer Lizzie Borden earlier in her life. "Nance O'Neil," 20 Feb. 2004 <www.lizzieandrewborden.com/Galleries/NanceO'Neil.htm>.

25. Pictured in *Fashion Digest* 11 (fall–winter 1954–55): 44.

26. Frazier published articles and a book under a pen name, but his nephew does not know what the name was. His work remains undiscovered.

27. A copy of the play's program lists Swan as "Pantomime Director" (SB).

28. The article, titled "Paul Swan Still Dances," is dated 27 April 1952. Forrest had begun his greeting duties shortly after he moved in with Swan.

29. The *Collier's* article was titled "Name Your Culture: A Visit to Carnegie Hall Studios." See SB for a notice from the exhibition, dated 10 January 1946.

30. Herridge to Swan, 10 July 1947, in possession of the authors.

31. The topics are listed on note cards in SB.

32. The program from the Adelphi event and letters of thanks are in SB.

33. The Forrestal bust is now owned by Princeton University, Forrestal's alma mater.

12. Holding On, 1951–1960

1. Helen's obituary appeared in the *New York Times* and the *New York Herald Tribune* on 15 June 1951.

2. The mural depicted Christ, surrounded by various biblical figures. A photograph of it and Helen Swan's telegram are in SB.

3. Swan told the story to Helen Swan (Mrs. John Swan).

4. This story of Helen Swan's influence is drawn from interviews with Helen Swan (Mrs. John Swan), Vince Grimaldi, and Richard Nealy. Helen Gavit Swan is buried in Forest Lawn Memorial Park, Glendale, California, internment space 2, lot 573.

5. Passages from Cluzel's book were translated from the French by Rolande Pinkerton.

6. Magruder refers to Swan's lecture "The Philosophy of an Artist," which he often presented after a performance.

7. Magruder sent Swan a transcript of the *Big Joe* broadcast, which took place on 16 January 1952. Collection of the authors.

8. A letter from the head of the testimonial committee is dated 7 May 1952 (SB). The event was held on 20 May.

9. One sketch by Yeats survived the fire. See Londraville, "Paul Swan" 333–34.

10. Edward C. Caswell, the artist who illustrated Edith Wharton's *Old New York*, published an article ("Paul Swan") in the *Murray Hill News* (New York) a month before the Grand National American Artists Professional League exhibition, calling Swan "legendary" and saying that he reminded Caswell of "Benvenuto Cellini as sculptor and craftsman": "I was amazed by the power of his paintings. . . . Paul Swan is a great artist who has made an art of 'Life.' "

The highest-priced piece was a bust of sculptor Antonio Salemme by Michel Werboff ($3,500). Works averaged $400. *Portrait of Sigvard*, collection of the authors.

11. Swan's scrapbooks contain several letters from Blanco to Swan. One dated 13 February 1958 praises Swan for "the richness of quality of your performances. . . . Did I hear correctly . . . were [Swan's original drawings] priced at only three dollars apiece? They are certainly worth a lot more . . . and the public should be thrashed with a bamboo stick on their roundest parts for not collecting them. Yet they will buy *contemporary misery*" (emphasis Blanco's).

12. A photograph of Swan's dog portrait appeared in the *Long Island Sunday Press* on 18 January 1959.

13. Seventy-six years old in 1959, Swan had by now reduced the number of dances he gave during an evening performance to between seven and eleven. Old favorites, including *To Heroes Slain* and *Bacchanal of the Sahara Desert*, were joined by newer dances such as *Forgotten Dreams*, *Nightingale and the Rose*, *Bon Jour Madame*, and *A Corner in Montmartre*.

14. Gregory Morris to Janis Londraville, e-mail, 8 Apr. 2004. Morris is an artist in Washington State.

15. Robert Barnes (b. 1934), winner of numerous awards, including the William and Norma Copley Foundation Prize for Painting (1961) and the Childe Hassam purchase prize from The American Academy of Arts and

Letters (1981), was elected into the American Academy of Design in 2001. See <www.levatodesign.com/robertbarnes/chrono_print.html>. Roberto Matta (1911–2002) is noted for his use of color "to create energized forms and space." Marcel Duchamp (1887–1968) was one of the most influential artists of the twentieth century. He is known particularly for his readymades and his celebrated work *The Bride stripped bare by her Bachelors, even* (1915–23, also commonly known as *The Large Glass*), a huge work in glass now at the Philadelphia Museum of Art. Alexander Calder (1898–1976) is famous for his sculptures and kinetic abstract mobiles.

16. Robert Barnes to Janis Londraville, e-mail, 4 Nov. 2003.

17. Robert Barnes, telephone conversation with Janis Londraville, 24 Feb. 2004. Barnes's work often suggests an autobiographical metaphor of his experience. Literature, poetry, mysticism—all are themes in Barnes's work, and his pastels of Swan easily fit into this context.

18. Robert Barnes, telephone conversation with Janis Londraville, 24 Feb. 2004.

19. Swan's dance was named *Bacchanal of the Sahara Desert*, the same title Barnes gave one of the pastels. Two color photographs of the Barnes pastels are at The Ringling Museum of Art, with Swan's scrapbooks.

20. Dallas Swan Jr., telephone conversation with Janis Londraville, 10 Feb. 2004. For Loos's quotations see <www.brainyquote.com/quotes/authors/a/ani ta_loos.html> (acc. 25 Feb. 2004); for Swan's, see his *Philosophical Musings*.

21. Colette was the pen name for Sidonie-Gabrielle (1873–1954).

22. The eviction notice indicates that Swan rented Studios 90 and 91 (SB).

13. Diminuendo, 1961–1972

1. Richard Nealy, phone interview with Janis Londraville, 24 Feb. 2004.

2. See *Life Magazine*, "A Hopeful Reprieve for Historic Hall" (25 Apr. 1960: 117–19), and a photograph of Swan in his studio (119). Carol Peters, a reporter for the *Chelsea Clinton News*, wrote on 25 August 1960 ("Art News and Notes"), "Paul Swan, the great dancer, will give his final performance. . . . Rents have now been raised and are so high that many like Paul Swan are forced to leave. In a few weeks, Mr. Swan will depart for Paris. If you have never seen this fabulous dancer . . . you'll have your last opportunity Sunday evening. . . . Paul Swan is noted as a great painter and sculptor." An article in the *New York Times* (28 Aug. 1960), "Good-bye for Now," by dance critic John Martin, is also about Swan's final Carnegie performance.

3. Richard Nealy accompanied Swan to the dinner. See chapter 1 for Swan's relationship with Aiken.

4. Richard Nealy, phone interview with Janis Londraville, 22 Feb. 2003.

5. Adela Roatcap to Janis Londraville, e-mail, 13 Mar. 2004. For the Albanian story see Roatcap 18–20.

6. Richard Nealy, phone interview with Janis Londraville, 24 Feb. 2004.

7. Flora didn't like being called by her real name. She chose to be called Dorcas, after a minor author, Dorcas Palmer. Her father hated the name. Some in the family never knew her real name was Flora.

8. Swan, who always designed his own ads, believed that a simple advertisement with one bold heading would draw more attention than wordy explanations. Richard Nealy, phone interview with Janis Londraville, 24 Feb. 2004.

9. Alberto Jaccoma, phone interview with Janis Londraville, 12 Dec. 2003.

10. Richard Nealy, phone interview with Janis Londraville, 24 Feb. 2004.

11. See <http://www.bfi.org.uk/collections/release/deathinvenice/synopsis.html> (acc. 15 Mar. 2004).

12. Harriet Spence died on 22 June 1962.

13. Jane Spence Peters (granddaughter of Harriet) to Janis Londraville, e-mail, 13 Mar. 2004. Harriet was a talented painter, primarily concentrating on oils and pastels.

14. *Forward*, 8 Dec. 1963. Although friends recall that the sculpture was donated, the Kennedy Memorial Library has no record of receiving it. Its location is not known.

15. Richard Nealy, phone interview with Janis Londraville, 24 Feb. 2004.

16. For additional information about these paintings see chapters 4, 6, and 11, respectively.

17. Swan had painted Nebraska governor Adam McMullen in 1926. See chapter 7.

18. Kay Anderson to Janis Londraville, e-mail, 19 Apr. 2004.

19. Helen Swan (Mrs. John Swan) to Janis Londraville, e-mail, 13 Mar. 2004.

20. Richard Nealy to Janis Londraville, e-mail, 24 Mar. 2004.

21. Both daughters faced serious trials during their lives. Paula's fifth husband, Dalton Coke, left her for a twenty-year-old at the time she received her cancer diagnosis. Her second husband, Walter Arnold, had left her in the early 1950s to marry her sister, Flora.

22. Collection of Vince Grimaldi.

23. Walter "Arnie" Arnold, from Paul Swan's memorial service.

24. Nealy remembers Warhol "laughing and giggling" at Swan's attempts to dance at age eighty-three. Richard Nealy, phone interview with Janis Londraville, 22 Feb. 2003.

25. Collection of Vince Grimaldi.

26. The painting *Nude on Couch* is in the collection of Dallas Swan Jr. and Margaret Swan.

27. Margaret Russell to Janis Londraville, e-mail, 14 Nov. 2003, 8 and 9 Mar. 2004.

28. Thomas Carlyle, "Sir Walter Scott," *Westminster Review* 28 (1838).

29. Gail Ambrose spoke to her friend Flora Swan for the last time in the spring of 1972 and recalls that she died the following year. Ambrose to Janis Londraville, e-mail, 10 Mar. 2004. Paula's cancer treatment was more successful, and she lived until 1991. Margaret Russell to Janis Londraville, e-mail, 15 Feb. 2004.

30. A friend of Swan's said he would find storage for the artwork, but after Swan died and Dallas Jr. retrieved them, a number of pieces were missing.

Bibliography

Anderson, Thom. "Camp, Andy Warhol." *Artforum* June 1966: 58.

Angell, Callie. "Andy Warhol: Filmmaker." *The Andy Warhol Museum.*
Pittsburgh: The Andy Warhol Museum, 1994. 125–26.

———. "Paul Swan." *The Films of Andy Warhol, Part II.* New York:
Whitney Museum of American Art, 1994. 23.

Arendrup, Bente. *Painting the Invisible.* Video, Klampenborg, Denmark:
Charioteer, Christiansholms Parkvej 4, DK 2930.

"The Art of the Mural Painter, the Portrait Painter, the Sculptor, and the
Caricaturist, Paul Swan." *New York Tribune* 21 May 1916.

Baldwin, James. *Giovanni's Room.* New York: Dell, 1956.

Biographical Dictionary of Dance. Edited by Barbara Cohen-Stratyner.
New York: Macmillan, 1982.

*Biographical Encyclopedia of American Painters, Sculptors, and Engravers of
the U.S.* Edited by Bob Creps. Vol. 2. Land O' Lakes FL: Dealers Choice
Books, 2002.

Blake, Robin. *Essential Modern Art.* Bath UK: Parragon, 2001.

Chauncey, George. *Gay New York: Gender, Urban Culture, and the Making
of the Gay Male World 1890–1940.* New York: Basic Books, 1995.

Cluzel, Magdeleine E. *Présences.* Paris: Maisonneuve, 1952.

Colacello, Bob. *Holy Terror: Andy Warhol Close Up.* New York: Harper Collins, 1990.

Corson, Orville. *Three Hundred Years with the Corson Families in America.* 2 vols. Burlington VT: Free Press Interstate Printing Corporation, 1939.

"The Dance as a Way of Life: An Interview with Paul Swan." *Dance Magazine* 18 Nov. 1944: 8–9.

de Pougy, Liane. *My Blue Notebooks: The Intimate Journal of Paris's Most Beautiful and Notorious Courtesan.* New York: Penguin Putnam, 1979.

Dictionary of American Artists, Sculptors, and Engravers. Edited by William Young. Cambridge MA: William Young, 1968.

Emerson, Ralph Waldo. "Nature." *The Harper Single Volume American Literature.* New York: Longman, 1999. 487–513.

Faderman, Lillian. *Surpassing the Love of Men: Romantic Friendship and Love between Women from the Renaissance to the Present.* New York: Morrow, 1981.

Fletcher, John. *Art Inspired by Rudolf Steiner.* New York: Mercury Art Publications, 1987.

Freud, Sigmund. *The Interpretation of Dreams.* New York: Avon Books, 1965.

Garber, Marjorie. *Vice Versa: Bisexuality and the Eroticism of Everyday Life.* New York: Simon and Schuster, 1996.

Girst, Thomas. "A Very Normal Guy: Robert Barnes on Marcel Duchamp and 'Étant Donnés.'" *Tout-fait* 4 (2002): 1–7.

Greenberg, David F. *The Construction of Homosexuality.* Chicago: U of Chicago P., 1988.

"Hailed in Greece as a Greek God Reincarnated: Paul Swan." *World Magazine* 17 Dec. 1912: 6–7.

Herridge, Frances. "Paul Swan Tries to Keep the Past Alive." *PM Weekly* 6 July 1947.

"Hidden Bohemia in Carnegie Hall." *Esquire* Aug. 1960: 48.

Hoberman, J. *On Jack Smith's Flaming Creatures (and Other Secret-Flix of Cinemaroc).* New York: Granary Books and Hips Road, 2001.

Jacobsen's Biographical Index of American Artists. Vol. 1, bk. 4. Carrollton TX: A. J. Publications, 2002.

Koestenbaum, Wayne. *Andy Warhol.* New York: Penguin Putnam, 2001.

Kurth, Peter. *Isadora: A Sensational Life.* New York: Little, Brown, 2001.

Lambert, Gavin. *Nazimova: A Biography.* New York: Knopf, 1997.

Londraville, Janis. *On Poetry, Painting, and Politics: The Letters of May Morris and John Quinn*. Selinsgrove PA: Susquehanna UP, 1997.

———. "Paul Swan: The Life and Art of 'The Most Beautiful Man in the World.'" *Prodigal Father Revisited: Artists and Writers in the World of John Butler Yeats*. Edited by Janis Londraville. West Cornwall CT: Locust Hill P., 2001. 331–47.

Londraville, Richard, and Janis Londraville. *Dear Yeats, Dear Pound, Dear Ford: Jeanne Robert Foster and Her Circle of Friends*. Syracuse: Syracuse UP, 2001.

Mallet's Index of Artists. Edited by Daniel Trowbridge Mallett. New York: Peter Smith, 1948.

"The Man behind the Current 'Wild Swan' Exhibit at Hosmer Gallery." *The Racquette* 29 Sept. 2001: 6, 8.

Mantle Fielding's Dictionary of American Painters, Sculptors, and Engravers. Edited by Glenn B. Optiz. Poughkeepsie NY: Apollo Books, 1983.

Martín, Benito Quinquela, and Fermín Fèvre. *Quinquela*. Buenos Aires: Editorial Ateneo, 2001.

Morris, Gary. "Gregory Markopoulos: Seconds in Eternity." *Bright Lights Film Journal*. Issue 20, Nov. 1997 <http://www.brightlightsfilm.com/20/20_markopoulos.html>.

Morrissey, Paul. "Paul Morrissey in his own words about his and Andy Warhol's movies." 24 Sept. 2003 <http://www.filmfestival.se/1997/war morkat97.html>.

Moss, Arthur H. "Paul Swan, Artist." *Shadowlands* 7.1 (1922): 22–23, 70.

Pater, Walter. *Studies in the History of the Renaissance*. London: Macmillan, 1873.

"Paul Swan, Dancer-Artist." *Art Digest* 1 June 1940: 18.

Roatcap, Adela. *Raymond Duncan: Printer, Expatriate, Eccentric Artist*. San Francisco: Book Club of California, 1991.

Said, Edward. *Orientalism*. New York: Vintage, 1979.

Schickel, Richard, and Michael Walsh. *Carnegie Hall: The First One Hundred Years*. New York: Harry N. Abrams, 1987.

Sontag, Susan. *Against Interpretation*. New York: Dell, 1969.

Strang, Lewis C. *Famous Actors of the Day in America*. New York: L. C. Page, 1900.

"Swan: An American Who Revives the Greek Ideal." *Theatre Magazine* May 1913.

Swan, Paul. *Philosophical Musings*. Paris [1939].

Taylor, Paul. "Andy Warhol: The Last Interview." *Flash Art*, no. 133 (Apr. 1987): 40–44.

Vickerman, Thomas. "Current Exhibits in Chicago: Nazimova Launched Paul Swan's Career." *Chicago Evening Post Magazine of the Art World* 29 Jan. 1929: 2.

Warhol, Andy. *The Andy Warhol Diaries*. Edited by Pat Hackett. New York: Warner Books, 1989.

———. *The Philosophy of Andy Warhol (From A to B and Back Again)*. New York: Harvest Books, 1975.

Warhol, Andy, and Pat Hackett. *POPism: The Warhol '60s*. New York: Harcourt Brace, 1980.

Who Was Who in American Art. Edited by Peter Hastings Falk. Madison CT: Sound View P., 1985.

Who Was Who on Screen. Edited by Evelyn Mack Truitt. 3rd ed. New York: R. R. Bowker, 1983.

Wilde, Oscar. *The Artist Critic: Critical Writings of Oscar Wilde*. Edited by Richard Ellman. New York: Random House, 1969.

———. "The Decay of Lying: A Dialogue." *The Nineteenth Century: A Monthly Review* Jan.–June 1889: 35–56.

Wilson, Robert Forrest. *Paris on Parade*. New York: Bobbs-Merrill, 1924–25.

Yeats, W. B. *The Collected Poems of W. B. Yeats*. Edited by Richard J. Finneran. New York: Macmillan, 1989.